Vermont's Land and Resources

Vermont's
Land and Resources

Harold A. Meeks

Introduction by
Charles C. Morrissey

The New England Press
Shelburne, Vermont

The New England Press
P.O. Box 575
Shelburne, Vermont 05482

Library of Congress Catalog Card Number: 86-50973
ISBN: 0-933050-40-2

Printed in the United States of America

Foreword

Geographers are concerned with the character of places. This is to say those features which in total make a particular place what it is. Would anyone care to try to list all the features that constitute Vermont? Or the United States? Like any regional geography, this book is selective.

Traditionally, all the component parts of a particular place can be grouped into two major categories: people and the land they occupy. Thus, a complete geography of Vermont should deal with both the human and the natural elements. In an earlier book, *Time and Change in Vermont: A Human Geography,* I focused on Vermonters themselves and traced the state's development from the earliest pioneers to the arrival of IBM and General Electric three centuries later. *Vermont's Land and Rosources,* on the other hand, is about Vermont's natural environment. While some chapters discuss how Vermont's resources have been used the emphasis is on the land itself.

For many the word "environment" means only one's natural surroundings. Actually the word implies everything, cultural and natural, that surrounds an individual. Vermont's environment includes everything from run down dairy farms and IBM plants, to glacial features and cold, wet northeast winds. For convenience, we separate this total environment into cultural (dairy farms) and natural (glacial features) parts, and here emphasize the "natural" parts of Vermont's environment.

This is not as easy as it sounds. Technolgically advanced societies, such as the United States and by extension Vermont, have been able to alter nature to such a degree that it is often hard to separate what is truly natural from what is man-made. Take the black and white Holstein—one of Vermont's greatest symbols. As a product of decades of selective breeding, artificial insemination, and culling of poor producing cows, the result may well be a human rather than natural creation. The same applies to Vermont soils which have been overturned, transported, added to and subtracted from for generations. Or to the natural piles of glacial gravel along Vermont valleys which are turned into landfills with little resemblance to what they originally looked like.

Our natural environment can be classified into several components, but we always have to keep in mind the modifications which we have impressed upon it. Major natural environment categories, however, generally conform to the chapters of this book.

Most obvious to all is the shape of the land—the hills, low mountains, river valleys and flat plains which give Vermont its distinctive character. The first four chapters describe how Vermont's shape came to be through the work of streams, glaciers, and great movements of the earth's crust.

But stopping with the forces which shaped Vermont would not tell the whole story, because generations of Vermonters have been using the land for a variety of economic activities. Aside from the present ski recreation industry, the changing colors of the trees, and the abundance of lakes and cleared farmland—with the silo monuments to a vanishing activity, Vermont historically has based its economy on the physical environment. The most direct impact of the state's geology has been in the various mineral industries which developed in granite, marble, slate, and schist. Chapters 5 and 6 review the development of Vermont's mineral resource industries and look at their current status.

Another obvious element of Vermont's natural environment is the constantly changing weather; the bitterly low winter temperatures, the scenic valley fogs, the hot humid days of summer, and the commonplace day to day and sometimes hour to hour changes. The essentials of local weather are detailed in Chapter 7. But like the origin and shape of the land, the ramifications of Vermont weather are as important as what it consists of. Water, a result of precipitation, causes floods (Chapter 8), but it also provides the force to drive turbines which drive generators to produce electricity (Chapter 9).

Vermont's climate is also responsible for what grows. Vegetation patterns have developed through a combination of moisture, temperature and topography. Chapter 10 describes the major forest-vegetation patterns, while Chapter 11 looks at the major use of the state's forests for sawlog, pulpwood, and fuelwood production.

Finally, the hodgepodge of Vermont's soils is a critical factor in influencing both agricultural and development patterns. In a national context, most of Vermont has poor soils for farming—one factor responsible for the long period of hill farm decline. Furthermore, most valleys in the state have heavy clays that are unsuitable for development and effective septic systems. The last two chapters describe Vermont's soil resources and the environmental legislation that has evolved through the poor use of that resource.

One does not need to be in Vermont for long to see that this state has a vocal and environmentally aware population. Many debates at both state and local levels are concerned with the use and misuse of our natural heritage. Sincere efforts on the part of many individuals and organizations are directed towards preserving and protecting that heritage. But in the rush to protect, some forget that it was the use of the environment which has made Vermont what it is. We strive to protect the small hill farm perched on a scenic hillside, forgetting that those steeply tilted fields often have a serious soil erosion problem. In a similar fashion, we strongly protest a new housing development proposed for a boulder strewn pasture, not realizing that such use just might be the highest and best use of that land. It certainly was not intended for commercial farming!

In this book I've tried to strike a balance. I don't plea for environmental preservation, and I don't defend flagrant environmental abuse. *Vermont's Land and Resources* is the story of Vermont's valuable natural heritage, and how it has been used—and sometimes misused—throughout the history of the Green Mountain State.

It has often been remarked that teaching is a learning experience. And that certainly has been true for me in my years at the University of Vermont. Much of the material incorporated here has come from my students who, over the years, have come from almost every town in Vermont. In many case, following their careful directions, I have visited old quarry sites, fine examples of the work of glaciers, and a host of other intriguing features on the Vermont landscape. I owe a considerable debt of thanks to my students for the things that they have taught me about Vermont.

My colleagues at the University have helped in innumerable ways, but I must thank Canute VanderMeer and Charles Ryerson of the geography department specifically for their assistance. Students who did research on topics covered here include Robert Hartnett, Alex Marshall, Peter Marshall and Dave Orr. Peter Hannah, Hubert Vogelmann, Phil Wagner, Frank Armstrong and Daniel Bousquet are faculty members who provided valuable help or who read portions of the manuscript. Their critical suggestions were appreciated. Many other individuals at UVM gave generous advice, and without their help this never could have been written.

Away from the University, I owe a debt of gratitude to Arthur Hogan and his staff at the Chittenden County Regional Planning Commission, Margaret Garland of the State Environmental Board and State Energy Office, William Gove, Wood Utilization Forester with the Department of Forest, Parks and Recreation, and Brian Stone of the same department. Charles Ratte, State Geologist, assisted me on the subject of mineral resources. The staffs of the Brownell Library (Essex Junction) and the Vermont Historical Society (Montpelier) were of great help, always available to seek out and loan materials. The National Weather Service in Burlington always welcomed me when I stopped by with questions.

Among close friends, William Flanders of Essex Junction helped me to appreciate the problems that many builders face when confronted with current environmental legislation. Hazen Wood's interest in old quarry sites and stone buildings matched my own, and we spent many delightful days together tracking down such features on the landscape.

With the writing of any book there comes a time when the

manuscript must be typed, arriving from the author with cut and paste corrections, typographical errors and undecipherable marginal notes and directions. Cindy Valetta was very patient with me as she typed what at one time I thought was the final draft of this book. But this project could never have been completed at all had it not been for the unstinting help provided by Rita Benjamin, Geography Department secretary.

This book was written at home in a small cubicle which serves me as an office. My family bore the greatest burden as they had to put up with someone who became a recluse as he slaved over his typewriter. There is no way that I can adequately thank my children, Charles and Lany Ann, or my wife, Milly, for their patience and support.

Introduction
Charles C. Morrissey

This book is an eye-opener. Because Harold Meeks explains why Vermont is shaped as it is, his narrative enriches everybody's understanding of the Green Mountain State as a special place of visual beauty and distinct essence.

Like countless others for several generations, I have often felt that Vermont exuded a noticeable character when entering this state from Massachusetts or New Hampshire, but even a deliberate sharpening of the eyes and a concentrated scrutiny of the world beyond the windshield left me puzzled as to why Vermont's topography, looming ahead across a man-made boundary, seemed curiously different. A particular aura seemed evident, but this quality seemed too elusive to be definable. Entering Vermont at Guilford, in the southeast corner, and driving northward on Interstate Highway 91, that mysterious trait seemed to emanate from the terrain. "There is something Vermontish about Vermont," I'd remark pontifically, even if driving alone, and then add humbly, with frustration, "but I can't figure out what exactly it is."

Now, having read Hal's *Vermont's Land and Resources* I know that my perceptions weren't induced by the imaginary figments of a self-confessed Vermont chauvinist who lets affection color his judgment. Discussing the undulating contours of Vermont's physiognomy in Chapter One, Hal notes that "The northern end of the Connecticut Valley Lowland comes to an abrupt stop at the Vermont state line in Guilford, one reason why travelers into Vermont on the interstate highway experience a remarkable change in the landscape as they enter the state." Reading this for the first time I exclaimed, "Aha! There's a valid geographic reason for why Vermont looks Vermontish as you enter at Guilford; I'm not as parachial or as foolishly romantic as I feared."

Hayden Carruth, the much-published poet who lived in Johnson, Vermont, for many years once observed that even the sand and gravel pits in Vermont looked different from similar excavations in adjoining states. Sure enough, Hal has the answer for this peculiarity on pages 38-40 of this book: when the continental glacier was melting 10,000 years ago the valleys were still full of ice as the highlands slowly emerged above the ice cap. Melt-water streams flowing down from these higher elevations carried quantities of sand and gravel across the ice tongues filling the valleys, depositing this glacial outwash on top of the ice along the sides of the valleys. Today these kame terraces, as geologists call them, provide the sandpits I salute with a fondness induced by Hal's explanation of their ancestry as I encounter them in my travels —east of the Passumpsic River behind the Big Boy Restaurant north of St. Johnsbury, west of the Winooski River and Route 2 when approaching Waterbury from the south, west of the Black River heading from Plymouth into Ludlow, and elsewhere.

My home in Montpelier is perched high above the capital city with an unobstructed view of Camel's Hump, Vermont's most dramatic mountain. Thanks to Hal (page 33), I now know why the view through my living-room window offers the craggy profile of a mountain that seems to be lofting itself, western-style, into the sky whereas most mountains in Vermont, unlike Camel's Hump, have rounded summits. "The peak is unusual in that it drops off very steeply to the south, or away from the direction of the ice movement," says Hal. "This appearance was caused by the plucking or quarrying action of the ice as it passed over the peak and worked on the lee side."

He also helps the unwary traveler in Vermont to see and understand features of the landscape that may otherwise escape detection. A drive eastward across southern Vermont, for example, on Route 9 from Bennington to Brattleboro, provides a geologic sight-seeing tour for those who are prepared by this book to recognize what they are seeing. "The motorist in the space of a few miles has ascended over 1,400 feet to the summit of the Green Mountains," Hal asserts. "But surprisingly, there is no concept of being on top of a mountain range. Instead, as the road continues beyond Woodford towards Stamford and Searsburg, the impression is one of a rolling surface of low hills stretching north and south to the horizon, with an occasional isolated higher summit such as Stratton Mountain and Glastenbury Mountain poking their heads up above the general elevation of the hilltops." Hal explains that here one is "crossing one of the most remarkable features in New England—an old erosion surface which is presently being carved up by streams but which still retains a remarkable flatness between 1,700 and 2,000 feet in elevation."

Other excursions throughout Vermont are made more meaningful by the knowledge imparted in this book. If you visit the Rock of Ages Quarry in Barre (actually in the well-named hamlet of Graniteville), you will see exhibited the steam engine of the Barre & Chelsea Railroad (which, ironically, never got to Chelsea, as Hal wryly notes), now an outdoor museum piece but in its era the technological wonder that transported huge blocks of granite down the steepest railroad incline east of the Rocky Mountains when this twisting railroad was constructed in 1888. Sculptors in the granite sheds, spread along the valley floor, transformed those granite blocks into statues and memorials now implanted across America that rightly caused Barre to become known as the granite capital of the world. Hal explains how this short but spiraling railroad was the crucial link between the inexhaustible granite deposits on the heights above Barre and the artistic stone-cutters in the bustling city below; not until the railroad conquered the heights was the granite exploitable, and Barre's rapid economic growth assured.

Despite all the times I have driven around Lake Fairlee, where both my children attended Camp Billings, a summer camp for youngsters operated by the Vermont YMCA, I didn't realize until I read this book that many of the vacation homes surrounding this beautiful lake were originally built to house miners in the nearby copper village at the Ely mine called—suitably—Copperfield. These structures were moved to the Fairlee lakeshore and converted into summer camps. Even the mansion of the owner of the Ely copper mines was transported overland to a new and dignified siting at the north end of Lake Fairlee.

Despite all the times I have driven through the apple orchards of Shoreham and Orwell in Addison County and the orchards gracing the Champlain Islands in Grand Isle County, I didn't realize until Hal educated me that these locations are perfect orchard-country—still cold enough in May so the trees won't bud until the threat of severe frost has passed, still warm enough in September to allow a late harvest before frost occurs in the fall. The surface water of nearby Lake Champlain retains its winter chill well into June and its summer heat well into September, providing apple-growers with the best of two climatic worlds.

Other correlations are revealed in this book. Hal points out that most of the split-rail fences in Grand Isle County are of northern white cedar because the incidence of this timber is especially common in non-glacial till areas, such as the Champlain Islands. The date when farmers abandoned their fields, decades ago, can often be determined by the height of a white pine now towering where once hay was mowed and farm animals pastured. From a low-flying airplane in the autumn, when the fall foliage is reaching its glorious display of beguiling colors, green patches of rectangles, squares, and odd-shaped pieces reveal land that was open until the forest reclaimed it, whereas fence lines are often marked by the yellows and reds of maple trees bordering old roadways. A century ago about two-thirds of the Vermont countryside was cleared of trees; today about eighty percent is forested again, but Hal carefully points out how today's forest is not similar to the one cleared by Vermont's early pioneers. Romantics may have some mental images corrected by this book, even while others, like the distinctive appearance of Vermont at the Guilford entrance, may be validated.

Truly, this book is an eye-opener. Anyone who enjoys Vermont will enjoy accompanying Hal on this geographer's tour of Vermont's natural environment. But in these pages, he goes one step further than a purely descriptive tour. Hal explains the features which he knows so well, not only how they came to be—as with Camel's Hump and kame terraces, but also how they are used. The history of sawmilling and marble and granite and other stones enriches these pages, as does his summary of floods, flood control and the use of Vermont's water for the generation of electricity. Reading this book provides a clear and comprehensive understanding of the environment Vermonters are so impressively eager to preserve.

for
Mom, Dad and Chet
— Many Thanks —

Contents

Vermont's Land and Resources

The Natural Landscape

I have stood on the summit of Mt. Mansfield many times and gazed westward towards Lake Champlain, always impressed with the scene before me, but equally impressed by the complexity of lakes, forests, hills, trees, farmland, highways, cities, and factories—the panorama spreading from Vermont's highest to lowest points.

I have enjoyed water sports on Lake Champlain. The view from the lake to the mountains often is spectacular, but except for the immediate shoreline (often lined with vacation cottages) and the bulk of the green mountain mass rising in the distance, little of the landscape can be enjoyed.

To appreciate the landscape most people like to get up and look down. This is one reason why I suspect that golf course clubhouses are invariably located on a hill rather than in a valley, and why golfers always hike uphill to the 18th hole.

The view from most hilltops in Vermont generally is the same, although the individual features are different. We always will see trees and forests, but their composition is different in the Champlain Islands than near Island Pond. There always is a valley, in most cases occupied by a stream and more often than not a dusty road. There may be a small pond, and if the view is in autumn or spring, perhaps a layer of fog partially obscuring the view.

These are common natural features (although the pond may be behind a dam). The road is man-made and along it there may be a white church and a general store with two dilapidated gas

The Champlain Valley is one of New England's finest dairy farm regions. The heavy clay soils require artificial drainage, as shown by the rectangularity of many fields in the foreground. The picture is looking east from Cornwall.

pumps in front. So suddenly one becomes aware that things are not so simple; nearly every view in Vermont will contain cultural features. And while they often blend gradually into the natural environment, as they tend to in rural areas, shopping centers represent a sudden intrusion into a blended scene. Vermont is still largely a natural landscape with carefully-blended cultural forms. On the other hand, New York City is nearly a wholly cultural landscape—a landscape that some may not like but others appreciate.

Perhaps the most obvious natural landscape in Vermont is the shape of the land—or the landforms. Steep and gentle slopes—undulating surfaces covered with pastures and deep valleys—are always with us. The best way to understand this landform diversity is to take a quick journey around the state. A good place to start is on Route 7, Vermont's major north-south highway on the western side of the state.

Landform Regions (Figure 1.1)

North of Bennington, old Route 7 is compressed into a small valley, especially north of Manchester. In Danby and Dorset almost vertical walls of rock rise on both sides. Close inspection reveals piles of waste rock marking the site of an old marble quarry. On the other side and closer to Manchester, the old roadbed of the Rich Lumber Company still can be seen where it ascended the Green Mountains in 1909. The highway follows a distinctive landform region, the *Valley of Vermont.* On the west side rise the *Taconic Mountains,* and on the east, the main *Green Mountain* range, here with a somewhat unusual flat summit.

Going north, on the west the Taconic Mountains become lower, so that in the vicinity of Brandon there are only a couple of low hills on the horizon. As the highway continues north through Middlebury and Vergennes to Burlington, the landscape is one of rolling hills, although flat stretches occur once in a while as one looks to the west towards Lake Champlain. The *Champlain Lowland* is another distinct landform region.

In some areas of the Champlain Lowland, the actual change to the Green Mountains to the east is hard to determine as the hills get higher and the mountains lower. This is especially true north of Burlington.

Our route now turns east towards the Green Mountains. The Winooski, the Lamoille and the Missisquoi are the only lowland passages across the two roughly-parallel ridges which form the core of Vermont and give the state its major physical identity.

Following the Winooski River on I-89, the highway gradually rises to Montpelier (elevation 520 feet). The Winooski did a good cutting job in making its valley, as the level of Lake Champlain is only 425 feet lower at its elevation of 95 feet.

The interstate highway turns due south at Montpelier and climbs to an elevation of more than 1,700 feet towards Brookfield and Randolph. While there are some flat upland areas, amazingly still supporting a few farms, nearly all the land is sloping, with hill upon hill stretching to the horizon. The Green Mountains tend to dominate the view westward, and are higher than the hills over which the highway winds. This is the *Vermont Piedmont* often called simply the "Vermont Hills." The largest and most diverse of Vermont's physical regions, it has deep river valleys such as the White, Williams, Ottauquechee, Ompompanoosic, Passumpsic and Black. Isolated mountains, such as Ascutney, and Spruce in Groton, are distinctive. The largest valley cut into the hills of eastern Vermont is the Connecticut, with its fertile flat bottomlands still supporting excellent dairy farms.

Tiring of the interstate, one can turn off the main highway and take a roller coaster-like ride across the hills, mainly following small valleys to St. Johnsbury on the Passumpsic River. St. Johnsbury has an elevation of about 600 feet at its railroad station.

Leaving I-89 at Randolph and following a mix of numbered and unnumbered roads across the Piedmont, one finds these elevations (in feet):

Randolph Center	1,384
East Randolph	606
Chelsea	820
Corinth Corners	1,507
Goose Green	823
East Topsham	1,018
Groton	780
Mosquitoville	1,004
Peacham	1,310
Danville	1,430
St. Johnsbury	600

This is truly an up and down journey through a region in which there has been wholesale abandonment of hill farms, and increasing conversion of that land to non-farm residential uses.

North and northeast of St. Johnsbury rises the most remote and isolated area in Vermont. Culturally an area of forest products, logging, poor farms and limited economic opportunity, it was so described and named the "Northeast Kingdom" in a speech by George Aiken in the 1940s. So as not to confuse the physical area with the cultural, the term *Northeast Highlands* is used. Indeed it is highland. Island Pond (elevation 1,191 feet) is on its western border, and several mountains rise to more than

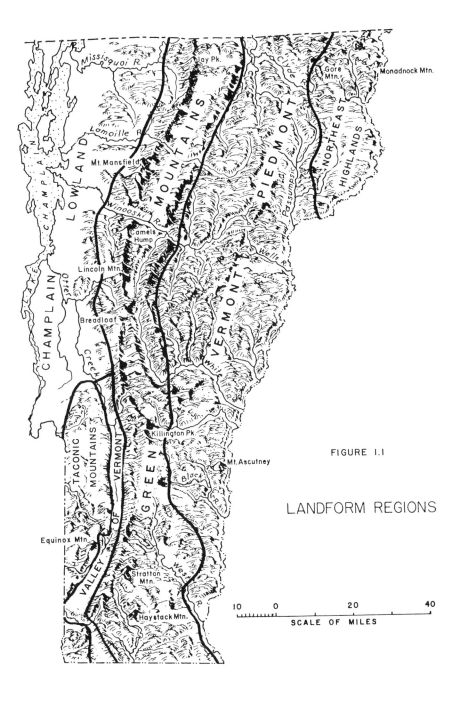

FIGURE 1.1

LANDFORM REGIONS

SCALE OF MILES

3,000 feet within the region. The Connecticut River drops from an elevation of 1,042 feet in the village of Canaan to less than 500 feet in Barnet. The area is so remote that Granby did not have electricity until 1963.

Vermont possesses six distinct landform regions. But the state does not have a monopoly on them because each region extends outwards far beyond the state's borders (Figure 1.2). In fact, all the regions come together in Vermont, giving its 9,609 square miles (15,461 square kilometers) the greatest diversity of landforms in New England.

The Green Mountains represent only a short segment of a mountain system which reaches from Mt. Mitchell, North Carolina to the tip of the Gaspe Peninsula in Quebec. With its Mt. Mansfield (elevation 4,393 feet) Vermont boasts the second highest elevation in the whole chain.* South of Vermont, the Green Mountains are continued in the Berkshires of western Connecticut and Massachusetts. In a similar fashion, both the Champlain Lowland and the Valley of Vermont are northern extensions of valleys farther south, the Champlain Valley in fact related to the famous Shenandoah Valley of Virginia.

The Taconic Mountains extend into New York State, although the actual division between them and the Berkshires is difficult to determine. The Vermont Piedmont of eastern Vermont is widespread throughout the entire New England region and is found even in the American Southeast, although there the topography is much more subdued. There is a remarkably flat area in the rolling hills of New England called the Connecticut Valley Lowland. It has isolated ridges rising above the valley floor. The northern end of the Connecticut Valley Lowland comes to an abrupt stop at the Vermont state line in Guilford. This is one reason why travelers entering Vermont on the interstate highway experience a remarkable change in the landscape as they cross the border.

Finally, the Northeast Highlands of Vermont are nothing but an extension of the great White Mountain granite complex of

---

*The White Mountains of New Hampshire (which contain Mt. Washington) are both geologically and topographically distinct from the Green Mountains.

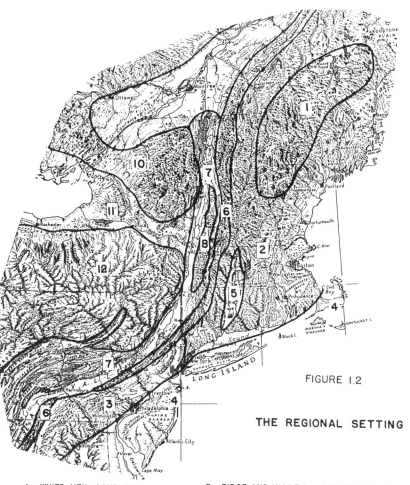

FIGURE 1.2

THE REGIONAL SETTING

1	WHITE MTN. COMPLEX	7	RIDGE AND VALLEY — CHAMPLAIN VALLEY
2	NEW ENGLAND PIEDMONT	8	TACONIC MTNS.
3	APPALACHIAN PIEDMONT	9	ST. LAWRENCE LOWLAND
4	COASTAL PLAIN	10	ADIRONDACKS — CANADIAN SHIELD
5	CONN. VALLEY LOWLAND	11	INTERIOR LOWLANDS
6	BLUE RIDGE — GREEN MTNS.	12	APPALACHIAN PLATEAU

BASE MAP: ERWIN RAISZ

New Hampshire. This is the main reason why the mountains in this part of the state are not arranged in a clear range-like form as are the Green Mountains which form Vermont's backbone.

Mountains

I am fascinated by what many consider trivial geographic details. "Quick, which state has the smallest capital city?", or, "How many towns in Vermont begin with the letter 'W'?" I think the answer to the first is Pierre, South Dakota—although I read recently that Montpelier has that distinction. The second question is easy. No less than 33 Vermont towns begin with the letter W. Winooski is a *city,* and Wells River is a *village* in the Town of Newbury, so they don't count.

There seem to be a lot of trivia buffs like myself. While trivia is a lot of fun, it can become addictive. It's surprising how many questions have been directed to me over the years about Vermont's lowest elevation, longest river, second-highest mountain, and biggest drainage basin. The next few pages, I hope, answer some of these questions.

Ask what the lowest point in Vermont is, and the most frequent answer would be the Connecticut River as it leaves the state in Vernon. Not so; Lake Champlain with a mean level of 95 feet is 105 feet lower. Lake Champlain also drains northward through the Richelieu River into the St. Lawrence.

At 4,393 feet, Mt. Mansfield is the highest peak in Vermont. Add the television antennas and it's a bit higher than that. But there are 100 named mountains in Vermont with elevations greater than 3,000 feet. The highest are Mansfield, Killington (4,235 feet), Mt. Ellen (4,083), Camels Hump (4,083), Mt. Abraham (4,052), Cutts Peak (4,020), Lincoln Peak (3,975), Pico Peak (3,957), Mendon Peak (Little Killington) (3,939), Stratton Mountain (3,936), Jay Peak (3,861), Bread Loaf Mountain (3,823), Mt. Equinox (3,816), Nancy Hanks Peak (3,812), Dorset Peak (3,804), and Big Jay (3,780). Mt. Ellen, Cutts Peak, Mt. Abraham, Lincoln Peak and Nancy Hanks Peak often are referred to simply as Lincoln Mountain. All but two of the elevations over

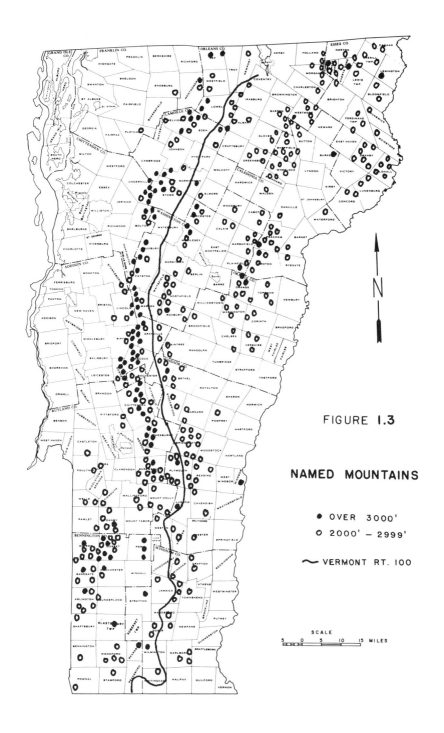

FIGURE 1.3

NAMED MOUNTAINS

● OVER 3000'

○ 2000' – 2999'

～ VERMONT RT. 100

SCALE

5 0   5   10   15 MILES

3,800 feet are in the Green Mountains. Equinox and Dorset are located in the Taconics.

The Green Mountains are actually two somewhat parallel ranges with the eastern range (Figure 1.3) more fragmented and discontinuous, and disappearing altogether in southern Vermont. The Lowell Mountains, Worcester Mountains, Northfield Mountains and Braintree Mountains comprise the main eastern ridge. Route 100 follows the valley between the two Green Mountain ranges.

Few peaks over 3,000 feet are found outside the Green Mountains or Taconics, but they are quite concentrated where they are found. While Mt. Ascutney (3,144 feet) sits in splendid isolation in Windsor, the others generally are located in a northeast trending zone beginning near Barre and ending in Norton and Canaan. Like Ascutney, the rocks here are harder and more resistant to erosion. This is also true throughout the Northeast Highlands.

Lakes

Vermont has relatively few lakes. There are 38 "lakes" (of which five are artificial) and 50 "ponds." The words don't mean too much since Lake of the Clouds on Mt. Mansfield is much smaller than Norton Pond.

Excluding Lake Champlain and its 322 square miles which are in Vermont, there are only 22 square miles of water out of a total area of 9,609 square miles. Not much. Including Champlain, the eighth largest fresh-water lake in the United States, 3.6% of the state is water. Compare this to Maine, 6.9%, New Hampshire, 3.0% and Massachusetts, 5.2%.

Lake Champlain is 107 miles at its maximum length and has a maximium width of about 10 miles in the Burlington-Plattsburgh area. Since the prevailing winds in the Champlain Valley are southerly the long expanse of the lake often can kick up quite a storm. Its maximum depth is about 400 feet, although south of Chimney Point the lake is very shallow, as it also is in the Inland Sea portion east of Grand Isle County. Both those areas have seen accelerated eutrophication in the last 20 years.

The total area of the lake, 490 square miles, is shared by Vermont (322), New York (159) and Quebec (17). There are 80 islands, most of which are in Vermont.

Compared to Champlain, other lakes in Vermont are minor. Memphremagog has 6,317 acres in Vermont and 17,920 in Canada. The other eight largest bodies of water in the state are Lake Bomoseen (2,364 acres), Harriman Reservoir (2,184), Seymour Lake (1,732), Lake Willoughby (1,692), Somerset Reservoir (1,623), Lake Carmi (1,417), Lake Dunmore (1,035), and Lake St. Catherine (910). Woodbury in Washington County has the greatest number of lakes or ponds in the state. The greatest concentration of water is in northeastern Vermont because of glaciation and the poor drainage which results from glacial deposition (Chapter 3).

In 1972 Vermonters were alerted to apparent unusually high levels of mercury in fish caught in the state. Further testing subsequently revealed that mercury levels were normal—fish caught in Sterling Pond near the summit of Spruce Peak in Stowe showed the same concentrations as fish caught in Lake Champlain. Water quality in the state's waters still is very good, although a deterioration has been identified in parts of Lake Champlain and rivers passing through urbanized or important agricultural areas.

Rivers (Figure 1.4)

"How long is Otter Creek?" or "How long is the Winooski River?" Sometimes it is hard to say where a river ends and its tributaries begin, or which tributary is the longest or the correct one.

Were it not for the fact that New Hampshire owns the Connecticut River, it would be easy to say that the Connecticut River is the longest in Vermont. From where it begins to parallel the state until eventually flows into Massachusetts, the Connecticut, with all its looping meanders, is about 200 miles long. In that distance it drops 850 feet and the tributaries feeding into it on the Vermont side drain an area of about 3,900 square miles, or about 41% of the state's area.

The longest specifically-named river wholly within Vermont is Otter Creek at 100 miles. This is followed by the Winooski (90), the Lamoille (85), the White (57), West (46), Passumpsic (43), Poultney (40), Ottauquechee (38), and the Black River draining into the Connecticut at Springfield, 35 miles long.

However, this hardly will solve many arguments because the Missisquoi River is 90 miles long, 74 of which are in Vermont. Is this the fourth longest Vermont river?

If we talk about "river systems," that is, the main river and all its tributaries, we find the Otter Creek *system* totaling 250 miles. That is considerably more than the Winooski (198), the Lamoille (143) and the White (139).

Size of the drainage basin? The Winooski drains an area of 1,080 square miles, and is part of the St. Lawrence drainage area. Otter Creek drains 936 square miles, also eventually into the St. Lawrence via Lake Champlain. Others are the Missisquoi (619 in Vermont), the Lamoille (706), the West (423), the White (710), and the Passumpsic (507).

Irrespective of the rivers, all the water that falls on Vermont runs into three major drainage systems. The Connecticut accounts for 41% of the state's area, while streams in the St. Lawrence drainage basin drain 5,275 square miles—more than 55% of Vermont. Only 429 square miles in the southwest corner are tributary to the Hudson River.

Vermont emerges as a complex piece of land; far more complex than Iowa or Illinois for example. Vermont can be divided into six regions, each with its own distinctive core characteristics. Add the landscape details—piles of gravel along the sides of the valleys, heavy flat clay expanses, distinctive mountain summits, and broad uplands—and the enormous diversity of the landscape is apparent.

How did this come about? The immensity of geologic time processes have been at work to create what we now see. What we see today will be far different in the distant future.

But we can look back and by deciphering past evidence

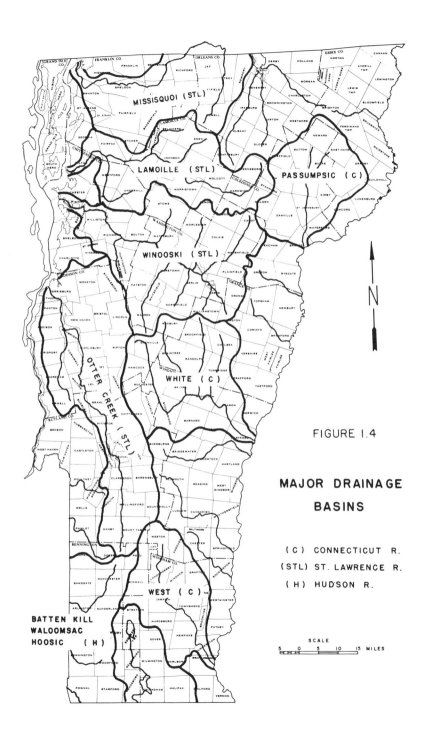

FIGURE I.4

MAJOR DRAINAGE
BASINS

(C) CONNECTICUT R.
(STL) ST. LAWRENCE R.
(H) HUDSON R.

SCALE

5   0   5   10   15 MILES

understand how the present has come about. We may possibly predict what will happen in the future, but that is not the purpose here.

Many forces have been at work. In the broadest sense there are those external forces of nature operating on the surface and the internal activity that is associated with great heat and pressure. Generally speaking, the internal (tectonic) forces are responsible for the rough outlines of the landform regions, while the external (gradational) forces like wind, water and ice are responsible for the detail of the surface.

What to do first is a moot question. Chronologically, rocks come before the forces which shape and carve them. On the other hand, individual valleys, rivers, and piles of gravel are more familiar to many people. Let's take a little hike in the town of Bolton and see where that leads us.

The Work of Running Water

Near the Bolton Valley ski area in the town of Bolton is a small trickle of water emerging between moss-covered rocks. Late in the summer it often dries up as the top of the groundwater table gets lower. Normally, if you hold a tin cup under the flat-topped rock, it will fill in about a minute. Have a drink of this crystal clear mountain water, then turn and follow the small trickle of water as it moves over some rotting leaves and across some small stones. Another trickle of water joins our little rivulet, and our little stream soon is big enough so that it takes a good step to get across it. Upon closer examination, one can see some leaves moving with the current and perhaps, especially after a shower, some movement of the sand and rock fragments over which the stream now is flowing. As more water is added, sands and even small stones are carried along as the water drops more and more as it reaches for the valley below. As the stones rub against each other they gradually become smaller, and as they bump and jump in the water they strike the rocks and soil on either side.

Soon it takes two steps to get across the stream, then three, four, until hip boots are recommended for fishing there. The first brook trout are very small here as their size is directly proportional to the food supply of the stream in which they live. The little stream may have a name now. In this case it is Joiner Brook, which is about four miles long, and in that distance drops 2,800 feet before it reaches the Winooski River in the large val-

ley below. In the summer the fishermen easily can see the sands
and even small rocks moving along in the current as it descends
steeply at about 700 feet per mile. The fishermen rarely see the
brook in March when it is fed by the melting snows. Then Joiner
Brook is a raging torrent, carrying along large boulders which
bang back and forth against its rock walls, and scouring out
some of the smaller stones and gravels which accumulated during
the previous summer.

The junction of Joiner Brook and the Winooski is a favorite
fishing hole. To get to it, walk along the stream by the Central
Vermont Railroad tracks until the river is reached. There is a
deep hole just underneath the railroad trestle where brook trout
often congregate, and the bed of the stream here generally consists of rather small stones, all rounded from their harrowing
passage from the heights above. Most of them are schist, but
there are occasional quartz pebbles from small dikes and, if one
is really lucky, a minute speck of gold might be found.

At the mouth of Joiner Brook is a gravel bar extending out
some distance into the main river. Closer to the bank the material
is coarse sand and gravel but further out on the bar the material
becomes finer in texture. Suddenly the shallow bar abruptly dis-
appears in a dropoff, and the clouded waters of the main stream
swirl by in marked contrast to the much clearer waters from the
brook.

Erosion by Streams

Joiner Brook now is gone, but it has done its job well. It has
carved away (eroded) the land to the best of its ability, and has
delivered the eroded material to its parent stream. The brook's
slope lessens and its flow slows in its last 100 yards, so it has a
harder time of moving the larger rocks in its bed. Many stay in
place, perhaps until the following March, but the gravels are carried further, and the sands, silts, and clays are carried all the
way to the Winooski.

The Winooski is a tired river. Much energy was expended in
carving its valley years ago as the mountains were rising on all

All streams begin as springs. Here water gushes forth at the old Brunswick Mineral Springs located on a kame terrace above the Connecticut River. Three hotels occupied the site, the last burning to the ground in 1930.

At 2,200 feet, this uninspiring church in Woodford is Vermont's highest.

sides, and now it flows serenely from Montpelier to Burlington with a drop of only a few hundred feet in nearly 50 miles. Its gradient is only eight feet per mile and it does not have the energy to move very much of the larger material delivered to it. But it does a reasonably good job of moving the fine silts and clays delivered by Joiner Brook. The Winooski is murky because of the load of silt. With far more water during the annual spring melt, the river moves some of the heavier material but this pace slackens by May so the gravels usually sit for ten months before they are moved along again.

Some of the material delivered by the Joiner Brook eventually will flow to Lake Champlain where the finest particles are spewed out by the Winooski to add sediment to the bottom of the lake. The remainder either end up in the bottom of the river itself, or are deposited on countless fields along the river's course during the annual spring meadowland flooding.

Running water, coursing for millions of years, has shaped the landscape dramatically. Through erosion, narrow valleys have been carved and the overall elevations of the land lowered appreciably. Through deposition, floodplains with many specific features have been formed, deltas have been created, and lakes have silted up and disappeared. Lakes Champlain, Memphremagog and others await the same fate.

All the valleys in Vermont have been carved primarily by running water. Glaciers have modified many of them subsequently but nearly every valley is formed by stream erosion.

As a region undergoes erosion by streams, it passes through stages which grade into each other. "Youth" and "old age" are flat surfaces, but with different characteristics and history. Rougher surfaces, like much of Vermont, are called "mature." Today, most of the state is an area of mature stream dissection (or erosion), but parts of the southern Green Mountains are a noteworthy exception.

The traveler crossing southern Vermont on Route 9 heading east between Bennington and Brattleboro follows the narrow valley of Roaring Brook up into the front range of the Green Mountains. The road twists and turns sharply as it follows the course of the rushing stream, all the time rising rather steeply. Woodford has an elevation of 2,200 feet, and thus boasts the highest church in Vermont, although the church lacks a tall steeple like those in Belmont and Windham. Together, these three locations contain the highest churches in Vermont, but only Woodford is over 2,000 feet. In the space of a few miles the motorist has ascended more than 1,400 feet to the summit of the Green Mountains. But surprisingly there is no concept of being on the top of a mountain range. Instead, as the road continues beyond Woodford towards Stamford and Searsburg, the impression is one of a rolling surface of low hills stretching north and south to the horizon, with an occasional isolated higher summit, such as Stratton Mountain and Glastenbury Mountain poking their heads above the general elevation of the hilltops.

One is crossing one of the most remarkable features in New England—an old erosion surface which is being carved by streams, but which still retains a remarkable flatness between 1,700 and 2,000 feet in elevation.

Figure 2.1 shows the origin of this striking region. At one time southern Vermont as well as much of the uplands of New England was probably a relatively flat plain with streams winding across the ancient landscape. This flat surface of millions of years ago, with few streams, was the beginning of the story, and the start of the erosion cycle through which the area passed. Since this flat plain is the beginning, it is called "youth," and the landscape is young and just starting its development. The present American Great Plains are a current feature of this type (Figure 2.1, No. 1).

As years pass, the streams gradually deepen their valleys and develop tributary systems which eat back into the flatness of the landscape between the major streams. The land is carved up by degrees. Erosion of the original plain into hills and valleys begins, and the landscape becomes rougher. Finally, perhaps only the scattered hilltops are left to represent the original elevation of the old plain. The streams have created the rough landscape of maturity (Figure 2.1, No. 2).

This is not the end of the story. The water still flows across the land, but now perhaps the rivers have cut down into the rock as deeply as they can. When this happens, the ancient streams begin to swing back and forth across their valleys wearing away the rock walls on either side. Over long periods, the valleys become wider, and the intervening hills between the drainageways become smaller until perhaps they disappear entirely. Again, the landscape becomes a flat plain, this time with old rivers winding back and forth across the surface they have created. This flatness is that of old age, not that of youth where it all began.

As the streams swing laterally in their valleys and continue to erode the valley sides, the drainage divides between the rivers become narrower. Most probably will disappear, but sometimes, often because there may be harder rock, or because a particular remaining hill is far from the horizontally-cutting streams, a few isolated remnants of the original youthful surface might remain. On the old-age plain a few hills may remain marring the flatness of the horizon. When the landscape of old age looks like this it is called a *peneplain* (from the Latin, "almost a plain") and the isolated erosional remnants on the surface are called *monadnocks* (Figure 2.1, No. 3).

There are at least two Mt. Monadnocks in New England. One is in northeastern Vermont, the other in southwest New Hampshire. Both are distinctive in that they rise considerably above the surrounding hilly landscapes. It was in New England that this concept of the erosion cycle first was worked out, and the use of the term monadnock is borrowed from Mt. Monadnock in New Hampshire, which is throught to represent a feature formed in the manner just described.

The story of the southern Green Mountains is far from finished. For all this to have happened would require that the earth's surface remain motionless for an eternity of time—a long period without any folding, earthquakes, volcanic activity or any sort of tectonic movement. This is hard to imagine, and the ideal cycle was interrupted many times by movements of the earth's crust.

Much of southern and central New England probably was moved upwards several times through internal forces, and after each period of upward movement the streams would attack the land again and attempt to re-carve it.

Figure 2.1 (No. 4, 1A, 2A) shows what happens if a peneplain with monadnocks on it is uplifted and subsequently eroded. Eventually, the stage of maturity might be reached in the second

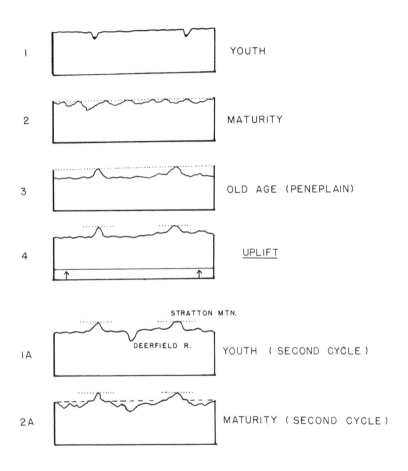

Figure 2.1. *The Cycle of Stream Erosion.* In (1) a youthful plain is begin-ning to be cut into by streams. By (2) the streams have been able to carve a rolling hilly surface of maturity. The tops of the hills are often of the same height and represent the original surface. In (3) the streams have cut sideways to create another plain, but in this case with two monadnocks ris-ing above. This is a peneplain or old-age erosion surface. Stage (4) represents the entire region being uplifted by tectonic activity, allowing the streams to renew their down-cutting activity. Stages (1A) and (2A) show the cycle beginning again, producing landscapes similar to those of the southern Green Mountains and parts of eastern Vermont.

cycle of erosion, with a rolling hilly landscape with nearly all the land in slope. The tops of the hills would represent the level of the old peneplain surface, but monadnocks from the uplifted peneplain would be rising above the hilltops, now looking like mountains rising above the lower-elevation hill summits. Mt. Monadnock looks exactly like this in New Hampshire, as does Stratton, Ascutney, Glastenbury, and several other peaks in southern Vermont.

Looking north, the traveler on Route 9 easily can recognize the surface described. Here, and along the Mohawk Trail in Massachusetts, are classic examples of a maturely-dissected landscape with deep valleys, hilltops of the same elevation, and isolated monadnocks rising above. The southern Green Mountains then are unique, and differ a great deal from the more linear ridge form found in the northern two-thirds of the state.

Deposition by Streams

What happens to all the material worn off the Green Mountains and the rest of New England through geologic time? Simply stated, it eventually ends up in the low points on the earth's surface. Joiner Brook was carving the sides of Bolton Mountain and delivering its material to the Winooski River. The West River is wearing away a good bit of southeastern Vermont, and in the same way supplying the Connecticut. In turn, the larger streams transport the finely-ground rock in the form of sand, silt, and clay to the bodies of water into which they flow.

On any stream there are two places where transported material will be deposited. One is at the mouth of the stream where it enters a large lake, a small pond, or even where a small brook enters a larger river. Depending on any water flow in the body of water that the river is entering, a delta might be formed. The other place is on the floodplain of the river itself (Figure 2.2).

As the word implies, floodplains are flat areas adjoining streams which are subject to periodic flooding. Not only are there individual features on typical floodplains, but the river itself usually has a distinctive course and pattern. Most common

Hogback Mountain on Route 9 west of Brattleboro offers one of the most spectacular views in Vermont. The point marks the place where the highway descends from the Green Mountain plateau into the Connecticut River Valley.

The best place to appreciate the flatness of the Green Mountains of southern Vermont is from the summit of Hoosic Mountain near North Adams, Massachusetts. Here the monadnock of Stratton Mountain can be seen faintly on the right skyline. The Deerfield River flows through the valley in the center of the picture.

in Vermont is the classic meandering stream with wide looping bends back and forth across the flat surface. Beautiful meanders (or loops) can be seen in most Vermont river valleys. Since the stream has a greater velocity on the outside of a bend, and thus a greater ability to erode, loops often will be cut off, and the old river channel left behind as a lake looking like a half moon. These very common meander loops that represent cutoff bends of the river are called ox bows (Figure 2.2 A). Over a period of time they will disappear, first to be swamp and marsh, then to just a softer earthen depression in a field. After the annual spring meadowland floods, the old ox bows often will show up once again as small lakes where the water collects as the flood recedes.

Another feature common to nearly all floodplains are natural levees. These are the tops of the river bank, often marked by a

The Lamoille River meanders through the countryside upstream of Cambridge Junction. Among typical floodplain features are abandoned channels, natural levees marked by trees, and even a drainage ditch or two in the backswamps. The highway in the lower right is Route 15 which avoids the floodplain. On the other hand, the Lamoille Valley Railroad travels on a low embankment through flood-prone areas.

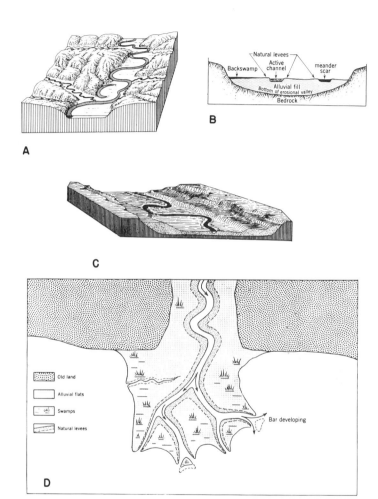

Figure 2.2. *Floodplains and Deltas. A.* shows a typical floodplain valley as is common in Vermont. Notice the ox bow lake and meandering stream course. *B.* is a cross section of a typical valley, and *C.* shows the appearance of stream terraces. *D.* is a delta. (*A* is from A. N. Strahler, *Physical Geography,* 2nd edition, John Wiley and Sons, 1960. *B, C* and *D* are from Finch, Trewartha, Robinson and Hammond, *Elements of Geography,* 4th edition, McGraw Hall, 1960. Used by permission.)

line of trees. The land here is slightly higher and better-drained and during annual floods the natural levees often are above the floodwaters which cover the meadows. It is here, right along the stream, where most deposition of sediment occurs when the river overflows its channel. With repeated floodings, the natural levees are built up higher than the surrounding land. They are bigger in Mississippi where most settlements are located on natural levees, but are distinctive on every Vermont floodplain. Away from them the elevation of the floodplain gradually becomes lower and poorly-drained backswamps are encountered (Figure 2.2 B).

In the backswamp, usually the lowest elevation in the floodplain, the soils often are heavy clays. Use of them normally requires drainage ditches, and sometimes the soils will not dry out until June, delaying the planting of corn which is the major crop on many Vermont floodplains.

Terraces are common floodplain features too. They are flat, better-drained surfaces often five, ten or even twenty feet higher than the backswamp. They represent former river floodplains into which the present river is cut (Figure 2.2 C). Many are used for hay crops, with the corn on the lower floodplain, but on some valley farms the crop patterns are reversed.

While deposition takes place on floodplains almost every year, some material always is carried farther by the river to be deposited at its mouth. In this way a delta is formed (Figure 2.2 D). The best Vermont examples are the streams draining into Lake Champlain, especially the Missisquoi and Lamoille rivers. The Winooski does not have a delta because the wide intervale of the river in the north end of Burlington acts as a settling basin for much of the silt and clay carried by the stream.

Several smaller streams draining into interior lakes have nice deltas. Possibly the best example is on Lake Dunmore where Branbury State Park is located. Modified deltas also are found where a smaller tributary enters a larger, slower-moving main stream. This occurs where the Black River enters the Connecticut.

The features of a delta are similar to those of a floodplain (Figure 2.2 D). Old courses of the river are common, marked by higher-elevation natural levees. In the deltas, the backswamps usually are more poorly-drained than are the floodplain back-

Where it enters Missisquoi Bay the Missisquoi River has built the finest example of a delta in Vermont. Natural levees and backswamps show clearly.
The area is a federal wildlife refuge.

swamps upstream. The Lamoille and Missisquoi deltas are important waterfowl refuges.

Deltas are rare south of Vergennes on Lake Champlain because
the northern end of the lake is rising relative to the southern
end, and the lake water is backing up the river valleys draining
into the lake and drowning them. That is beautifully illustrated
at East Creek which has a classic drowned valley.

Surprising as it may seem, some of Vermont's finest deltas
are not even in water, but sit at higher elevations along the sides
of present valleys. This is due to glacial events, which also account for Lake Champlain's tilting. These events are very recent
when compared to millions of years of stream activity, but are
extremely important in interpreting the present landscape.

The Work of Glaciers

Compared to the millions of years that running water has been cutting into Vermont's bedrock, the work of glaciers is much more recent. Lingering ice masses probably still existed as recently as 10,000 years ago. While there were several major ice advances and retreats during the Pleistocene epoch (the Age of Glaciation), the latest glacial maximum over New England was about 20,000 years ago when ice sheets extended as far south as Long Island—and indeed created Long Island. In the Middle West the ice nearly reached the Ohio and Missouri Rivers. In human perspective, about 10,000 years ago there already may have been almost 20 million people on earth. Many plants and animals had been domesticated, and copper and bronze implements were being produced in the Mediterranean basin.

Vermont mountains usually show rather smooth, rounded summits. In scenic grandeur the serrated peaks of the Colorado Rockies or the Tetons often produce exclamations of awe in comparsion to the reactions to Round Top Mountain in Plymouth. The profile is smooth because ice sheets in Vermont were so thick that they buried even the highest summits. Estimates of the actual thickness of Pleistocene glaciers vary, but they probably were not as thick as the 13,000 feet of ice now covering central Greenland. Whatever the thickness was, the ice was heavy and hard, and it ground away (or scoured) any knife-edge peaks that the Green Mountains once possessed. Studies have suggested that the *average* thickness of rock removed from New

England might have been about 15 feet, but this figure probably is conservative.

The ruggedness of the mountains in the western United States is a result of their not having been buried by an ice sheet. Instead, smaller local glaciers developed in higher valleys and, through plucking and quarrying at the bedrock, ate into and etched the sides of the mountain masses. Left behind today are sharp and jagged peaks, and spectacularly scoured deep U-shaped valleys.

Glacial Erosion

Like running water, glaciers will erode the land and the material eroded will come to rest or be deposited someplace. The farmer clearing his land of the stones which "grow" every spring is well aware of glacial deposition, just as the hiker walking across the smoothly-polished bedrock between the nose and chin of Mt. Mansfield is aware of glacial erosion.

Glacial erosion scours the underlying land. All loose material is removed as the ice grinds across the bedrock. Harder boulders incorporated into the bottom of the ice mass act as pieces of grit in sandpaper. Glacial scratches (striations) are common on nearly every piece of exposed bedrock throughout the state. Lack of striations probably indicates that the bedrock itself was harder than the boulders dragged across it. This often is true in areas of hard granite.

While the overall effect of glacial erosion was to smooth the existing stream-dissected topography, there are some individual features directly attributable to ice scour. Probably the most striking are glacially-scoured valleys, best shown by Lake Willoughby which occupies a glacially-scoured trough nearly 3,200 feet deep. Mt. Pisgah, on the shores of Lake Willoughby, has an elevation of 2,751 feet, while the lake has a depth of more than 300 feet. This is almost as deep as Lake Champlain. Smugglers Notch between Mt. Mansfield and Spruce Peak is a glacially-enlarged-and-deepened former stream valley. Lake Groton occupies a similar glacial trough as does Gillett Pond in Richmond. While the glacially-scoured valleys of Vermont often are not as dramatic

Glacially-scoured bedrock in the Winooski Valley. Glacial striations (scratches) can be seen running from right to left.

Occupying a glacially-deepened trough, Lake Willoughby is one of the finest examples of a finger lake in New England.

A 1924 U.S. Army photograph of Mt. Mansfield clearly shows the effect of glacial scour. Smugglers Notch is to the right. (Courtesy of Noel Ring.)

as the Finger Lakes of New York or Crawford Notch in the White Mountains, there are enough of them to give character to certain parts of the state. Many Vermont lakes, especially those in the northeast, occupy glacially modified basins.

Another distinctive feature is illustrated by the profile of Camels Hump (elevation 4,083 feet). The peak is unusual in that it drops off very steeply to the south, or away from the direction of the ice movement. This was caused by the plucking or quarrying action of the ice as it passed over the peak and worked on the lee side. There are smaller features of this type scattered around the Champlain Valley.

The gouge on the flank of Mt. Washington, New Hampshire, known as Tuckerman's Ravine, more properly is called a cirque. The Great Gulf just to the north of Tuckerman's Ravine is another one. A cirque also is found on Mt. Katahdin in Maine. A cirque is formed through the erosive action of a smaller glacier lodged on the side of a mountain. The Rockies are full of such features. They are most typical of areas which did not experience continental ice sheets as did New England. In Vermont a possible cirque is on the east side of Mt. Mansfield near the Moscow settlement in Stowe. A private lake sits in it and a towering headwall rises to the summit of the mountain. Another one may be on the flank of Belvidere Mountain farther north, and there may be a few others in the state. None, however, are as spectacular as those of the west, or those in the White Mountains and Maine.

Aside from a few glacially-scoured valleys, features like Camels Hump, and possibly a few cirques, specific individual features associated with glacial erosion are rare in Vermont. The main effect of the scouring ice sheets was to smooth and polish the bedrock.

Glacial Deposition

The story is told of the city person who stopped along the road and watched a farmer laboriously picking up stones from his steeply-tilted field. "What are you doing?" the traveler asked. The farmer turned and replied, "What the heck does it look like I'm doing?" The traveler then asked, "Where did all those stones come from?" "The glacier brought them," the Vermonter said, looking rather disgusted. Looking around, the visitor asked, "Where's the glacier?" Now more than a bit irritated, the farmer turned his back and said over his shoulder, "Gone back up to get some more."

As the ice grinds over the landscape it acts as a gigantic plow. But unlike the plow, there is no side of the road on which the material can be deposited. Everything not pushed along by the ice is incorporated into the snout of the glacier, and eventually into the lower layers of the ice itself. Therefore, a moving glacier, like a moving stream, is carrying enormous quantities of material, but unlike the stream, the material can include boulders larger than many homes. These largest boulders, left behind when the ice melted, usually are different from the bedrock on which they come to rest, and are called erratics. Countless large boulders in Vermont fields originated thusly.

Ice sheets move at different speeds depending on their location, depth, underlying topography and a host of other factors, not least of which is the amount of pushing which is going on further north. In 1936 the Black Rapids Glacier in Alaska began to move at a rate of about 100 feet a day, or, if extrapolated, almost seven miles a year—perhaps a world record. If ice sheets covering New England moved at that rate, all of Vermont would have been covered in less than 30 years. Continental glaciers seem to move very slowly, and only after many years of careful measurement in Greenland and the Antarctic will the answer to glacial speed be known. It is easier to determine how long it took a glacier to melt or "retreat."

Glacial deposition often is hard to understand. The glacier is *always* moving if force is exerted in the source area. Even if the front of the ice is melting backwards rapidly because of warmer conditions, the ice mass may still be moving forward delivering material. If, for example, the ice front was at Bennington, and there was a sudden warming of the climate, the *front* of the ice might retreat rapidly to Manchester. But even as the front moved north, the ice *mass* continued to move south and consequently to leave materal even as the location of the terminus was changing.

When the ice melts under conditions of warmer temperatures, the debris lodged in the ice is left behind. Various-shaped deposits composed of different materials dot the New England landscape and have a bearing on present land use. Areas of clay are poor to build on, but often are fine farm areas. Areas of sandy materials are excellent for development, but excessive drainage may hinder agricultural use. Fields studded with large boulders may be highly scenic, but are a continual frustration to anyone who has to plow the fields. Gravel and sand mounds along Vermont valleys provide excellent road-building and fill material, as well as grit to spread on highways after an ice storm.

All glacial deposits are called drift, and parts of Vermont are covered with hundreds of feet of glacial drift. Drift is of two types depending on its composition. Till is glacial drift—a jumbled mass of material containing everything from large boulders to fine clays. On the other hand, outwash is material that has been size-sorted by running water associated with glacial melting. Most sand and gravel areas in Vermont originated as glacial outwash. Outwash usually will be stratified, that is, the material will occur in layers showing the orientations of the water currents that laid down the material.

Glacial drift takes many different shapes, each related to the methods by which it was deposited originally. In the Middle West glacial forms on the landscape are easy to identify because of the general flatness of the bedrock underneath. But throughout New England the surface beneath the glacial drift is rugged and even mountainous. This makes it difficult to identify certain glacial forms easily seen elsewhere, and difficult to unravel the glacial history of Vermont. Furthermore, while the ice retreated over places like Iowa and Illinois in a regular manner from south to north, its New England recession from its southernmost limit on Long Island was characterized by a simultaneous melt back from the front and a melt down from the top as well. This meant that there were tongues of ice in New England valleys long after mountains and hills stood as islands in a sea of white. In the Midwest there were no hills to stand above the retreating and down-melting ice, thus the whole process there is much less confusing.

The most common forms or shapes which glacial drift takes upon deposition are moraines, sheets of glacial till, kame terraces, kettle holes and eskers. There also were many glacial lakes in Vermont, whose history clearly is marked by shoreline features, chiefly glacial deltas. The following pages try to explain what these features are, where they can be found, and what their present importance is.

Moraines are hilly belts with a local relief of about 100 feet containing many poorly-drained depressions. In the Midwest they are commonly distinct features extending over many miles, but they arc hard to find in Vermont. There are three reasons for this: (1) the ice melting down from the higher elevations, (2) ice melting back from south to north, and (3) the rugged landscape. Where moraine landscapes have been identified in Vermont they usually are areas with less slope and relief than the bedrock hills. In Michigan, on the other hand, they are generally areas that are more rugged than the surrounding flat landscapes. In Vermont, therefore, the moraines often are better agricultural areas than in the Midwest.

A moraine is formed when the rate of melting of the front of

The city of Newport at the south end of Lake Memphremagog sits on part of a moraine which once spanned the area between Back Bay (at the top of the photograph) and the main lake. Hummocky topography both east and west of Newport is typical of glacial moraine areas.

the ice mass is just equal to the speed at which the ice is being pushed forward. This means that the ice front will stay in one place for some time; perhaps a few hundred years, and considerable quantities of glacial debris will be delivered by the moving ice to that particular area. On Long Island, the two finger-like projections at the east end represent two belts of hills or moraines. The southernmost point (Montauk Point) is the Ronkonkoma Moraine, and to the north, Orient Point represents the Harbor Hill Moraine. That moraine complex goes under Long Island Sound, but is expressed by Block Island, a range of hills along the Rhode Island coast, and part of Cape Cod. The Ronkonkoma Moraine is responsible for Martha's Vineyard and Nantucket Islands and another part of Cape Cod. This is all very clear on nearly any map.

Dig into any part of the Ronkonkoma Moraine, perhaps at Forest Hills or where the moraine crosses the Hudson River to form the narrows at the entrance to New York Harbor, and there will be a mass of glacial till. Moraines, deposited directly by the conveyor belt ice mass, are composed of unsorted material of different shapes and sizes. Go south of the moraine to Coney Island or Southampton and the material will be uniform sand. The beaches of the south coast of Long Island are composed of glacial outwash (sandy material washed out of the moraine by the large quantities of melting water), and spread out in a gently-sloping apron of material. Later wave and current action has produced the beaches and lagoons of the south shore of Long Island.

Scattered throughout the outwash along this south shore are many holes (or depressions) in the sandy material. Sometimes these are occupied by small ponds, often fairly stagnant. These are kettle holes which represent the spot where a large block of ice became detached from the retreating glacier and became covered by outwash in the same manner that square blocks of ice used to be cut from Vermont lakes and covered with sawdust to prevent melting. Over a period of time the sawdust-covered ice melts and as this happens, the sawdust collapses and a hole is formed. So it was with the buried ice. There are a few kettle hole lakes in Vermont. Miles Pond in Concord, Harvey Lake in Barnet, Danby Pond in Danby and Brunswick Springs Pond in Brunswick probably originated thusly.

At best, moraine areas in Vermont are patchy in occurrence (Figure 3.1). There is a concentration in the northeastern part of the state, and a large area extends along the Green Mountains south of Rutland. Many other small patches of glacial moraine exist but are local in extent. Remember that the ice not only was retreating north but was melting down as well. Several studies have suggested that there was a small halt and then re-advance of the ice in the St. Johnsbury area. The map suggests that this may well have happened.

Kame terraces are common glacial features in nearly all Vermont valleys. They are composed of glacial outwash, usually sand and gravel, but some larger kame terraces along the Missisquoi River and other streams have finer silts and provide excellent farmland. Flat land is at a premium in the state, and the flat tops of such terraces often are an important resource.

As the continental glacier was melting, many valleys remained

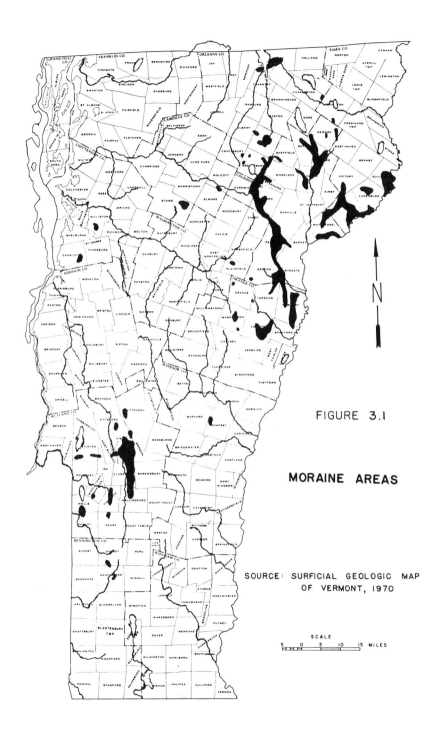

FIGURE 3.1

MORAINE AREAS

SOURCE: SURFICIAL GEOLOGIC MAP
OF VERMONT, 1970

SCALE
5   0   5   10   15 MILES

full of ice as the highlands were being uncovered. Meltwater streams flowing down from these higher elevations carried quantities of sand, gravel and other materials (Figure 3.2). Finding the valleys still full of ice, the streams flowed out on top of the ice tongues, laying down their materials through the normal processes of stream deposition (see Chapter 2). Most of this outwash material was deposited on top of the ice along the sides of the valleys. When the ice finally melted from underneath, the stream-deposited sand and gravel was let down gently as the underpinnings were pulled out. These deposits of loose materials can be found along the margins of most valleys in the state. Important as a source of sand and gravel, the kame terrace is an obvious feature in Vermont. There are few valleys without glacial debris lining their sides, the best examples of which probably are along the White River in South Royalton and Sharon, and along the Winooski in Waterbury and Duxbury. Other kame terraces are common along the Connecticut River in Brunswick, and throughout the length of the West River.

One other outwash feature is found in Vermont, but it is rare. Eskers are long sinuous ridges perhaps 50 feet high and maybe 100 or so feet wide that mark the course of former streams encased in tunnels beneath the glacial ice (Figure 3.2). The longest in Vermont extends along the Passumpsic River between St. Johnsbury and Lyndonville, its course marked by a series of gravel pits and by a stand of pines, frequently found growing on sandy well-drained sites. There are a few small ones in the Champlain Valley near St. Albans, one in Shaftsbury, and another just north of Island Pond. A large esker crosses the Connecticut River in Norwich and generally parallels the river north into Thetford. What few eskers there are in Vermont are rapidly disappearing because their stream-washed gravels are excellent fill material.

Kame terraces are very common along the sides of most Vermont valleys. Eskers usually are located at lower elevations but are rather rare. Glacial till is the most common glacial deposit, mantling about three-fourths of Vermont. It is spread out in a sheet, thicker at lower elevations, and thin and sometimes entirely lacking on the summits of hills and mountains. Where the till is thinner, the rocks normally are larger. Some till is predom-

A large kame terrace being used as a gravel pit in Bolton in the Winooski Valley.

Kame terraces line the sides of most Vermont valleys. They are most commonly composed of sand and gravel, but sometimes finer-sized materials are found. The sandy terrace here along the Connecticut River in Brunswick was cut away in the middle to provide a site for the Brunswick Mineral Springs Hotel. This picture is taken from the New Hampshire side of the river; the Connecticut itself flows at the base of the terrace out of view.

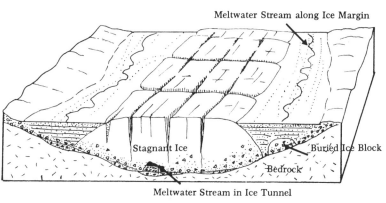

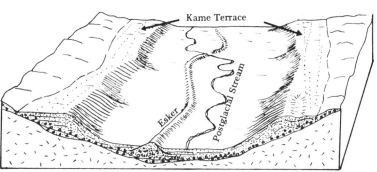

Figure 3.2. *Glacial Deposition in Valleys.* Kame terraces are common along the sides of nearly all Vermont valleys. The diagrams do not show the glacial lakes which often were common to many valleys. From Neil Jorgensen, *A Guide to New England's Landscape,* Globe Pequot Press, 1977.

inantly clay, while other mostly is sand. Till was laid down directly by the retreating ice and dumped indiscriminately on the underlying landscape.

Glacial till "grows rocks" every spring and is a constant problem to anyone trying to farm above the relatively stone-free valleys. While not all till is full of large boulders, its distribution can be seen in the old stone walls which snake across the New England uplands. Till is one of the reasons why there is little upland farming left in Vermont.

Away from the valleys with their floodplain deposits and lake clays, most of Vermont is covered by rocky glacial till. Most farms have long ago retreated to lowland areas, but this farm still exists in East Charleston.

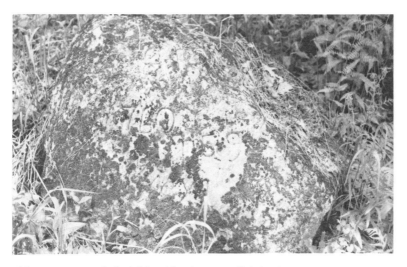

This moss-covered glacial boulder in Cavendish is the original eleven mile marker of the Crown Point Military Road constructed in 1759-1760 between Crown Point, N.Y. and Charlestown, N.H. The inscription reads: "CP 1760 1759 Mile XI".

Some glacial till is so full of large boulders that the resulting stone "wall" is more often than not just a random pile of large stones. This farm is in Middlesex.

The striking glacial delta in South Hinesburg is disappearing rapidly because of gravel extraction. Notice the flat top of the feature.

Glacial Lakes

Most of Vermont that is not covered with sheets of glacial till was once buried beneath extensive deep lakes. Lake Champlain, or its ancestors, may have been deeper than present Lake Superior (1,200 feet). At one time almost half the state was under cold glacial lake water (Figure 3.3).

Conditions of formation varied, but all the old lakes were lowland areas in which glacial meltwaters were impounded because normal drainage was blocked either by a tongue of ice or perhaps a temporary moraine. Rivers had different courses than they have today, and at one time the large lake in the Winooski Valley may have drained south through Barre and into the Second Branch of the White River. Similarly, water impounded in the Lake Memphremagog basin drained into the Lamoille system to the south. Route 14 through Craftsbury follows a striking old glacial drainage channel. Other channels can be seen along the Canadian Pacific railroad along Route 5 south of Crystal Lake.

Some of the lakes were short-lived and features associated with them are obscure and difficult to find. Old shorelines, glacial deltas, and heavy clay soils are the major evidence of these lakes.

There is an old sand beach running through a pasture in Williston, and on a hill just south of St. Albans is a beautiful beach and cliff at an elevation of almost 700 feet; more than 600 feet higher than the present level of Lake Champlain only six miles away. Almost every hill in the Champlain Valley will show shorelines, and they often can be traced along the edge of the Green Mountains. Similar features can be found in many other parts of Vermont, but no bodies of water have been studied as much as those in the Champlain basin and the Connecticut River Valley.

The Champlain Lowland, because of its size, retains old lake features more than smaller valleys, including that of the Connecticut. Smaller valleys have seen more erosion and cutting by the streams occupying them, and many of the shorelines are fragmentary and difficult to find. Old deltas are the best indicators, and there are many flat, rather sandy areas along the sides of river valleys which represent places where streams once flowed

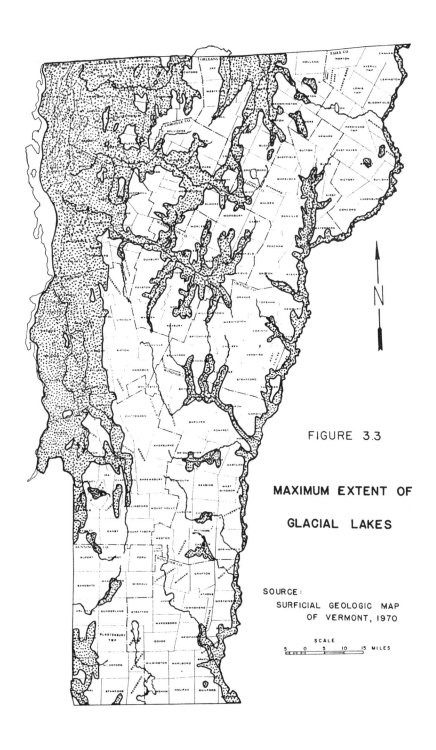

FIGURE 3.3

MAXIMUM EXTENT OF

GLACIAL LAKES

SOURCE:
SURFICIAL GEOLOGIC MAP
OF VERMONT, 1970

SCALE
5   0   5   10   15 MILES

into much higher-level lakes. Some of the best glacial deltas in the state are in North Springfield, Bristol, Hinesburg, Jericho, Essex, Burlington, Williston, Milton and along the Connecticut Valley where most present streams drain into the river.

From Middletown, Connecticut northward there were a series of glacial lakes at various elevations and at various times during the waning of the ice sheets. The series of lakes between Vermont and New Hampshire have been called collectively Lake Hitchcock after the first geologist to unravel the glacial history of the area.

What happened in the Champlain Valley is typical of the history of glacial lakes in general. As the tongue of glacial ice retreated northward it formed a dam blocking drainage in that direction. Higher land to the south, and perhaps moraine deposits, blocked drainage into the Hudson Valley. With the Green Mountains on the east and the Adirondacks to the west, there was nothing for the meltwaters to do but form a lake in front of the glacial mass. The general sequence of events is shown on the accompanying maps which were worked out many years ago (Figure 3.4). Recent studies have modified the details of the history, adding new names for additional lake stages and identifying some of the old shorelines more precisely.

During the early stages in the evolution of present Lake Champlain the waters drained into the Hudson. The earliest outlet was at Coveville, New York, and a deep gorge there shows where waters of ancient Lake Vermont once drained. This early stage is called the Coveville stage of Lake Vermont. There may have been an earlier stage (Quaker Springs) at an even higher elevation in the Champlain basin, but restricted to the southern part of the valley. Shoreline features of the Coveville stage can be found at about 625 feet in the Burlington region, at 600 feet in Hinesburg, and about 400 feet in Brandon.

Notice how the elevations of the shoreline slope to the south. Natural law dictates that a body of water has a level surface, yet it appears that the old lake had a sloping surface. This is because the land has been rebounding from the weight of the ice since its final disappearance. At the Canadian border the earth has risen about 800 feet above what it was some 10,000-12,000 years ago, and the upward movement continues. In another few thousand

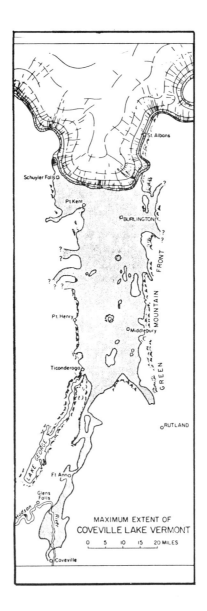

MAXIMUM EXTENT OF
COVEVILLE LAKE VERMONT

0   5   10   15   20 MILES

Figure 3.4. *The Evolution of Lake Champlain.* Three major events in the Champlain basin are represented. The Coveville stage of Lake Vermont is the oldest, the Marine Invasion (Champlain Sea) the most recent.

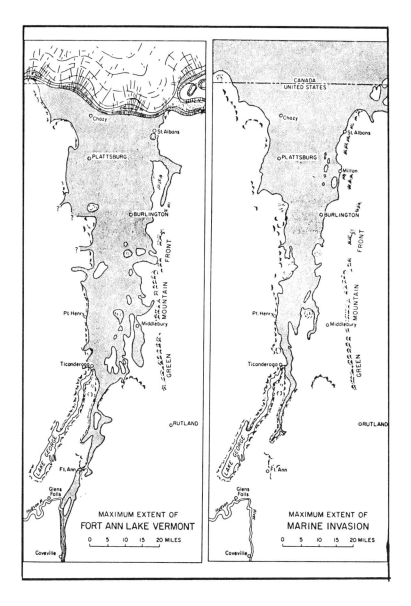

(From William D. Thornbury, *Regional Geomorphology of the United States*, 1965, adapted from D. H. Chapman, *American Journal of Science*, 1937. Used with permission.)

The edge of the Coveville Lake Vermont delta on which the village of Bristol is located can be seen beyond the modern dairy farm in the foreground.

years it may be that Lake Champlain will reverse its drainage once again and flow into the Hudson.

After a period of time, the high water levels of the earlier stage dropped rather suddenly, controlled by a new outlet at Fort Ann, New York. Lake Vermont still drained southward, but the new outlet was lower than that at Coveville. The Fort Ann stage of Lake Vermont has left features in Milton at 580 feet, Essex at 500 feet and on Snake Mountain in Addison at 380 feet. The ice continued its retreat northward, the basin filled with water, and streams continually drained into the lowland from both sides. Finally the glacier melted back far enough to allow salt waters from the Atlantic to flow around the edge of the ice, mix with, and finally dominate the fresh waters of the Fort Ann stage of Lake Vermont. The Champlain basin no longer was occupied by a fresh-water lake; instead, it was now an arm of the sea. No other body of water in Vermont had a salt-water stage, and in this the Champlain Sea is unique.

The skeleton of a whale was excavated in Charlotte many years ago while farmers in Addison County used to uncover marine shells in their plowing. The Marine stage in the valley was unusual but to be expected since the northern outlet of the valley was perhaps 800 feet lower than it is now. Beaches, deltas and other shoreline features were formed around the sides of the Champlain Sea and give an excellent record of this time in the natural history of the region. The shoreline is found at 400 feet in St. Albans, 370 feet in Milton, 300-350 feet at Burlington, and in Colchester Village at 355 feet. In the vicinity of Middlebury, the Champlain Sea shoreline is about at the present level of Lake Champlain (95 feet) and cannot be identified.*

The various stages of Lake Vermont lasted for a millenium from approximately 11,000 B.C. to 10,000 B.C. The Champlain Sea was in existence nearly 2,000 years, finally disappearing around 8,000 B.C. Most sites of the earliest aboriginal occupancy are found on the shorelines of the Champlain Sea.

The history of events is interesting, but pales in significance compared to how these ancient happenings affect present land use in Vermont. Flat sandy delta soils have a great importance as do the heavy clays associated with the old lake bottoms. Other deltas besides those in the Champlain and Connecticut Valleys can be found on the road between Jeffersonville and the Smugglers Notch ski area, and high up along the Gihon River above Johnson in the Lamoille valley. Throughout Vermont most high, level sandy areas along the sides of valleys are either the tops of old deltas or kame terraces. They usually are composed of sand and gravel, and many have been excavated for that resource, or for sanitary landfills as in Williston, Essex, Swanton, South Burlington and other places.

Extensive flat sandy areas are excellent sites for development; construction is easy, and soil percolation is such that septic systems normally operate efficiently. Bristol developed on top of a Coveville delta of the New Haven River is a good example of the association of development and delta surfaces. Better ex-

*See Figure 4.2 for a diagrammatic representation of delta surfaces as they are encountered along Route 15 going east from Burlington.

amples are the mobile home developments in Milton; all again on a flat delta surface. With a few important exceptions, excessively sandy areas are less desirable for farming than areas of heavier soil which retain water better; thus concentrated development is often the optimum use of such sites.

As the streams built their deltas, the finer materials were carried out into the ancient waters. There the silts and clays filtered to the bottom and accumulated, with the finest material in the deepest waters. With the final draining of the old lake basins, these flat, heavy-clay areas have become common and represent the old lake floors. Mud season in Vermont is an annual tradition and the worst mud is found in these areas. Daniel W. Cady celebrates Addison County clay in a poem that first appeared in *Rhymes of Vermont Rural Life.*

ADDISON COUNTY, VERMONT, CLAY

The North Vermonter who would fain
The Equinox Hotel attain;
The South Vermonter, who, in turn,
Would see some Swanton powder burn;
The East Side habitant who tries
To view Vergennes before he dies,
Are each and all compelled to share
The same intensive wear and tear,
And cross, to their extreme dismay,
The Addisonian wastes of clay.

Each time my fliverette goes through
New Haven on the double skew,
Each time my touring chariot skids
Amongst the Dunmore dogs and kids,
Each time I stop to set a tire
In Middlebury's classic mire,
I ask myself, What in the deuce
Can be the town or county use,
The rhyme or reason, anyway,
For such a monstrous mess of clay?

And answers two have come to hand
Which absolute respect command;
The first one says, "These lofty hills,
Which give your motor man the chills,
These hills that make the soul recoil,
The spark plug swoon, the water boil,
Require to hold 'em where they b'long
And underpinning stiff and strong,
And nothing else will make 'em stay
In place but Addisonian clay."

The others says, "That when the snow
Makes up its April mind to go,
When runners scrape and sleds cut through,
And girls get red and "fellers" blue;
When Lincoln teams throw off their loads
And you'd be stuck on other roads,
This pasty blueness acts like grease
And slides you on your way in peace;
Your harness holds, your heart is gay—
You're saved by Addisonian clay!"

These reasons sort of disagree,
But either one will do for me;
For when I'm told a thing is so
It's all I ever want to know;
I now can slip and skip and slue
Through Weybridge and through Waltham, too,
And 'long the heights of Hancock hump,
In Bristol bump and Shoreham slump
And feel I'm favored all the way
In travelling over first-class clay.

Most heavy clay in the Champlain Valley is called Vergennes clay by the Soil Conservation Service and is widespread south of Burlington. With its ability to retain moisture, clay often does not dry out until well into May. Drainage ditches are common as farmers attempt to make the land more workable earlier in the growing season. An advantage of the clay is its ability to retain moisture during a dry year, and its freedom from the stones and boulders of glacial till. The location of farmland in Vermont almost mirrors the land which is *not* glacial till, and the lake basin areas, floodplains and moraine areas probably contain 80% of all the best agricultural land in the state.

In the Connecticut Valley and other smaller lake basin valleys unique laminated clays often can be found exposed along banks and roadcuts. These clays, with laminations called *varves,* once were used in attempts to unravel the time sequence of glacial retreats. Typically, a varved clay will show lighter and darker layers, usually a half-inch or so in width. Each pair represents a year of deposition; the lighter layer being laid down during the winter, the darker layer (containing more organic material) laid down during the summer. So a pair represents one year, and by counting varves from one location to another, an approximate number of years can be calculated. Varve counts now have been replaced by more refined radiocarbon-dating techniques.

Good exposures of varved clays are common in the Lamoille Valley and at many locations along the Connecticut River. Varves can be found along the west shore of Lake Memphremagog, along the Connecticut River in Putney and Dummerston, in Williston along the Winooski River and in White River Junction. Lakes in the interior of the state often were shallower and smaller and had sufficient current so that the clays did not settle out. Also, subsequent erosion of the material by streams may have washed the clays downstream and the deposits have disappeared.

The events of Pleistocene glaciation have had far-reaching effects on the appearance and the land use of Vermont. Agricultural patterns reflect glaciation as do development patterns in densely populated parts of the state. Sand and gravel excavations and sanitary landfills owe their locations to the ice sheets, as indirectly do the wildlife refuges on Lake Champlain. The soil we

In the Champlain Valley and other glacial lake lowlands the lack of stones created problems in fencing the land. Until barbed wire came into widespread use in the 1870s split rail and stump fences were common. Above is a stump fence south of Vergennes, and below a split rail fence in Grand Isle.

Varved clays in many Vermont valleys were once used in attempting to date glacial events. This exposure is in Jeffersonville in the Lamoille Valley.

work, both good and bad, is a legacy of the ice. Vegetation patterns often reflect the character of what is underneath, as does agricultural land use. In short, the recent ice sheets, in scouring the landscape and in covering it with rubble, probably have a greater bearing on what people are doing now with their land than any other natural processes operating throughout geologic history.

Vermont Geology

Several years ago I took a troop of Brownie Scouts on a mineral-hunting expedition along the shore of Gillette Pond in Richmond. As usual, I found their questions more difficult to answer than those of college students. One scout showed me a jagged piece of mica schist she had extracted from a fresh road cut where the town road grader had sheared off some rock. I explained that what she had was a common rock that forms the bedrock of much of the Green Mountains, and I showed her how the minute pieces of mica would reflect the sunlight and glisten when held at a certain angle.

Her satisfaction pleased me, and I became more confident about answering the scouts' questions until another youngster approached with a dull rounded piece of rock scavenged from a small beach. I explained that she also had a piece of mica schist. "But why isn't my piece like Jenny's? Mine doesn't shine like hers does, and it's much smoother."

It was obvious to me that I had to explain weathering, erosion and glaciation all at once to an eight-year old, a task that I attempted, but judging from her expression, failed miserably at. I tried to tell her that there is a great difference between the bedrock in place, and the weathered pebbles, stones and boulders resting on top of it. The loose material is there because of much more recent geologic events. The bedrock itself holds the key to understanding the geologic evolution of what was to become Vermont.

The oldest bedrock on earth may be almost six billion years old; some of these most ancient rocks may form the core of the Rocky Mountains and be widespread through portions of Canada. As far as is known the rocks of Vermont, while very ancient, are more recent in geologic age.

We know that the earth's primary rocks were formed by the cooling of liquid material and that any sort of life on the planet dates from about 600 million years ago—relatively recently geologically. But the stones being picked up from the field by the scouts were placed there within the last few million years, a drop in the bucket of geologic time.

The period in earth history before the appearance of lifeforms is called the Precambrian. Rocks of this age are found in the central and southern Green Mountains, but most of Vermont is younger. In the Champlain Valley, rocks of the Cambrian (500-600 million years old) and Ordovician (425-500 million years old) periods are widespread. The northern Green Mountains contain rocks of the same age, but these differ considerably from those in the valley.

The bedrock of eastern Vermont is younger, but geologically is still very old when compared to that of the western United States. Most of the Vermont Piedmont is from the Ordovician and Silurian (405-425 million years old) periods. The most recent bedrock in the state is represented by the granites scattered throughout the eastern regions. They are from the Devonian age and were formed between 345-405 million years ago.

Nearly all the bedrock of New England is as ancient as the foundations of Vermont. The White Mountains of New Hampshire, related to the granites of eastern and northeastern Vermont, are from the same Devonian period. The youngest series in the entire region are the Triassic shales and sandstones of the Connecticut River Lowland, dating from 230-270 million years.

Given the nearly 400 million years since the last rocks were formed in Vermont, it is difficult to unravel the geologic history of the state. There have been 400 million years of squeezing, breaking, buckling, heating, cooling and altering of most New England rocks. The bedrock is complex. This is in contrast with the much more recent and undisturbed geology of the western United States.

Bedrock Geology

What was eventually to become New England was once the bottom of an ancient sea. For millions of years streams poured their loads of sediment into this ocean, the materials' weight creating great pressures. Cementation took place gradually, and the sediments became hard rock. In its simplest fashion, sand becomes sandstone upon compaction, while clay and silt become shale. If the original sediments were red, yellow or black, the resulting rocks reflect that color. The Triassic sandstones and shales in Connecticut are dark red. Since tropical soils are red and yellow, sediments of that hue indicate ancient tropical climate conditions. Other materials become cemented; gravel is represented by conglomerate while limestone reveals the skeletal remains of ancient marine life.

Depending on the conditions and the nature of the original sediments, compaction produces siltstone, magnesium limestone, dolomitic limestone (or dolomite) and other rocks. It does not occur in Vermont, but bituminous coal is a sedimentary rock formed through decomposition of organic material in swamps.

It is likely that all of New England once was a sedimentary rock area, with many layers of sandstone, limestone and shale. Well over 20,000 feet of limestone alone accumulated throughout the immensity of geologic time. Yet today, relatively undisturbed sedimentary rocks are found only in a few widely-scattered places. In New England the two largest regions are the Champlain Valley and the Connecticut Valley Lowland, and even here the rocks are broken and altered.

What happened is that most of the bedrock of New England has been changed since the sediments became rock. This tectonic activity not only caused the original limestones and sandstones to become metamorphic rocks, but also folded the Green Mountains, created the Taconics and produced spectacular overthrust faults in the Champlain Valley. In western Vermont, many of the original limestones were changed (or metamorphosed) into marble in the same fashion that sandstone becomes quartzite and shale becomes slate. In these cases the alteration produces a harder rock than the original.

Somewhat metamorphosed sedimentary rocks are exposed in this road cut in Shaftsbury in the Valley of Vermont.

In central and eastern Vermont, metamorphism has been extreme, and the predominant rock is a metamorphic one called schist. Vermont easily could become the "schist state" as New Hampshire is the Granite State! Depending upon the minerals in the schists, there is garnet schist, mica schist, and more commonly, chlorite schist. A close relative to schist is a soft, fibrous flaky rock called phyllite.

The last sediments probably were laid down during the Ordovician period. The Ordovician limestones and shales in the Champlain Valley are rich in fossils which indicate the age of the rocks.

At the end of the Ordovician period crustal deformation took place. Great pressures developed, culminating in a mountain-building period in geologic history called the Taconic Orogeny after Vermont's Taconic Mountains.

The tectonic activity began in the east and moved west, constantly increasing in intensity. The former sedimentary rocks of

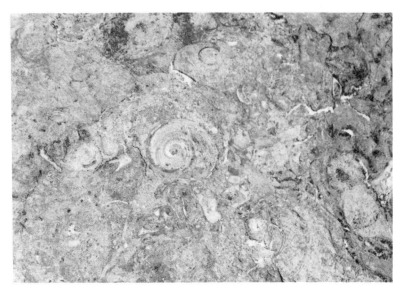

Some Vermont limestones contain many fossils. This is one reason for the enduring popularity of "Black Marble" from the Isle La Motte quarries.

eastern Vermont were metamorphosed by pressure and heat, and localized folding and breaking (faulting) of the rocks occurred. The copper deposits in Vershire, Corinth and Strafford may have been formed at this time, and the zone of slate from East Montpelier to Northfield represents shales which were metamorphosed close to the eastern border of the Green Mountains.

One of the most difficult lines to draw on a map is the true eastern boundary of the Green Mountains. One reason is that there is seldom a sharp break in the metamorphic rocks, and the surface topography changes only gradually. The basic structure of the Green Mountains, however, probably was formed at this time. The mountains generally represent a very complex anticline, or upward-folded mass. But because of the scale, there are many small anticlinal and synclinal (downward-folded) structures throughout the whole area. The valley followed by Route 100 is

The Glen Lake fold near the west shore of Lake Bomoseen shows how the rocks of the Taconics were subjected to great pressures as the mountains were being formed.

mostly a synclinal valley, while the mountains on either side represent complex anticlines.

One of the most catastrophic events in geologic history took place in southern Vermont and geologists still are trying to determine exactly what happened. The geologic map (Figure 4.1) shows that the summit of the Green Mountains from north of Rutland to the Massachusetts line consists of Precambrian rocks, while the rest of the system is largely Cambrian or younger.

What happened to the Cambrian rocks of the southern Green Mountains? Study the map. The Taconic Mountains, now separated from the main Green Mountain mass by Route 7 and the Valley of Vermont, represent the old top of the southern Green Mountains. Whether the Taconics slid off the Green Mountains, or were pushed still is not entirely clear. Some experts even suggest that the Taconics are upside down! Any geologic feature which was shoved, pushed, folded or otherwise put on top of

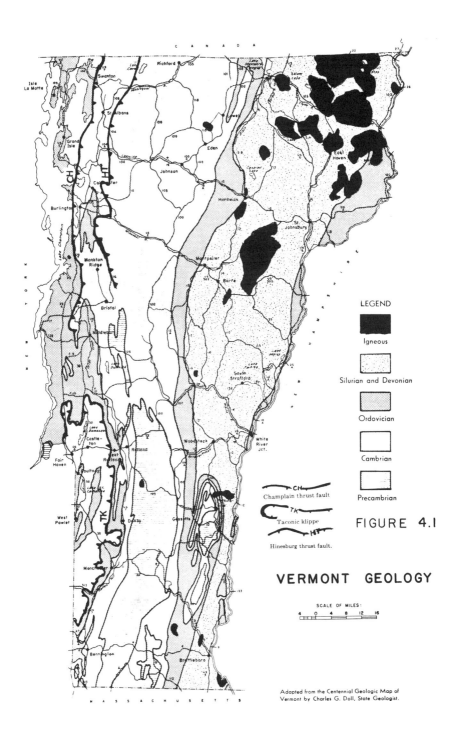

LEGEND

Igneous

Silurian and Devonian

Ordovician

Cambrian

Precambrian

CH
Champlain thrust fault

TK
Taconic klippe

HT
Hinesburg thrust fault.

FIGURE 4.1

VERMONT GEOLOGY

SCALE OF MILES:
4 0 4 8 12 16

Adapted from the Centennial Geologic Map of
Vermont by Charles G. Doll, State Geologist.

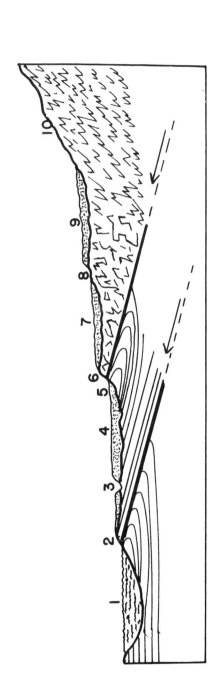

Figure 4.2. *Diagrammatic cross section of geology and surface deposits, Lake Champlain to Mt. Mansfield.* 1: Lake Champlain 2: Champlain thrust fault 3: Winooski River 4: Champlain Sea delta 5: Essex Junction 6: Hinesburg thrust fault 7: Fort Ann delta 8: Jericho 9: Coveville delta 10: Mt. Mansfield. Not drawn to scale. Numbers 4, 7, and 9 are discussed in Chapter 3.

rocks of a different age, usually younger, is called a klippe. The Taconic klippe is world famous.

The northern part of the Green Mountains did not suffer the indignity of losing its top as happened to the southern part. Instead, the waning tectonic pressures pushed parts of the mountains on top of the sedimentary rocks in the valley to the west. These low-angle or overthrust faults are classic and their effect produces many of the hills and local relief in the Champlain Lowland.

Two major faults distinguish the northern Champlain Valley, each representing where older rock from the east pushed over the younger sedimentary series in the lowland (Figure 4.2). Farthest west and bordering Lake Champlain for much of its length is the famous Champlain fault, best exposed at Rock Point in Burlington. Here older Cambrian rocks (the Dunham dolomite) sit on top of younger shales of the Ordovician period.

The overthrust fault at Rock Point in Burlington is one of the best examples in the world of this type of feature. Older and harder Dunham dolomite rests on top of younger Utica shale.

Snake Mountain (1,287 feet) rises in splendid isolation above the town of Addison in the fertile Champlain Valley. It marks the location of the Champlain fault and can clearly be seen from Route 22A (below).

Shelburne Bay dominates the center of this photograph. Burlington is in the upper right. The Champlain fault runs from Shelburne Point on the left to Lone Rock Point in the center background.

Up and down the Champlain fault are isolated hills representing places where the overlying harder Cambrian rock has not disappeared. These klippes are represented by Arrowhead Mountain and Cobble Hill in Milton, Pease Mountain and Mt. Philo in Charlotte, and largest of all, Snake Mountain in Addison. Snake Mountain was called Grandview Mountain when it had a hotel and observatory on its summit.

East of the Champlain fault is the Hinesburg fault (once called the Mountain Border fault). Along this line, the metamorphic rocks of the Green Mountains overlay the younger Cambrian and Ordovician of the Champlain Lowland. Sometimes the western border of the Green Mountains is drawn along this line since it separates the sedimentary and metamorphic rocks. Yet in topography there is little change. Going east of Burlington on Route 15 the fault can be seen as a cliff-like hill in Essex Junction, but there is little change in the appearance of the land.

The Green Mountains are a complex anticlinal structure of metamorphosed Cambrian and Precambrian rock, largely schist. The Taconics, sliding off the Green Mountains years ago, are Cambrian metamorphics, with associated slate areas and marbles in the Valley of Vermont. The Champlain Lowland, with gently-folded and broken sedimentary limestones, shales and sandstones is of Ordovician and Cambrian age. The Vermont Piedmont defies generalization. Most of it is metamorphosed Ordovician with some Silurian rocks.

What causes the confusion in eastern Vermont is volcanic activity, and while Vermont probably never had any classic volcanoes, volcanic activity was important in shaping the appearance of this part of the state.

Hills of Granite

In the Connecticut Valley Lowland the traveler on route I-91 always is conscious of angular hills that rise directly from the flat floor of the valley. Just north of Holyoke, Massachusetts, the highway itself cuts through the edge of one of these elevations (Mt. Tom). Meriden Mountain and East Rock and West Rock in New Haven, Connecticut are similar features. Most of these ridges represent lava flows which were spewed out on an ancient landscape. Subsequently deeply buried with sediments (to become sedimentary rock), the land was tilted, erosion occurred, and the flows are now exposed at the surface. This hard rock forms the major relief features of central Connecticut and Massachusetts.

Any rock which cooled and solidified from a molten condition is referred to as an igneous rock, and lava, because it cooled originally on the earth's surface, is described as an extrusive igneous rock. Because the material cooled fairly fast, the individual crystals in most lavas are very small, thus the rock is very fine-grained and homogeneous in appearance.

On the other hand, most molten material never reached the surface, but cooled very slowly deep within the earth. Granite is the most widespread intrusive igneous rock and is common throughout eastern and northeastern Vermont. With slow cooling, mineral crystals become larger so that in most granites the appearance is much coarser than with fine-grained lavas.

There are many varieties of granitic-type rocks, mainly related to their chemical composition and the size of the crystals. Some granites, such as those at Barre, are rather fine-grained; others are much coarser and therefore somewhat weaker and unsuitable for monumental work. Most granites, however, are usually harder and more resistant to erosion than surrounding rocks. In eastern Vermont most higher-elevation areas are predominantly granite. The geologic map shows this well. Northeast Vermont is an offshoot of the New Hampshire granite areas, and its generally higher elevation and mountainous topography reflect the harder rock of which it is composed.* Similarly, the higher elevations around Lake Willoughby, in Craftsbury, and extending through Woodbury, Groton, and Orange are related to granite. Mt. Ascutney is an isolated granitic mountain in southern Vermont, and granite was quarried for many years on the side of Black Mountain in Dummerston near Brattleboro.

The Devonian period may have seen the formation of the major granites, but the constant metamorphism of Vermont's rocks was an ongoing process throughout the Cambrian and Ordovician periods, and possibly the Silurian as well. The pressures associated with the Taconic Orogeny, the thrust faulting in the Champlain Valley, and the folding of the Green Mountains involved an incredible amount of heat. Rocks were melted, and pressures were intense. As a result throughout the brittle crust of the state small igneous intrusions are common. There is hardly a road cut in Vermont without a finger-like projection of quartz or other material intruded into the surrounding rocks.

Many rocks were melted and remelted, and those close to the major granitic intrusions altered so as to become undecipherable. In many cases, mineralization occurred, with the mineral formation in the metamorphics of subsequent use to mankind. Gold, lead, silver, iron, copper, and uranium all were formed in Ver-

---

*The great Nulhegan Basin of Essex County is an exception. Here the granitic rocks are weaker than the surrounding metamorphics.

mont's metamorphic rocks. Asbestos, soapstone and talc are associated with metamorphism. For many years certain localized areas were important for a variety of mineral resources. The following chapters look at the history and present development of Vermont's mineral industries.

Metallic Minerals

Like those in other New England states, the hard metamorphic rocks of Vermont have been mined relentlessly in a never ending search for their hidden treasures. Although little of much value ever has been produced, mining and quarrying have contributed their share to Vermont lore over the years. Today certain towns and villages derive their present economic and social characteristics from the mineral industries.

In 1845, C. B. Adams, the first official Vermont state geologist, wrote this introduction to his *First Annual Report:*

> Vermont, unlike the neighboring states, being deprived by nature of foreign commerce, must look within herself for the sources of wealth. Already has the enterprise of individuals developed mineral treasures, which have, while enriching their possessors, conferred prosperity on several of our villages. Marble, iron and manganese have richly rewarded skill and enterprise, while most of our mineral wealth yet lies concealed beneath the surface, to be revealed, not by any mysterious and unintelligible arts, but by simple methods, which are the result of practical knowledge. . . .

Adams proceeds to give a sketch of the then-understood bedrock geology of the state, with several pages devoted to discussing mineral resources, their occurrence, production, and use.

Minerals are classified as either metallic or non-metallic. The difference is largely one of the luster of the mineral after separation from the rock. Metallic minerals will show a metallic sheen; iron, copper, lead, gold, and silver do this. One the other hand, a lump of asbestos or talc hardly glistens. The only metallic minerals to have much importance in Vermont were iron, copper and gold. Non-metallic mineral production still is important, as witnessed by the asbestos operations in Lowell and several talc mines.

Metallic minerals are associated normally with areas of metamorphic rock. In Vermont, that means the whole state except for the largely sedimentary Champlain Lowland and the generally granitic (igneous) Northeast Highlands.

Mines and Minerals

In the *First Annual Report of the State Geologist,* Mr. Adams notes the existence of anthracite coal in Norwich, earlier reported in *Thompson's Gazeteer.* He then says that:

> Dr. Davis, who has given much attention to the minerals of this vicinity, informed us that about half a bushel (of anthracite coal) was obtained from thin layers . . . of slate in the northwest part of the town.

As is common in the early reports, the discussion is continued in the *Second Annual Report* (1846), with the following quoted verbatim:

> Norwich. We mentioned last year, giving the authority of Dr. Davis, that a small quantity [of anthracite coal] had been obtained in thin layers. Since then we have received the following statement from a gentleman, whose name, if we considered ourselves at liberty to give it, would be regarded as ample guarantee for what he actually states.
>
> "About eight or nine years since, I heard the rumor of anthracite having been found in Norwich, Vt., and in company with Prof.——, visited the farm and 'locality,' where it was said to have been discovered. The rock is bright mica slate; on the general declivity of the hill, a few miles back from the Connec-

ticut river; the locality right *at* the surface—with enough of digging to shew some fresh fractures of the rock—but we found
there nothing that bore any resemblance to anthracite. On our
return to the farm house, we were shown specimens of genuine
Pennsylvania anthracite in a box. There can be no doubt whatever, that the whole matter is a gross deception, and we learned
then, there was a close connection between the discovery of
the coal and a desire to sell the farm, preparatory to a removal
west."

On the other hand, however, we have received the following
account from Dr. Davis.

"The statement I gave you, was from *my own personal* examination, at two or three different visits to the location, and
I can say decidedly, that the specimens which I dug from the
rock could not have been placed there by human agency, unless there is some more subtle and mysterious slight of hand
than has hitherto been exhibited to the public. Every appearance indicated to me, that the fragments of coal were forced
into crevices by subterranean combustion, and they had evi-
dently occupied the position in which they were found for a
series of years.

"Mr. Smith, who was owner of the place at the time, and
who made the discovery, was a member of the congregational
church, and a very candid and respectable man, altogether
above any suspicion of intrigue or speculation, and at the time,
had no anxiety to sell his farm, but actually leased this location
to an agent of the copper company, for a term of years to be
wrought upon shares, and afterwards sold the place to another
person at a moderate price previous to the expiration of the
lease."

Whether we have cleared up the subject by introducing these
communications may admit of some question.

There is no anthracite coal in Vermont today and probably
there never was any. But the record books tell a different story.
Nearly 1,000 mineral occurrences have been reported, most of
which never amounted to much or were a figment of the then-
land-owner's imagination. While historic records show gold in
Shoreham next to Lake Champlain, we now know that such an
occurrence is impossible.

The following mineral resources have been reported at one
time or another over the years:

Metallic	Non-Metallic
Manganese	Garnet
Iron	Mica
Copper	Graphite
Lead	Talc
Tin	Asbestos
Gold	Kaolin
Chromite	Pegmatite (a complex igneous
Silver	intrusion with large mineral
Uranium	crystals)
	Oil
	Natural Gas

Iron was important in the era before railway communication made the state less dependent on its own resources. Copper was mined intermittently from the late 18th century until the 1950s. Vermont once was an important copper producer. While small amounts of most of the other metals listed above either were located or actually mined, gold deserves special mention because of the romance associated with its occurrence.

Gold in the Hills

Over the years, gold has been reported in at least 50 Vermont towns. No other metal has been so widely, and probably erroneously, reported. Extremely improbable occurrences have been noted in the sedimentary rocks in the Champlain Valley towns of Bridport, Shoreham, Benson and West Haven. In the other 46 towns, gold perhaps is a possibility since they are all in the metamorphic or igneous areas, but the reports probably are more wishful thinking than an actual occurrence. What was reported as gold in many areas probably was pyrite, or "fool's gold." Curiously though, a map of reported gold findings correlates with the most probable area for the metal and maybe some of the old sightings should not be disregarded impatiently (Figure 5.1).

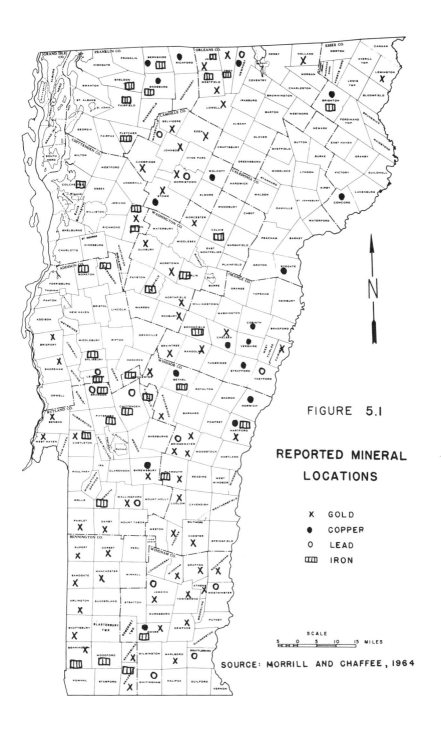

FIGURE 5.1

REPORTED MINERAL
LOCATIONS

X   GOLD
●   COPPER
O   LEAD
▥   IRON

SCALE

5   0   5   10   15 MILES

SOURCE: MORRILL AND CHAFFEE, 1964

In 1845 the state geologist apparently suggested some caution when he reported that, "Iron Pyrite is frequently mistaken for gold. . .", and in discussing a reported discovery of gold in Somerset, noted, "It has been suggested that the gold had been placed there for purposes of speculation." Adams concluded his brief three-paragraph treatment of the subject by trying to quash speculation of a major gold find in Newfane:

> A specimen of gold weighing several ounces was lost in Newfane many years since, by a gang of counterfeiters, when suddenly routed, as is now supposed by those best acquainted with the facts; and having been subsequently found, it has been quoted as an example of the native gold of Vermont.

After the 1845 and 1846 *Reports of the Vermont State Geologist* there was no complete inventory of the state's geology and mineral resources until an epic two-volume report produced in 1861. Nearly a thousand pages were devoted to an exhaustive compilation of all the known knowledge of Vermont's natural resources, even to a discussion of the relative value of human and cow manure for fertilizer. This report was referred to often as *Hitchcock's Geology of Vermont* because three of the four authors commissioned by the State Legislature were surnamed Hitchcock. The report actually was done under the direction of Mr. Albert D. Hager who compiled the many reports, probably did the editing, and saw to the publishing of the work. Hager, of Proctorsville, Vermont, also wrote much of the material, although his name seldom is mentioned.

In contrast to the earlier work, the 1861 *Report* devotes more than seven-and-a-half pages to gold, obviously in response to the awakening public interest in the subject born on the westerly winds from California where many Vermonters had gone to lose their shirts. Lead gets two pages, silver two, and copper, which was far more important, deserves all the ten pages assigned.

The first reported gold in Vermont was the aforementioned Newfane Lump, discovered in 1826, and the reported weight in the 1861 *Report* is 8½ ounces—no mean nugget by any standard.

In 1851 real gold was discovered in Plymouth and neighboring Bridgewater, which led to a locally important gold rush. The discovery of reasonably large amounts of the precious stuff in

Vermont awakened interest, and there were a few years of feverish activity as every farmer became an amateur prospector in his free time. Most reports of gold in the state came after 1850. It is easy to imagine how appealing the visions of quick wealth must have been to the farmer struggling on his rocky hillside. Gold was reported quickly at Stowe (where Gold Brook testifies to this), Granville, Worcester and, as the 1861 *Report* says, "and etc." The "and etc." includes another 35 or so towns in Vermont. A source as official as the Vermont state geologist specifically encourages prospecting in the "talcose-slate" areas of the state:

> That gold is scattered over extensive districts in the State, and will be found in other places than those now known to contain the precious metal, is very evident; and it is not at all improbable that other nuggets may be found, equaling in size and value the one found in Newfane.
> The largest lump found in Plymouth was valued at fourteen dollars, and was found in Reading Pond Brook, on the claim of Messrs. Sawyer & Eddy; and the largest one found at the Five Corners was valued at nine dollars and thirty cents, and was from the claim of Wm. Hankerson, Esq.
> (1861 *Geology of Vermont,* page 849)

While the Plymouth Gold Rush may have been blown a bit out of proportion, the discovery of gold in the region probably is the best-publicized event in the Vermonter's constant attempt at trying to find the full bucket at the end of the rainbow.

The actual date when the Plymouth region reported gold is a bit questionable. In 1851 probably a nugget was found in Buffalo Brook which drains into Echo Lake near Tyson Furnace. In any event, by 1855 Buffalo Brook had become Gold Brook and had lured a '49er by the name of Virgil Woodcock. Woodcock put in a sluiceway and is reported to have taken out more than $2,000 before he died.

While the sands and gravels of Buffalo Brook were being worked, others were looking for the mother lode, and there was a great deal of digging in the "Five Corners" area. The Plymouth Mining Company, established in 1853, had extracted some gold there before it failed in 1858. In 1860 it was reported that seven companies were working Buffalo Brook and there were 16 dams and sluiceways. It got so bad that year that some town roads were being washed out by the operations. Persistence was the lot of the treasure seeker, and a poor Mr. Allen who had returned recently from California complained that "he hadn't had a dry foot in ten days." But Allen also confided that he was averaging $1.25 a day and had "high hopes." With the prevailing wages of time, he could have been earning more in a local tannery. The same year another Vermonter, deeply mired in Gold Brook, proudly affirmed that he had taken out $7,000 worth of gold in the past year. That prosperity, which worked out to something like $19 a day, was enough to help continue the frantic activity.

Random digging and panning continued in the area for many years, with little profit being shown by most of those so engaged. In the 1880s the Rooks Mining Company was incorporated by Charles Rooks and several others to look for the mother lode. A large boarding house was built to lodge the prospectors. A shaft more than 50 feet deep was sunk. It promptly filled with water and a 300 foot horizontal drift had to be dug, mainly for drainage, to intersect the bottom of the shaft. A small mill was constructed, and rails laid for the tram cars. In 1884 the Rooks Mining Company of Plymouth reported that in six months it had taken out $13,000 worth of gold at a cost of only $5,000 and dividends were paid at the rate of 17¢ a share. Since this was a better balance sheet than any California company ever had reported, the figures were obviously inflated. It is probable that the Rooks Mining Company was broke, and hoped that favorable publicity would lure some unwary speculator. It must have worked because in 1885 Boston interests bought the property after documenting that profits of 131% on capital investment indeed had been realized. This venture soon collapsed and in 1887 the entire property was sold for $12,500 to Henry Fox. Mr. Fox died in Brattleboro in 1919 and had lived alone on the old workings for almost 40 years. Perhaps he made enough to keep himself in food and clothing, but with his death, the romance of the famous (for Vermont) gold rush died.

No one ever will know how much gold was taken out of the talcose-slate rocks of Windsor County. Not much probably, but quite possibly more than ever was extracted from any other place in Vermont. There still is gold in the hills, but little to satisfy the modern treasure seeker who might find a few flakes after several hours of work. Any stream in the broad north-south zone of gold reports possibly will yield a few grains. For income, however, it might be more profitable to pick up discarded beer cans and bottles with a five-cent deposit along Vermont roadways.

Silver and Lead

There is an old story about Richard Lawrence of Chester. As a boy, he was reputed to have helped an aged traveller going through town on horseback. Grateful for the help, the traveller, who claimed to be Spanish, told the boy that someday he would be rewarded richly. He said that his saddle bags were full of silver dollars that he had taken from a cave in Wallingford. The traveller added that when he was young, he and other Spaniards came to Vermont and discovered a large lode of silver in a mountain in Wallingford. They worked this for a long time, smelting the ore and coining the metal. They replaced the silver coins in the excavation, then sealed the adit to secure the treasure.

They carried what they could in their saddle bags and returned to Spain, leaving behind large amounts of silver bars and coins. The treasure was to remain there until one of them needed more silver, when he would return for another load. The old Spaniard claimed that he was the last living member of that hardy crew and would never return. Young Lawrence was sworn to secrecy, and told to wait a reasonable time to be sure that the old Spaniard had died. Then he could claim the buried treasure.

After waiting a reasonable time, Lawrence told some friends and they went to find the treasure. But horrors! The mouth of the adit could not be found, probably having been covered by a rock slide. Money was raised, powder purchased, men employed, and repeated blasting attempts were made in the area of the "White Rocks" in search of the elusive silver. To no one's great surprise, it never has been found. Other stories, stemming from the same or some different yarn, involved Captain Kidd and Bristol (substituting for Wallingford).

In 1861, the state geologist informed the reader that: "Notwithstanding the many reports of silver mines that reached our ears during the progress of the survey, we have never been able to learn the precise locality of even one workable mine of silver in the State." But, "before closing our remarks upon silver, it may be well to say that it is usually found associated with the ores of lead that are found in metamorphic rocks, and that in the lead from Thetford, traces of silver were found. . . ." An analysis of lead ore from Morrisville showed it to contain four *pounds* of silver per ton of lead. Since lead ores in Cornwall, England, were running about four ounces to the ton, some optimism was expressed that if indeed Vermont lead deposits had so much silver, extraction could be paid for easily on the basis of the silver alone.

Lead once was mined at Thetford. Six openings were made along a small vein which rapidly pinched out, and a 100 foot shaft was dug at one time to the ore body. All lead appears to have been removed well before 1860 at which time the works were full of water. Another small lead mine was opened up in Norwich along the Thetford line, apparently on the same narrow vein, but never amounted to very much. In 1861 the "mine" in Morristown consisted of an "excavation about 10 feet long and eight feet deep," hardly enough to be dignified by such a term. Lead has been found in Bridgewater, associated with the gold workings, and has been reported from Brattleboro, Whitingham, Jamaica, Chittenden, Waterville, Belvidere, Brandon, Leicester, Wallingford and Newport.

Traces of many common metallic minerals can be found in Vermont's metamorphic rocks. There have been reports of tin, and a tin "mine" was once located in Westport, New York across Lake Champlain, giving rise to early speculation that the ore body also would outcrop in Vermont. If there is, or was, any tin in Vermont, it probably is associated with the copper deposits because the two metals often are found in the same ore body as in the case of Cornwall. The copper deposits worked in Vermont often produced negligible amounts of tin and silver.

Copper and Copperas

There are two Copperas Hills in Vermont: one in Shrewsbury, and one in Strafford. There were copper mines in Vershire, Corinth, Strafford and Richford. While the mine in Richford never was too important, those in the three towns in Orange County once may have accounted for a good proportion of total United States copper production before the famous Lake Superior mines opened in the 1840s. Copperas and copper are two very different things, but copperas, as in the case of Strafford, may indicate the existence of a body of copper ore.

Copperas is iron pyrite (FeS_2), and often occurs in the crystal form as "fool's gold." It contains no copper. The two major areas where pyrite actually was mined were in Strafford and Cuttingsville, the latter in the town of Shrewsbury which contains the hill of the same name. In the 1850s the pyrite mining ceased in Cuttingsville, although reports held out hope that a body of copper ore might be discovered as had happened in South Strafford.

Copperas is an interesting substance. If reduced to a powder, then heated, it will emit a rotten-egg odor and turn black. The fumes from any large-scale copperas operation will choke the unwary, and the sulfur, if combined with rainwater, will form dilute sulfuric acid and wreak havoc with local vegetation and soils.

Current acid rain damage to Vermont and New York lakes and to the entire ecosystem on Camels Hump and other Vermont mountains is insignificant compared to the concentrated effects which accompanied copperas and copper production in Orange County. Birch forests have grown up on the highly-acid soils, and even today trout cannot live in the high-acid waters of the Ompompanoosuc between West Fairlee and Thetford and on its West Branch below South Strafford.

Once thought to be a valuable source of iron ore, a large quantity of copperas was taken from the deposit in Strafford to an iron furnace in Franconia, New Hampshire to be smelted. There it was mixed with rich iron ore and fed into the furnace with disastrous results. In the words of the state geologist, "instead of getting a supply of iron from the Strafford ore, the disengaged sulphur prevented even the flow of iron from the Franconia ore, and the result was that the furnace was blocked up, and no more ore could be smelted therin till the sulphurous mass was removed, which was done at considerable expense."

In the manufacture of copperas, large masses of crushed ore were piled upon planks with an air space beneath. The pile of crushed pyrite ore then was washed with water for a period of time, the water percolating downward through the mass and flowing out in a trough. The weak sulfuric acid was collected in reservoirs. The liquid was taken to large boilers and heated so that through boiling, the copperas became more concentrated. This is the weak sulfuric acid given off in the process. With sufficient boiling a crust of copperas salts collects on the sides of the vessels. The crystalline material then is packed for shipment. It is basically a crystal form of sulfuric acid, and still is used in the western states to make the alkaline soils more acid.

In the case of the copper mines in Strafford, the copperas led to the copper: "Upon entering the bed at greater depth, by the removal of the sulphate of iron for the manufacture of copperas, valuable copper ore was found to exist, and in such quantities as to induce the proprietors to again resume the copper mining business. . . ." Almost pure accident, but for many years copperas was regarded as an indicator to copper deposits, and this partly explains some of the confusion between the two terms. The Vermont copper ores are sulfur ores, that is, the copper is associated with that material as in chalcopyrite ($CuFeS_2$), the most common copper ore in the state. After mining, the ore must be processed to extract the copper, a complex process which proved to have a lasting negative impact on the mining areas. Along the railroad tracks by the Dog River in Northfield a piece of native copper (i.e., pure copper) was found many years ago, but it probably fell from an ore train carrying the native copper of the Lake Superior mines to eastern refineries. No other native copper even has been reported in the state.

Vermont's real copper belt was in a north-south zone in the towns of Vershire, Corinth and Strafford in Orange County. It is said that this area once was the largest copper-producing area in the country. It is impossible to find data to substantiate such a claim because it would have been before 1840 when the Lake Superior ores became important, and so in an era when few, if any, records were kept. Other important eastern producing areas were in Maryland and in Connecticut, especially in Chester. The Vermont deposits were most productive after 1870. In 1880 about 5.5 million pounds of metallic copper probably were produced, compared with more than 20 million pounds from the Lake Superior region the same year, and about 7 million pounds from the vast Anaconda deposits at Butte, Montana. In 1870, about 1.5 million pounds were produced in Vermont, compared with 4.5 million in Michigan.

The earliest development in the copper belt was at South Strafford on Copperas Hill where the earlier copperas mining (1793) had led to the discovery of the copper ore body. This was a large open-pit operation. Underground copper mining began in 1833 when Isaac Tyson, Jr. bought the mineral rights just north of the open cut and began operations.

However, while Strafford experienced the first mining activity in the region, the first mining for copper (rather than copperas) occurred in Vershire, the next town north, in 1821. Here, a company called the Farmers Copper Company began intermittent mining and smelting in a crude furnace. There are no records of the production from this era, but it probably was very small. This company was succeeded by the Vershire Copper Mines, and in 1853 by the Vermont Copper Mining Company. This latter company was the first to issue stock, but production continued to be small and erratic.

Corinth, the third town to the north, was the last to see development of copper ores. The Union, Cuprum and Eureka mines all were operating on Pike Hill by 1866. The Union had been opened that year, the other two somewhat earlier. The exact dates are unknown, but it is reported that in 1860 the Corinth Copper Company took over the Cuprum Mine, so it must have been active before that date. Indeed, the 1861 *Geology of Vermont* notes that: "In 1854 the Corinth Copper Company commenced their labors upon the bed. . . ."

Actual copper mining apparently first started in Vershire in 1821 in the village of Copperfield. Mr. Tyson began operations in South Strafford in 1833, with the Corinth enterprise apparently dating from about 1854. Tyson later developed the iron ores in Plymouth, for whom Tyson Furnace and Tyson were named.

Over the years the least important of the three major Vermont towns was Corinth. Production peaked probably around 1880, when 5.7 million pounds of copper ore fron the Union mine were shipped to the smelting works in Copperfield in Vershire. The area then declined in importance. In 1917 almost 510,000 pounds of copper and 2,000 ounces of silver were produced. In 1917 the Michigan mines produced 52 million pounds of copper. Operations ceased in 1919. There was some renewed interest during the second World War and again in 1984 when the New-mont Mining Company surveyed some of the old properties.

Vershire Copper

In contrast to the somewhat desultory operations on Pike Hill, the developments to the south in Vershire led to the major copper center in Vermont. The Vermont Copper Mining Company, chartered in 1853, knew only low and intermittent production for ten years until the name of Smith Ely of New York City began to appear among the names of the stockholders. In 1864, Ely was the owner of 2,600 shares. As the majority stockholder, aside from the owners who never had profited from the mine, Ely was elected president in 1865. He then bought most of the company's shares and became full owner of the property. A retired furniture manufacturer, Ely had little knowledge or understanding of copper operations in New England.

Many of the limited successes of the pre-Ely years were due to Thomas Pollard, the local superintendent. He was fired in 1863 in a company squabble and his loss was felt for several years.

Pollard, a Cornishman with a background in the copper and tin mines of his native land, saw to it that many of the miners were from Cornwall. Skilled in mining, the Cornish of the Vermont copper regions, joined by large numbers of Irish, complemented the Italians in Barre and the later Welsh miners in the slate quarries of western Vermont. Many Finns from the granite quarries of Quincy, Massachusetts were attracted to the Vermont copper mines, and there performed services that far greater numbers of their kinfolk were doing in the Lake Superior region. In 1880, the census counted 209 Cornish and 281 Irish in Vershire. Payroll records for November 1880 listed 851 workers, 205 of whom were Cornish.

Between 1865 when he became president, and 1882 when he deeded the property to his grandson, Smith Ely invested a lot of money and time in Vershire. A $100,000 dividend was declared in 1868. Production of copper metal increased from 943,000 pounds in 1870 to 3.2 million pounds in 1880.

Between 1872 and 1882, 25 million pounds of copper were given up by the metamorphic hills. That averages 2.5 million pounds a year, no mean production average. While national copper prices fluctuated widely during the period (21 cents a pound in 1870, 35 cents in 1872 and 21 cents again in 1880), the Vermont Copper Company remained relatively prosperous. For example, the 1880 production of 3.2 million pounds, the highest yearly production of the company, with a prevailing price of about 21 cents a pound, meant an income of about $670,000. Smith Ely once was offered $1.2 million for the property but turned it down.

The prosperity of the Ely years, and that of the whole copper belt from the early 1850s on, was related directly to the Connecticut and Passumpsic River Railroad, completed up the Connecticut Valley just east of the mineral belt during that period. Without the railroad it was very difficult to get the copper out. In 1854 the railroad made it possible for Pollard to ship a concentrated ore, averaging about 10% copper, to the smelters in Boston, Humphreysville, Connecticut, and Baltimore where the metal was recovered from the concentrate. Down in South Strafford, Tyson had tremendous difficulty in the 1830s getting his copper out, and is reported to have negotiated lower Connecticut River boat fees, and lower canal tolls through the locks at Bellows Falls.

Realizing the importance of railway connections, Smith Ely made many attempts at getting a railway spur built up to Vershire. In 1872, the branch almost became a reality, only to be buried in a financial crash. Ely settled for a new section of highway from Lake Fairlee to Ely Station, previously called Wares

Crossing, and now just called Ely.

Vershire had the second highest population of any town in Orange County in 1880. Thanks to the 1,500 people who lived in the company homes and boarding houses in Copperfield, the population of the town stood at 1,875. Few people lived outside the mining community. That same year, Corinth had a population of 1,627 and Strafford, 1,181. All three towns experienced their previous maximum populations in 1840, before the lure of California and the west had reached the hills of Orange County.

The ores from the Ely mine on the hill north of Copperfield originally were sent out of the region for smelting. Connecticut was the most common destination, and the barren hills around Waterbury, Connecticut attest to the early importance of copper smelting in the Naugatuck River valley. Rarely was all the material mined sent to the smelters. Before shipment the ore was concentrated. This was done by first "cobbing" or breaking the mined material into smaller-sized pieces by hand hammers. These pieces all were nut-sized lumps which were "jigged" on tables with screens beneath. The heavier material, the richest ore, would settle to the bottom and the lighter rock, or "gangue," material would be skimmed off. The richer ore then was ready for shipment for actual smelting where the copper metal itself was separated from the concentrate. The Ely ores ran about 3.31% copper, or about 66 pounds of copper metal from a ton of ore. The concentrate which was sent out usually averaged up to 10% copper content, so only 90% had to be thrown away at its destination, compared to 97% if the ore was shipped as it came from the ground. The Vermont copper companies desperately needed local smelting facilities. The wisdom of shipping a product which could be 97% waste was questionable economically.

As early as 1857, a German mining engineer had advised the Vermont Copper Mining Company to erect smelting furnaces to avoid shipments of large tonnages of waste rock to smelting plants on the coast. Finally, in 1867 Smith Ely hired William Long to start work on a smelting plant. By 1868, Long had roast beds, four furnaces in a 106 x 62 foot building, two blacksmith shops, a coke and coal house, and a lumber shed ready for operation.

The roasting beds were the earliest form of copper smelters.

The main street of Copperfield Village in Vershire as it looks today. Birches can tolerate the highly acid soils created by the old smelters.

There the concentrated ore from the jig tables was burned (or roasted) in heaps enclosed by rectangular walls open at the top. Enormous amounts of wood initially were required before anthracite coal was brought up from Pennsylvania. Thousands of acres of forest land were cleared for fuel for the roast beds, with much of the wood subsequently converted into charcoal. Many denuded hillsides in Vermont reflect not the clearing of land to plant more crops or provide more pasture for cows, but the need of the era's railroads and industries for a source of energy. When coal became available, generally in the 1870s, Vermont's forests began to regenerate themselves, but had a hard time of it in the copper belt. Even today the forests around Copperfield bear the imprint of the roast beds and smelters of another era.

The sulfur dioxide fumes from the roasting beds partly were responsible for the desert-like landscape which appears in early photographs of the Vershire mines. The land already had been cleared for its wood. The fumes, combining with normal precipitation, produced acid rainfall, rendering the soils in the immediate vicinity exceptionally acid. Birch, a species tolerant of acid conditions, has grown back, but most other softwoods and hardwoods are rare in and about old Copperfield.

Smelting is a common operation in the processing of all ores. In a smelter (for example, an iron blast furnace) the idea is to subject the ore to great heat. This separates the metal desired from the gangue material and a reasonably pure product is produced. The blast furnace, used most commonly with iron ore, is an upright smelter. The smelters used in Vershire were horizontal reverberatory furnaces, but they did the same job as the blast furnaces. In 1868 Long constructed four furnaces or smelters. By 1880 the Copperfield operation had grown tremendously. It included a structure 700 feet long containing 24 individual furnaces.

The copper content of the material eventually produced by the reverberatory furnaces averaged about 96-98% pure copper. The remainder was usually gold, silver, lead and zinc, metals which could not be smelted out. At this point the material went south to the refineries. Shipping a product more than 95% copper made much more sense than shipping a product which was 97% waste. The smelters were successful, and Vershire prospered.

Data relating to the Vermont copper industry is sketchy at best. Various totals are reported for copper production, quality of the ores, and the nature of the ore bodies. By contrast, records of the Lake Superior copper production on the Keweenaw Peninsula of Michigan are accurate, well-documented and complete.

In 1880, the peak year of 19th century Vermont production, the Calumet and Hecla Company, working the Michigan deposits, reported that the total cost per pound of eventual copper delivered to their smelters was five cents. In other words, prospecting, drilling, hoisting, breaking (cobbing) and milling cost that amount of money. Since the Lake Superior ores were native copper, these initial development costs probably were somewhat lower than the costs for the delivered ore at the Vershire smelters. While comparisons are hard, probably little Vermont copper ore, dug from the ground at 3.3% copper, could be ready for the smelter at a cost of only five cents a pound of eventual copper produced. This was the basic problem with Vermont copper and with any expansion of the industry after the boom year of 1880.

In 1882 the price of copper fell to 16 cents a pound, production was nearly one million pounds less, and as the shafts went deeper the quality of the ore was lessening. The Vermont Copper Mining Company was nearly $200,000 in debt because the expansion of smelting facilities had been a drain on the available resources. In addition, Ely's popularity had been falling ever since he had tried to have Vershire renamed after himself. Things were going from bad to worse and the company saw the first of several reorganizations.

One of the new owners was Ely-Ely Goddard, grandson of Smith Ely. The only member of the Ely clan ever to spend much time in Vermont, he became paymaster of the Vermont Copper Mining Company in 1876, after a quality European education.

A controversial individual, Ely-Ely Goddard attempted to maintain a quality lifestyle by building a mansion on Copperfield's main street and bringing in city orchestras to entertain the Cornish miners and their wives at dances in the third-floor ballroom. He drove an English dogcart drawn by purebred Morgan horses and commonly rode to the hounds through the Vershire hills. There was widespread resentment towards Ely-Ely and his manners, including his insistence on having his name hyphenated in the English manner.

He was a poor money manager and the final blow fell on June 30, 1883 when his workers, who all were owed back pay, watched a stop work order posted. Copper prices were now 15 cents a pound and falling. Only 300 miners and smeltermen were still on the payroll; many already had departed for greener pastures.

Worker frustrations culminated in what has become known as the "Ely War." On July 1, 1883 the non-operating company store was ransacked and Ely-Ely Goddard's mansion was surrounded by angry miners. As Ely-Ely was retreating to Newport, Rhode Island, the Vermont National Guard was called out to quell the uprising. Troops disembarked at Ely Station in the wee hours of the morning of July 7 and marched up the highway through Post Mills to Copperfield. There was no resistance, perhaps because the miners were still sleeping off the effects of the contents of the company store. The ringleaders were rounded up, and workers and their wives poured out their grievances. The Ely War became a part of Vermont history.

The glory years of Vershire copper were over. In 1884 the entire property was sold at auction for $36,000. The new Copperfield Mining and Smelting Company soon expired and in 1889 George Westinghouse acquired the property and invested considerable money in it. But by now the ores were lower in copper content and Arizona, Michigan, Montana and Utah could produce at a lower cost. Total copper metal production in Vermont in 1906 was only 240,000 pounds. Westinghouse gave up in 1905 and Copperfield was demolished that year.

The smelter was destroyed, and many of the town's houses became summer camps on Lake Fairlee after they were moved or dismantled and then rebuilt. The greatest home of them all, Ely-Ely Goddard's mansion "Elysium" now stands on a knoll at the north end of Lake Fairlee, and the birch forest is pitted with former cellar holes that once lined the main street of old Copperfield. When the leaves are off the trees the old smelter foundations can be seen, and the acid earth is yellowish-red, a legacy of the roasting beds of long ago. A driver who takes the partially-paved road due west from Post Mills passes through one of Vermont's few ghost towns.

After 1905, only one house and the store remained. The store burned in 1917, and the house about 1970. While the property passed to Agnes Bennett in 1917, to the Vermont Copper Company in April 1942, and is presently posted by the Ely Mines Sportsmans Club, the hill north of old Copperfield has seen no activity for 75 years.

Mining always has involved a boom-and-bust psychology, and nowhere can it be illustrated better than by what happened in Vershire. The Cornith mines to the north always were marginal, and except for a brief flurry of activity during the second World War, the South Strafford mines shared the same fate. Vershire, Copperfield, and Ely represent the epitome of boom-and-bust-mining activity in the state. Copper production boomed in 1880, and was bust by 1883.

South Strafford Copper

Isaac Tyson, Jr. was active in South Strafford. A metallurgist from Baltimore, Tyson came in 1830 to superintend both the

Copperfield Village in Vershire was a flourishing place in this 1880 photograph. The Ely mine, out of view to the left, supplied copper ore to the furnaces shown as the source of smoke. All the employees lived in the village. Ely-Ely Goddard's mansion is the one in the center with the cupola and spire.

The mansion of Ely-Ely Goddard as it now appears overlooking the north end of Lake Fairlee.

old copperas works and the newly discovered copper deposits. He found his interests focused on the copper ores as well as the iron operations going on at Plymouth, Brandon and other places.

With capital available, he soon had an interest in several mining areas in Vermont. The South Strafford copper deposits reportedly yielded 250,000 tons of ore through 1883. At an average copper content of 3%, probably 15 million pounds of copper metal were produced up to then. This was less than the Ely mine in Vershire, but considerably more than ever was squeezed out of Pike Hill in Corinth. But the glory days of the South Strafford operations on Copperas Hill were still far in the future. Geologists totaled the lifetime production of the Vermont copper mines and calculated that South Strafford yielded a total of 105 million pounds, Vershire an estimated 31 million pounds, and Pike Hill probably nine million more. Perhaps 145 million pounds of copper in total were taken from Vermont during the lifetime of the mines. That compares with 52 million pounds of copper produced in 1915 in Michigan, and 107 million in Butte, Montana in 1884.

While developments in South Strafford were less exciting than those in Ely, the South Strafford mines proved to be far more important. When he arrived at the copperas works Tyson found four small furnaces and roast beds in existence. When he left, probably about 1837, there were eight furnaces on Copperas Hill. The technical and transportation problems were considerable, but Tyson learned enough to establish his iron furnace in Plymouth after the collapse of the South Strafford operations.

Between 1837 and 1870 various companies and individuals tried their luck at the ore body. Several shafts were sunk, but no one reached the main ore vein which eventually put the South Strafford deposits on the map. In 1881, Isaac's son James, who had inherited part of the property, came to try his luck. He incorporated the Elizabeth Mining Company, named after his wife. Two new shafts were sunk north of the old open-cut copperas workings. The mine, too, was named after his wife. The 1880s saw sporadic mining, intermittent production, and several recessions. Tranquility prevailed in South Strafford during the boom-and-bust cycle in Vershire. James Tyson was relegated to having the ore cobbed as had been the practice in Vershire, bringing the copper content up to 5%, and then sending it by rail to Connecticut smelters.

The Elizabeth Mining Company failed around 1885. Copper prices had dropped to nine cents a pound and the operation could not continue without smelters, and with the high cost for shipping a mass of material to Connecticut that was only 5% copper. Nevertheless, small operations continued into the 1890s.

The Elizabeth Mine remained in the Tyson family and in 1896 James W. Tyson, Jr. entered the picture. He drilled a 1,400 foot adit into Copperas Hill and found the long-suspected rich copper vein. A concentration mill, roast beds and a smelter were erected and the future looked promising, but the fluctuating price of copper hindered much development of the new ore body. In 1907 the Elizabeth Mine passed from family control. James W. Tyson, Jr. sold out to August Heckscher of New York, known far and wide as the New Jersey zinc tycoon.

Starting operations in 1907 under the name of the Strafford Mining Company, Heckscher sank a lot of money into the property which included a hydroelectric plant at Sharon, on the White River, with lines to carry the power to his mines. (The electric plant disappeared in the 1927 flood.) At the mine he built a mill, magnetic separators, a new blast burnace, new tramways and, being perhaps environmentally conscious, a 125 foot high chimney to carry away the noxious fumes. In February 1909 a disastrous fire destroyed the structures (although the chimney stood until 1945 when it finally was demolished). South Strafford was quiet again, but in these two short years, a few pounds of copper had been produced at an undoubtedly incredible price.

Undaunted, Heckscher built another large blast furnace in 1909. This operated for two weeks before the main flue collapsed, and with it Heckscher's interest. The property remained idle until 1916, which year saw some diamond drilling, and in 1918 some copper actually was produced. The property passed from owner to owner and occasionally a hardy soul would invest a few thousand dollars and get a few pounds of copper as a return. One investor was the American Metals Company of Vermont which acquired the Elizabeth Mine in 1927 and mined about 20,000 tons of ore. In that year it reported that 1,800 tons of 18% copper concentrate were shipped. Low copper prices caused this enterprise to fail. The same thing happened to the National Copper Corporation which operated the property in 1929-1930.

The 1941-1942 *Report of the Vermont State Geologist* concludes its discussion of the Elizabeth Mine and the South Strafford workings with this comment:

> As one reads the history of operations on the Elizabeth ore body, he is impressed with the many vicissitudes that attended production and marketing operations. It would seem that the mine has never had a fair chance to show its commercial possibilities.

As that was being written, the Elizabeth Mine was being reopened once more. In April 1942, the Vermont Copper Company was organized with private capital to make a systematic study of the Vermont copper belt, and to develop and start operations on that portion deemed worthy of attention. The company acquired full ownership of all three properties—the Elizabeth Mine, as well as the land in Corinth and Vershire. This venture was stimulated by the copper shortage caused by World War II, but it also was the result of the improved ore-treatment processes whereby ore concentrated to 25% to 30% could be shipped economically for smelting and refining.

During the spring of 1942, the properties were studied carefully, and it was decided that they could be productive once again. Original plans called for mining in all three areas, but only South Strafford actually was mined. Private funds of $1.3 million were available, and a $550,000 loan came from the Metals Reserve Company an agency of the federal government. Government geologists had estimated that the Elizabeth ore body itself could produce 16.5 million pounds of copper in two-and-a-half years from the commencement of mining operations.

The mine began production in the spring of 1943 after a new incline shaft had been drilled to the 600 foot level. All the old buildings were demolished. A new mill (to crush the ore), and a concentrator using the flotation process were built. Other new structures for storage, blacksmithing, etc. were constructed. Old houses that once accommodated the workers were refurbished, where possible, to house the personnel needed for both construction and actual operation. New accommodations, including a boarding house, were built near the mine.

Production was a bit below four million pounds in both 1944 and 1945, lower than anticipated because of labor shortages. The mine was deepened to the 975 foot level, and in 1946 six million pounds of copper were produced, a record for any Vermont copper deposit in any year. Production dropped in 1947, but with a further deepening to a depth of 1,053 feet, subsequent production went way up and stayed there for a few years.

After the war, the price of copper remained high, but not high enough to keep the company solvent. In 1948 the mine almost closed but Washington came to the rescue with a contract that guaranteed a price of 19.25 cents a pound for 30 million pounds of copper if the company could produce it.

But problems were far from over. In 1948, when production was over four million pounds the company was losing more than $15,000 a month, and had been for two years. And 1949 was a recession year. A new consultant was hired by the company in hopes that expenses could be shaved. The 200-man work force was pared, the work week reduced, development work ceased, and a general belt tightening ensued. In 1949, even with curtailment, production topped six million pounds again as the ore mined was somewhat richer.

Things began to improve after the fat cutting of 1949. The price of copper was rising, and the Korean War created another demand situation. Seven million pounds of copper were produced in 1950, and in 1954 and 1955 the old Elizabeth Mine gave up more than eight-and-a-half million pounds—a record never repeated, and probably never to be seen again. In 1956 prices of copper peaked at 46 cents per pound. Coinciding with government aid and high production, explorations again traced an extension of the ore body. The prosperity of the 1950s led to its sale. Nipissing Mines Company Ltd. of Toronto acquired a 25% share of the company in 1951 and full control in 1954.

The old mine's peak year probably was 1955. In that year the employment rolls reached 220 from 16 surrounding towns. (Miners no longer lived on the premises, but commuted to work.) The annual payroll exceeded $1 million and a profit of $1 million was reported by Nipissing Mines, or more correctly, Appalachian Sulphides, a subsidiary of the parent company. Things went down, down and down from here.

Appalachian Sulphides, while controlling eight thousand acres

The concentration mill at the Elizabeth Mine in South Strafford operated until 1958. Beyond the mill lie piles of tailings, the product of many years of copper mining.

in Orange County, had exploration rights to 50,000 acres near Mt. Katahdin, Maine, and considerable speculative property in North Carolina. The North Carolina deposits were far richer than those at South Strafford, Vershire or Corinth. In 1958 operations ceased at the Elizabeth Mine.

There certainly is much more copper in Vermont. The ore body in South Strafford goes down much further than was mined. But unless the metal is exceptionally valuable, underground mining by shaft method cannot be done now. If the Vermont copper deposits lent themselves to open-pit operations as do the finely-disseminated copper ores of the west, copper mining in Vermont still would be with us. If the price of copper escalates considerably, mining of the Vermont copper ores might take place again. But that is highly doubtful. Even the old underground mines of once-mighty Michigan are still and deserted, the result of low copper prices and the great expenses of underground mining.

Iron

If Vermont ever had a "boom" it was with copper. Gold was exciting for a short time, and lead was mined in small quantities. Minute traces of silver were a curiosity. Iron goods were a basic ingredient to an evolving pioneer settlement, so iron manufacturing was very important in Vermont's early years of settlement and industry. Iron played the same role in every New England state because it was common, necessary, and required little technology in its processing. Vermont is not unique in its old ironworks and mines. Brothers to the presently-standing old iron furnaces in Bennington, Dorset, Brandon, Pittsford and Troy can be seen at Saugus, Massachusetts and Cornwall, Connecticut, as well as at a hundred locations throughout the Appalachians.

The story of Vermont iron mining and iron making is hard to unravel, not so much because of the manufacturing operation, but because of what was used as the raw material. Iron occurs in so many forms that even the old geology reports seem confused when talking of this or that "bed" of ore.

The means of iron manufacturing are relatively simple. A quantity of crushed material containing a significant percentage of iron was (and still is) dumped into the top of a vertical furnace (a blast furnace). Beneath the iron-bearing ore was charcoal. Charcoal originally was made from roasting hardwood and many acres of Vermont's forests were cut for this purpose. In modern iron- and steel-making, coal in the form of coke is substituted for the charcoal.

The charcoal or coke is ignited and the ore melts. Limestone is added as a flux in the process, so early iron furnaces had to have a supply of it. The concentration of old ironworks in the Champlain Valley and the Valley of Vermont is partially a result of the need for either crushed limestone or marble. After a period of time, the melted iron, now separated from the rock, is drawn off and cast into molds as required. Slag, a combination of the limestone and gangue material in the ore, is thrown away. Downstream of many old iron furnaces a dark glassy-looking rock often can be picked up from the stream bed.

Ideally, an iron furnace had to be located where there was

limestone or marble, water, iron ore, and charcoal. The latter was usually no particular problem because Vermont abounded with forested land, and thus charcoal availability never became of paramount significance to the location of the early industry. The same was true of water; there are no shortage of streams in Vermont. The most important considerations involved the availability of a calcium carbonate rock like limestone or marble, and the proximity to a source of quality ore. The typical charge each time ore was smelted was 30 bushels of charcoal, 1,500 pounds of ore and 150 pounds of limestone.

Forges were also a part of the iron industry. A total of 51 are shown in Figure 5.2, most in close proximity to the blast furnaces. Many actually were smaller-scale blast furnaces, although with a greatly different process. These forges, called bloomery forges, manufactured iron in smaller quantities than the furnaces and went a step further in fashioning the iron into various usable shapes. Most forges were generally in areas not served by a blast furnace, such as those in Swanton.

Some forges, however, were finery forges (or refinery). They would take the cast iron of the blast furnace, reheat it, and then fashion it into the required shapes and sizes. Finery forges had a "cupola" furnace to accomplish this task, and most were located close to the blast furnaces. In many cases records do not indicate whether a forge was a bloomery or refinery operation.

At least 18 blast furnaces operated in Vermont at one time or another. Figure 5.2 clearly shows the pattern of both forges and furnaces in the western part of the state.

Besides the natural resources affecting the locational development of the early iron industry, there was a cultural force as well. The hills of western Connecticut were one of the great centers of early iron manufacturing. This area sent many young pioneer families north into New England's 18th century frontier, most eventually settling in western Vermont. Many of these early settlers had a knowledge of iron manufacturing gained in Connecticut, and were quick to apply that knowledge in their new surroundings. The correlation of early Connecticut settlement in western Vermont and the distribution of iron furances and forges is striking.

The first ironworks in Vermont was in Fair Haven and pro-

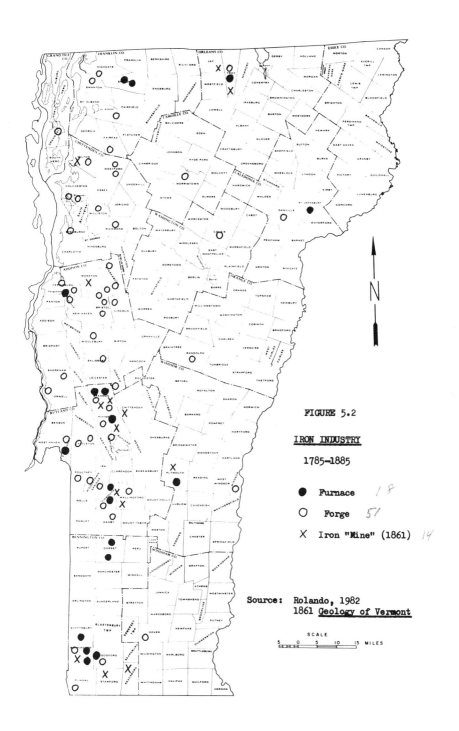

FIGURE 5.2

IRON INDUSTRY

1785-1885

● Furnace / 8

○ Forge 5/

X Iron "Mine" (1861) /4

Source: Rolando, 1982
1861 Geology of Vermont

SCALE
5 0   5   10   15 MILES

duced pig iron as early as 1785. Pittsford was in production by
1791, and the furnaces at Sheldon were operating in the 1790s.
The earliest Bennington furnace was constructed in 1788 by
Moses Sage. In 1816 Mr. Sage moved to Pennsylvania and built
a blast furnace with the knowledge he had gained in Vermont.
That place is now known as Pittsburgh. The other furnaces in Vermont date from the 1800s, one of the latest being the furnace
and forge at Phelps Falls on the upper Missisquoi River in Troy
in the 1840s. Here the Troy and Boston Iron Company may have
cast the iron used in the International Boundary markers (1842),
but by 1851 the furnace no longer was in use. The longest-lived
ironworks in Vermont was one in Brandon which operated into
the 1890s.

Even today, as it was nearly 200 years ago, the iron industry
is acutely conscious of raw materials. Requiring large amounts of
bulky material with a low value per unit of weight, any successful iron industry has to be situated where the materials are available easily and cheaply. But there also must be a market. The
dearth of iron furnaces in northern Vermont reflects this problem. The ideal spot is where there is limestone, a bed of iron, a
stream, and an easy source of charcoal. Few locations are perfect,
but the early Vermont industry tended to reflect these locational
requirements pretty well. In his *History of Pittsford* (1872), A.
M. Caverly writes of the waning years of the iron industry:

> For some years after this furnace was built it was a source of
> considerable profit to the owners, while it also furnished work
> for a large number of individuals who were enabled, thereby,
> not only to pay their current expenses, but to lay aside a por-
> tion of their earnings, with which some of them afterwards
> purchased farms and made themselves comfortable homes. But
> in the process of time the ore bed, from which the furnace was
> supplied, ceased to be productive, and the company had to re-
> sort for their supply to another deposit of ore, some six miles
> away. The extra cost of transportation, and the increased ex-
> pense of other materials required in the manufacture of iron,
> have exceeded the rise in the price of the metal, so that latterly
> the furnace could not be operated remuneratively.

In terms of tonnages used, iron ore was the most important
raw material, but describing Vermont ores is not easy. They

This iron furnace in East Dorset is the most accessible one left in Vermont. Most of the others are deeply buried in forest growth and much harder to find and photograph.

were variable, including both secondary iron as limonite and primary ore such as magnetite and hematite. The local beds of secondary iron were soon exhausted.

The subject is complex, but in general, what was used fell into two categories. "Bog ore" and "vein ore" are mentioned constantly in the early reports. In addition, there are references to "lodestone," "pyrite," "ocher" and a host of related iron-bearing or associated materials.

Everyone has seen streaks of reddish rust on rocks. This is iron deposited by water seeping from the ground and oxidizing when exposed to the atmosphere. Considerable incrustations of iron can develop in this manner, and these deposits of bog ore were the first to be used because they almost could be dug from the ground and were relatively high-quality material. Technically the ore is limonite, and in its purest state runs about 60% iron. Limonite is therefore a surface occurrence of iron rather than an underground occurrence as with the other major ores. Ocher really is loose limonite which is not in a solidified state. It was used sometimes as iron ore, but with poor results. Its major use later was as a base for paints.

Ocher and limonite usually occur together, and often kaolin (china clay) is found as well. The first report of the Vermont state geologist (1845) separates "brown iron ore," "magnetic oxide and specular oxide of iron," "chromic iron," and "manganese" as the major occurrences of iron. The 1861 report is equally vague and unhelpful but understandable in view of the confusion as to what the material actually was. Because iron occurs in so many different forms, in the early days of local iron production nearly any nearby source of the material, good or bad, could be used in the primitive furnaces and forges.

Any generalization has exceptions. An early report of the use of manganese as a source of iron ore in a furnace is given below:

> On finding that black pure manganese, he put a large quantity into the furnace to get better iron from this pure ore as he had thought it; that when they tapped the furnace, the liquid stream took fire and burned with fury in all directions, driving all hands from the building, so that it was not possible to proceed till the manganese was removed from the furnace, at no little expense.

Not everything containing iron would do, but most iron manufacturers were willing to take a chance on any material that contained reasonable quantities of iron.

The earliest iron works were based on limonite or bog ore. It was easier to extract, occurred frequently, and was obvious on the landscape. It also was mined out quickly—one reason why the modern explorer can find few concentrations of the material. There are so many confusing reports of iron ore in so many different varieties that the map (Figure 5.1) only shows places where "iron ore" was reported.

Most of the early iron development in the Champlain Valley probably was associated with limonite; certainly that was true at Highgate, Swanton, Sheldon, Ferrisburg and Monkton. What was referred to at one time as "brown oxide" probably was actually bog ore. The 1861 report notes that "in Vermont, the brown oxide . . . is not imbedded in the rocks of Vermont, but reposes on them, and immediately below the drift deposits associated with the iron are beds of kaolin, oxide of manganese and yellow ocher. . . ."

Continued speculation on exactly what material was used at various times to feed the early iron industry is fruitless. In these years there was a desperate need for iron tools, implements and household goods for an expanding population remote from manufacturing areas. Much ironware came from Canada in return for the potash and pearlash sent north; and when the Champlain Canal finally was completed in 1822-1823, manufactured goods from the south could reach the northern frontier. But in the interim, several places developed as important iron-manufacturing sites, primarily to satisfy local needs, and later, to send manufactured iron products out of the region.

Vergennes was the most important iron-manufacturing location in Vermont until the boom ended in the 1820s. In 1813 the Monkton Iron Company in Vergennes was reputed to be the largest iron manufacturer in the United States. It is a hard claim to substantiate without data, but Vergennes was very important in any case. During the War of 1812, the first battleship in the U.S. Navy was launched just below the falls. And ore was coming in sloops from Highgate, Swanton, and most importantly from the rich ores of New York just across the lake.

The most long-lived of Vermont's iron manufacturing centers were at Pittsford and Brandon. As late as 1856, the Pittsford industry (the Granger Furnace), produced 1,600 tons of pig iron. The Brandon industry lasted well into the 1890s because of a favorable set of circumstances, in many ways similar to the operations in Pittsford. In both places, a bed of iron ore was unearthed practically under the surface limonite deposits on which the developments had started. And, in the case of the Brandon-Forestdale complex, a patch of lignite coal was discovered on the property.

Forestdale and Brandon, close together, shared much of the production history of the Brandon area. In 1854 some 200 workers were employed, probably in Brandon, but possibly in nearby Forestdale. Production of the famous Conant stoves was important, and the Brandon Iron and Car Wheel Company (1858) grew to be a major U.S. manufacturer of railroad wheels in a time of tremendous demand for them. The first furnace at Brandon was built in 1820 by John Conant, and was long known as "Conant's furnace."

In the 1860s the Brandon Company owned more than 2,500 acres of woodland in Brandon, Chittenden, Hancock, Ripton and Goshen, which supplied whatever charcoal was needed in addition to that from the lignite beds. In 1860 the property included over 100 acres of mineral land which, according to *Hitchcock's Geology of Vermont* (1861), "embraces an enexhaustible supply of the valuable variety of iron ore known by the name of brown hematite; also, distinct therefrom, an extensive deposit of pure white kaolin, of porcelain clay, and fire clay, and fire sand, and many thousand tons of pigments. . . ." Indeed, in 1860 the proprietors of the Brandon works were sitting on a veritable "gold" mine.

The easily accessible Vermont ore beds soon were exhausted, and as railroads improved transportation there was little competitive advantage in working the small scattered iron deposits in Vermont. Tyson's enterprise in Plymouth was decaying by 1850. Brandon kept going because of its raw-material position. Another important factor in the demise of the industry was the increasing shortage and price of good-quality hardwood suitable for turning into charcoal. By the 1870s Vermont was nearly two-thirds cleared land, and most of the remaining forests were softwoods at higher elevations.

For all intents and purposes the early iron-mining industry in Vermont was pretty well finished by the 1860s. It served its consumers at a time when the commodity was needed and there was no way of importing iron goods cheaply. Transportation improvements helped end the iron era and helped the development of the non-metallic mineral industries which could exist only when there was a means of getting their bulky and low-value (by weight) product out of the Vermont hills.

Non-Metallic Minerals

Every *Annual Report* of the Vermont state geologist contained a section on mineral resources: what was being produced,
where produced, and the worth of the production. For example,
the 1907-1908 report, written after the temporary demise of
the South Strafford copper operations, noted that the value of
marble produced was $7.5 million, an estimated 11.34% of total
U.S. production. The figure for building-and-monumental-quality
granite was $2.9 million. Mr. Perkins, the state geologist, noted,
". . . to this should be added the large amount sold in the rough
and the much smaller amount sold as crushed stone. So far as I
can ascertain, the total amount is not less than $4,000,000. . . ."
The value of lime produced from the native limestones was
$367,000, but no estimates in the report give the value quarried
for building material. It probably was very small. A list of 55
slate-producing companies is shown in the report, but the value
of slate produced is not revealed. The 1909-1910 report notes
that sales of slate in Vermont amounted to $2 million.

The 1907-1908 report discusses the clay industry, noting that
in 1906 the Rutland Fire Clay Company sold $54,000 worth of
firebrick. As regards talc and soapstone "the total amount of
talc and soapstone sold annually in this state is not large, a little
more than $100,000 but apparently it is likely to be greater in
the immediate future." Asbestos mining was in its infancy, but
the report was optimistic in its outlook for this mineral.

The state geologist devoted 55 pages to marble, granite, limestone, slate, talc, soapstone and asbestos. The total value of these commodities was probably about $13 million. Two pages in the 1907-1908 report were devoted to the subject of metals. Silver was mentioned briefly, and its value estimated at $886. The future of copper was so bleak that no figures were given.

Except for the brief rebirth of the South Strafford copper industry during World War II (it closed in 1958) Vermont no longer was a metals-producing state. The total historic copper production of Vermont was about 150 million pounds, with a considerable amount of that coming after 1942. With an overall value of perhaps 25 cents per pound, the entire value was a little more than $37 million. But in 1906 the sale of Vermont *rocks* accounted for more than a third of that total. Including the small amounts of gold, silver, and lead produced, and the greater amounts of iron, it is very unlikely that the total value of metals mined from the Green Mountain State ever came to more than $55 million.

Marble

Probably the first rock quarried commercially, marble led all other non-metallic mineral production until at least World War I when in value of sales it was replaced by granite and more recently by slate.

Details of the first marble quarrying are sketchy. Some marble gravestones bear inscriptions as early as 1785 when Isaac Underhill began operations in Dorset.

Jeremiah Sheldon too opened quarries in Pittsford in 1785. Depending upon how marble was defined, the earliest quarrying probably was at the south end of Isle La Motte as early as 1761. But that material was not really marble at all, but Chazy limestone, marketed, however, as Black Marble. Here certainly was the oldest quarry in Vermont, with quicklime made by the French as early as 1644.

Four separate rocks were quarried and sold as marble during the colorful history of Vermont marble. The true marbles are metamorphosed limestones, and occur in a belt from Dorset and Manchester in the south to Middlebury in the north (Figure 6.1).

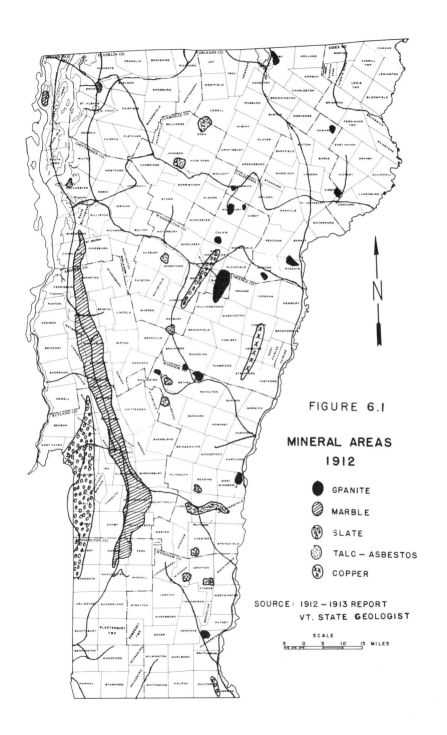

FIGURE 6.1

MINERAL AREAS
1912

GRANITE

MARBLE

SLATE

TALC – ASBESTOS

COPPER

SOURCE: 1912 – 1913 REPORT
VT. STATE GEOLOGIST

SCALE

5   0   5   10   15 MILES

They are normally pure white to off-white in color with few blemishes or other colors. Many companies invented a variety of fanciful names for their products, including American Yellow Pavanazzo, Baronial Antique, Colonial Cream Statuary, Light Cloud Italian, Pink Listavena, Northern Pearl and prosaically, Mahogany, which actually was a pure white stone.

A second group of rocks quarried and sold as marble included the dark Chazy limestones found close to Lake Champlain. This belt extends from Shoreham through Shelburne (just west of Shelburne Pond) to Isle La Motte in Grand Isle County. The limestones at Shoreham were quarried primarily for use as a flux in the iron blast furnaces across the lake at Port Henry, New York. The Shelburne Marbles never were very important. Swanton Dove Marble was quarried by 1848, but was more important as a source of lime. The Black Marble from the Fisk and Goodsell quarries on Isle La Motte enjoyed an enduring popularity. These "marbles" take a polish well, and since the limestones are fossiliferous, it is possible to see small fossils in the polished surface.

The Fisk quarry was important because of its location on the lakeshore, not for any particular attribute of the limestone. Rock is a low-value product per unit of weight, and to succeed there has to be inexpensive transportation from quarry to market. Before 1850 and the coming of the railroads, the Isle La Motte limestones were better located with respect to their market than any other quarry in Vermont. The Champlain Canal, completed in 1823, provided a water link south with New York, while in the north the Chambly Canal, constructed after 1835, bypassed the rapids of the Richelieu. More than one million cubic feet of stone from Isle La Motte went into the construction of the Victoria Bridge in Montreal in 1855-1858. The fortifications at Isle aux Noix took 484,000 cubic feet, the locks for the Chambly Canal itself 136,000 cubic feet. Large quantities of stone went into the abutments and piers of the bridge over the Richelieu at Chambly, into the barracks of the fort at St. Jean and even into Fort Montgomery (Fort Blunder) at Rouses Point.

Between 1850 and 1860, 60,000 cubic feet of Black Marble were sawed into hearthstones and sent to New York, Boston and Philadelphia. Since each cubic foot of stone makes about seven

At least three abandoned quarries are on Isle La Motte. Water now fills the old Fisk Quarry which for many years sold a black marble which really was a limestone. Possibly the oldest quarry operations in the state were carried on by the French along the lakeshore some 100 yards from this quarry.

feet of hearth when sawed, there probably still are a great many Fisk Quarry hearths around the northeastern United States.

The importance of low-cost transportation to the Isle La Motte quarries was significant. Mr. Fisk reported the following in 1861:

Expense of Quarrying 1 Cubic Foot of Stone	6 cents
Transportation, Duties, Canal Tolls/Cubic Foot. . . .	9 cents
TOTAL COST	15 cents
Price Received when Delivered.	21 cents
Net Profit per Cubic Foot	6 cents

This refers to stone delivered already cut to the St. Lawrence and Atlantic Railway bridge over the Richelieu near Beloil, Quebec. Fisk also reports that hearthstone was more profitable, with a net profit of 12.5 cents a cubic foot. Wages in 1860 ranged from 80 cents to $1.50 a day. Since quarry costs probably varied little from place to place, transportation was certainly the most critical factor, and explained why some quarries prospered and others did not.

Related to this second group of "marbles" were the scattered marbles of eastern Vermont. Mainly associated with the Waits River limestone, some quarrying occurred in Plymouth, Athens, Washington, Cavendish, Dover, Jamaica, Johnson, Moretown, Topsham, and even Readsboro along the Massachusetts border. The rock quarried in Plymouth and Topsham once was billed as marble. The other quarries, mostly short-lived, produced lime. There was a lot of interest in these limestones in the early 1900s, but little came of it. These areas are not shown on a 1912 map prepared during a period of maximum mining and quarrying activity in Vermont (Figure 6.1 is adapted from this map).

A third group of rocks also was sold as marble. Originally called "Winooski Marble," the name was changed to "Champlain Marble" when many of the properties were acquired by the Vermont Marble Company about 1901. Champlain Marble is closer to sandstone than anything else, and the quarries were in the Dunham dolomite, a slightly metamorphosed sandstone equivalent. Reddish in color, and veined with white quartz, the rock was decorative when polished and appealed to Victorian taste. Many mantles, table and counter tops, and other interior decorations were made from the stone, and in many respects it resembles the popular Mexican Onyx of the post-1860 period.

Champlain Marbles were quarried in a north-south zone from Monkton through Colchester (Mallets Head) to St. Albans and Swanton (Swanton Junction). The remains of an old Champlain Marble quarry and mill can be seen from the highway just across the Canadian border in Phillipsburg, Quebec. The zone was just east of the Chazy limestone quarrying; Swanton produced both kinds of marble and added to the confusion.

A complex rock called serpentine is the fourth rock which has been quarried as marble. Found in a long north-south zone along the eastern border of the Green Mountains, serpentine provides Vermont talc, Vermont asbestos, Vermont soapstone, and of all things, Vermont Verde Antique marble. Its character can vary widely in a small area, and a quarry digging the stone out for soapstone suddenly might find a vein of asbestos, and alternately, a talc deposit may degenerate into Verde Antique marble.

Technically, serpentine is not a rock at all, but a mineral with the chemical composition of $H_4Mg_3Si_2O_9$. A popular guide book to rocks and minerals says that "Serpentine rock is serpentine with more or less impurities such as pyroxene, amphibole, olivine, magnetite, chromite, calcite, magnesite, etc. . . Serpentine always occurs in and with metamorphic rocks, and was originally a metamorphic rock, but has since been changed by the hydration of its silicates, when it came into the zone in which water was present."

Probably the first quarry in the United States to work serpentine for marble was in Cavendish in 1835. In these early years quarrymen found this an exceedingly difficult stone to quarry, cut, and polish without fracturing it. It was realized only later that gunpowder was not the best method of quarrying blocks of stone. The Cavendish quarries closed after a few years but were reopened in 1932, only to close again shortly thereafter. Rochester and Roxbury long have been the most important centers for the production of Verde Antique marble. The Rochester Verde Antique was quarried after its talc mines were developed. Production continues today under ownership of the Vermont Marble Company. Roxbury has been worked intermittently since its opening before 1850. A beautiful polished piece of Verde Antique marble rests in front of the small railroad station in Roxbury at the summit elevation of the Central Vermont Railroad. Also the base of the statue of General Warren on the top of Bunker Hill in Boston is of Roxbury Verde Antique marble. The Verde Antique series extends as far north as Lowell, but no rock for marble purposes has been quarried in this northern zone.

The true calcite-marble belt between the Green Mountains and the Taconics always has been the most important district in Vermont, but development here, as elsewhere, depended on transportation. A large order of Dorset or West Rutland marble was hauled overland to Troy, New York in 1812 where it was loaded for shipment to Charleston, South Carolina for a new government building under construction. A small marble mill existed in Tinmouth after 1821 and the cut stone had to be hauled 30 miles to Comstock, New York and loaded onto canal boats. There were only 16 marble companies in business in 1840 which represented probably twice that number of holes in the ground. By 1860 the number of companies had more than doubled; there were more than 50 individual quarries, and more than 550 men were employed in extracting the stone.

When the Bennington and Rutland and the Rutland and Burlington railroads were built in 1849-1852, there was very little activity in the marble belt. The 1850 U.S. Census reported that only 60 quarrymen (including those working granite, slate, talc, soapstone, marble and limestone) were employed in Vermont. An additional 265 people worked in various finishing mills, but the business had been dogged by the lack of accessibility to markets.

After 1860, the marble industry increased rapidly in importance. The value of marble sold went from $500,000 in 1860 to $1.3 million in 1880, $2.3 million in 1890 and to $3.6 million by 1900. After the turn of the century competition from other areas of the country and the increasing use of Barre granite instead of marble had a depressing effect on the industry. The quantity and value of marble output continued to grow, but not at the rate of the previous 50 years. The value of marble produced in 1920 was $4 million while granite was $6.5 million.

Consolidations began to occur rapidly after 1860. Many old quarries were abandoned as marble veins were worked out, but others took their place. It is impossible to give any count of the actual number of individual marble quarries in Vermont. A map of the West Rutland marble area in the 1913-1914 *Report of the Vermont State Geologist* shows 18 active quarries and five inactive. Figure 6.2 shows these 23 quarries in the most concentrated quarry zone in Vermont.

Marble was quarried originally by simple prying "sheets" loose from a ledge with crowbars. Using chisels, workmen the1. attacked the block and worked it smooth and to the desired shape. In 1804 Eben Judd of Middlebury sawed the first piece of Vermont marble with a smooth strip of soft iron, and sand and water. Marble mills soon developed in the marble regions. Since polishing did not come until later, all the early mills were purely sawmills that cut the rough blocks from the quarries to customer specifications. The earliest was in Middlebury at the falls of the Otter, but other early mills developed in Tinmouth (1821), Brandon (1828), Proctor (1838) and West Rutland (1844).

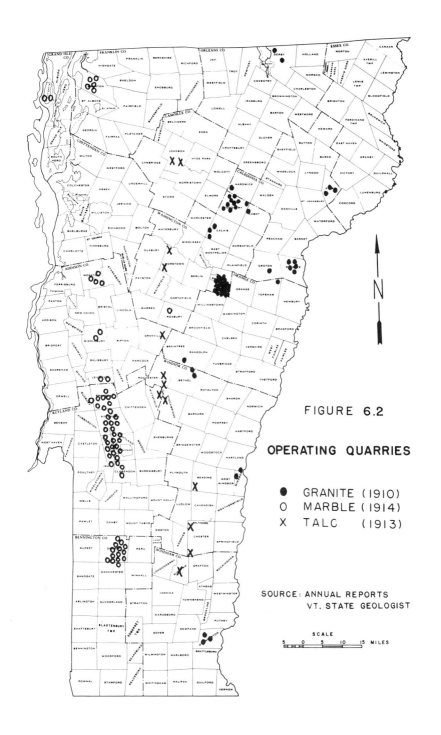

FIGURE 6.2

OPERATING QUARRIES

● GRANITE (1910)
O MARBLE (1914)
X TALC (1913)

SOURCE: ANNUAL REPORTS
VT. STATE GEOLOGIST

SCALE
5 0 5 10 15 MILES

Beginning in the 1830s Isle La Motte marble was sent by boat to Swanton for cutting, and as a result it often was sold as "Swanton Marble." It was not until 1863 that the first mechanical (steam-powered) channeling machine was used in the quarries to cut out the blocks. Before that, all quarry work was a laborious hand operation. The 1861 *Geology of Vermont* describes the early process:

> Channeling is done with long drills with chisel shaped edges. The channel, or groove is from one to two inches wide, and long and deep enough to extend the length, width and depth of the block to be raised. This being done, wedges are inserted in accessible points at the bottom of the block; in front or at the sides . . . the block is cleaved from its bed. With the derrick which is found in nearly all quarries, these blocks may be readily moved and loaded upon cart or car . . . .
>
> At this quarry it costs twenty-eight cents a foot to get these channels cut. A good workman will cut from five to ten feet— that is, a groove one foot deep and from five to ten feet in length—per diem, which yields a daily income to the workman of $1.40 to $2.80.

To earn this wage, good by the standards of the time, a quarryman had to spend 10-to-12 hour days, six days a week, 52 weeks a year working with a drill-chisel imbedded in hard marble. With no respite from the tedious hammering, it is incredible that the 19th century marble worker managed to survive long under such conditions.

After 1805, the rough stone went to the mill after quarrying. Here the block was squared off and cut to specified dimensions. In 1860 a six-inch square marble post sold for 30 cents a foot. A five-foot marble hitching post cost $1.50. (No wonder there are so many around.) A headstone two inches thick cost 5 cents a square foot without the inscription. A two-foot-by-six-foot high memorial (12 sq. ft.) could be secured for $6. It's not surprising that so many marble headstones dot early New England cemeteries, but marble was to be replaced soon by granite with its greater durability.

With the expansion of the marble industry after 1860, smaller producers were absorbed soon by larger companies, marginal quarries closed, and the overall number of companies continued to shrink. In 1870 Redfield Proctor organized the Sutherland

U.S. Route 4 swings to the south to avoid the marble town of West Rutland. The old marble sheds lie just north of town and appear as a white area in the photograph.

Falls Marble Company, combining the mill and quarries close to the falls of the Otter Creek in the then village of Sutherland Falls. Proctor acquired additional quarries and small companies, and in 1880 formed the Vermont Marble Company. In 1883 he welded all the larger companies into the Producers Marble Company. While this early cooperative venture lasted but four years it was an attempt to produce a united front with united prices against outside competition. Four companies joined with Proctor, their share of total production of Vermont marble being as follows:

Vermont Marble Company	54.7%
Sheldon and Sons	23.0%
Dorset Marble Company	5.9%
Ripley and Sons	7.3%
Gilson and Woodfin	7.0%
	97.9%

The entrance to the Vermont Marble Company Imperial Quarry in Danby. From here trucks haul marble blocks to the finishing works in Proctor.

The rise of this company dominated by the Vermont Marble Company eventually sounded the death knell to smaller companies operating elsewhere in Vermont. The first quarries in Danby were started in the 1840s and all were closed by 1870. In 1899 the properties were purchased by the Vermont Marble Company. One acquisition was the large Imperial Quarry at an elevation of 1,690 feet on the flanks of Dorset Mountain.

Vermont Marble Company commercial production from the Imperial Quarry commenced in 1907 and has become the premier source of Vermont marble. The underground operations now cover more than 16 acres and several varieties of white and off-white marbles are quarried. Annual production is more than 200,000 cubic feet. The only other marble production in Vermont is one Vermont Marble Company quarry in West Rutland (Pavanazzo Marble), a Verde Antique quarry in Rochester, and an old Goodsell quarry on Isle La Motte (Champlain Black or Radio Black Marble).

Maximum development of the quarries in Pittsford came after 1901 under ownership of the Rutland-Florence Marble Company. The "Florence" part of the company's name was in honor of Florence Smith, whose father owned the property. A Mr. Fowler of New York subsequently purchased the land, and changed the company's name to Rutland-Fowler. The Vermont Marble Company bought the company in 1911, and reverted to the original name at the request of the townspeople.

The Manchester, Dorset and Granville Railroad (the "Mud, Dirt and Gravel"—a name longer than its five-mile length) was built in Dorset in 1903 to haul marble from the quarries in South Dorset to the mills in Manchester. The operation passed to the Vermont Marble Company in 1913.

Sales figures became unavailable after the mid-1930s as the Vermont Marble Company came to dominate the business. This data is withheld from published reports because it would disclose private operating data for a single company. This is a common problem in Vermont because of the small number of concerns operating in any one product area.

With marble a depressed industry, the Vermont Marble Company ceased its marble operations during World War II and went into metal working at its plant in Proctor. Employment reached 1,250 in 1945. With structural marble no longer in great demand, granite being used for memorials, and plastics competing for counter top space, the company launched a diversification program after the war. While the Vermont Marble Company remained a producer of specialty marble items, two new divisions were established.

In 1940 the company realized the developing markets for fine-ground marble and for industrial extenders and fillers. It combined with the Thompson Weiman Company of Carterville, Georgia to form the White Pigment Corporation with plants in Vermont and in Pennsylvania. The Vermont plants are at Pittsford (Florence) and at New Haven Junction in the old Vermont Kaolin Company plant. Another plant is along Route 7 in South Wallingford. Calcium carbonate extenders and fillers for a wide range of products, including tires, chewing gum, plastic, caulking compounds and floor tile are produced.

The Ground Products Division primarily produces finely-

The once bustling marble works in West Rutland is now still as the Vermont Marble Company has concentrated all its marble finishing operations in Proctor.

ground marble for agricultural purposes, but also markets marble chips for a wide range of home landscaping uses and white "sand" for childrens' sandboxes. These two operations today are more important than the traditional marble products for which Vermont is most famous.

Summarizing the importance of the marble industry to Vermont is difficult at best because of the problem of statistics. Total sales (value) figures are as follows:

1860	$ 500,000
1880	$1,340,000
1890	$2,284,000
1900	$3,562,000
1908	$4,664,000
1916	$3,063,000
1921	$4,200,000 (estimate)
1935	$1,207,000
1945	$ 800,000 (estimate)

Col. James Fisk, Jr. was one of Vermont's most flamboyant individuals. Associated with Jay Gould in the manipulation of Erie Railroad stock, he was shot dead in 1872 over the affections of a mistress. Here his weathered visage carved in highly soluble marble looks out over a cemetery in Brattleboro.

Brigham Young, a founder of the Mormon Church, was born in Whitingham. This marble marker has withstood the ravages of time better than most.

More recent figures are less informative because of withheld data.

From about 1880-1930 Vermont was the leading producer of marble in the United States, first or second in granite, and second in slate. Georgia has challenged Vermont consistently in both marble and granite, and Pennsylvania always has produced much more slate than Vermont, which in turn always has produced considerably more than neighboring New York with whom the slate belt is shared. In the middle 1970s, Vermont ranked 21st in the nation in the production of "stone." In 1976, the Bureau of Mines ranked the state first in talc, second in marble, slate and asbestos, and third in granite, but a distant 38th in the category of "crushed and broken stone." In that year the total value of all mineral production (stone, sand and gravel) was about $35 million. Granite, marble and slate together amounted to some $11 million, talc approximately $1.7 million, and asbestos probably about $7 million. Sand and gravel production was worth $3.8 million and crushed and broken stone almost $11 million, much of which was agricultural limestone.

With information now woefully inadequate, 1983 Vermont non-metallic mineral production figures can only be approximated. Total value of production was $51.8 million. Marble, granite and slate dimension (cut) stone was $30.6 million; talc, asbestos and soapstone another $9.5 million, crushed stone (mostly agricultural limestone) $6.5 million, and construction sand and gravel $5.2 million. The state ranked second nationally in total dimension stone production, second in asbestos, and first in talc. Total tonnages quarried (in 1980) were: granite 94,565, slate 56,656, and marble, a low 18,055.

Granite

Vermont's granite industry, now the most important mineral industry in the state, developed only with the coming of the railroads. Those interested in the granitic intrusions of eastern and central sections of the state desperately needed a means of working the stone and then transporting it. Marble, on the other hand, was hewn from the rocks of western Vermont, along Lake

Champlain and in the Valley of Vermont.

Granite is the most resistant of all stones to weathering and, depending on its composition, takes an excellent polish. But its hardness, its advantage, is also its disadvantage as regards the cost of extraction. In 1916 the state geologist reported that for exterior work, granite was far more expensive than either marble or limestone. Both Massachusetts and Maine had a considerable advantage over Vermont in granite production because both possessed low-cost schooner transportation from quarry to market. Vermont granite came of age only after transportation was available and after the many small companies finally were welded into a few larger ones. (Rock of Ages, for example, was formed in 1930.) These larger companies could afford the advertising which sold the general public on the advantages of Vermont stone.

Nearly every mass of granite in Vermont has had a working quarry at one time. Bethel, Woodbury, Windsor, Derby, Dummerston, Barre, Kirby, Ryegate, East Haven, Calais, and Chester have all produced granite, but just as with marble, definition of the stone is sometimes a problem.

Seven pages in the 1861 *Report of the Vermont State Geologist,* are devoted to the subject of granite, and 28 to marble. Half of the granite discussion deals with gneiss, a metamorphosed granite important as a building material in the Proctorsville-Reading-Cavendish-Chester area. The report comments on the rather small knowledge and lack of importance of granite at the time, but urges greater attention to this resource: "The occurrence of workable granite of superior quality being so common in the State, it seems desirable that efforts be made to bring it into notice. In many instances, in the construction of buildings, persons have gone abroad to obtain granite, when an abundance was near at hand, but not being quarried, was lost sight of, and considered valueless."

For years people in many areas of eastern Vermont where the stone was found had managed to flake off occasional chunks for millstones, and word-of-mouth advertising spread knowledge of this hard and useful rock. Millstone Hill in Barre, now called Quarry Hill, received its name after Robert Parker and Thomas Courser first started quarrying there about 1812. Nowhere in

Vermont was granite much quarried, except for millstones and occasionally for doorsteps and window lintels. A firmer start to the granite industry came in the 1830s when Vermont's State House in Montpelier was being planned. The nearest place for stone was on top of the hill in nearby Barre. Before railroads, the closest stone available would be the one chosen. The capitol building, finished in 1838, was the second major building built of Vermont granite.* The quarries now developed on Millstone Hill needed other customers.

In the 1840s the city of Troy, New York needed paving blocks. Quarries on Millstone Hill provided 10 million of them. The expense of transportation must have been horrendous in this pre-railroad era. Barre had a market but no railroad. In 1849 the quarry workers on Millstone Hill watched with frustration as Charles Paine and his Vermont Central bypassed both Barre and Montpelier. For 40 more years Barre granite had to be carted to Montpelier Junction, then to Montpelier when the Vermont Central built a spur to the state capitol. It was not until 1888 that a railroad finally ascended the hill. The Barre Railroad, later the Barre and Chelsea (never to reach Chelsea), had a grade of 250 feet per mile, but at least it was a railroad. After this rail connection Barre rose to its prominent position as the granite capital of America, although Barre granite had become increasingly well-known after 1870, and more so in the '80s.

Ethnic Groups

As the fledgling industry grew with dynamic local leadership, Barre became world famous, especially in the granite areas of Carrera in northern Italy. Skilled artisans began to migrate from there in large numbers after 1880. These craftsmen helped establish Barre as a granite center and a major producer. Soon Barre had outdistanced Georgia's production.

---

*The first was Athenian Hall in Brownington, built 1834-1836 by the Rev. Alexander Twilight, the local schoolmaster and an 1823 graduate of Middlebury College.

The ethnic heritage of Barre's skilled granite craftsmen can be seen on the monuments in the Hope Cemetery in Barre.

Traditionally homogenous Vermont Yankees looked with wonder on the boisterous Irish who built the railroads and easily accepted the Cornish of the copper mines and the Welsh of the slate quarries because they spoke the same language. But as Italians began to appear in the quarry towns, mixing with smaller numbers of other southern and eastern European immigrants, degrees of ethnic tension often developed. Ethnic diversity developed in growing 19th century industrial and quarrying towns as local inhabitants could not furnish the unskilled and skilled labor needed. Springfield and Burlington drew their share, but in absolute numbers the greatest concentrations of newcomers were in the Rutland area and in Barre. The Italians were dominant in both places, although far more concentrated in the granite city. By 1910, 5.2% of the total population of Washington County (including Barre) was of Italian heritage (2,160) and 2.6% of the population of Rutland County was so classed (1,300).

There were (and some say there still are) *two* Italian communities in Vermont. Northern Italy furnished the skilled stoneworkers in such demand, and southern Italy supplied the mean bull work—the human horses deep in the quarries. The latter group came originally to work on the railroads with the Irish, but after the rails were laid soon gravitated to places where unskilled labor was needed. They were the earliest group, small in numbers compared to the later arrivals. After 1890, the northern Italians began to arrive, bound exclusively for the quarry towns. The first in this group was recruited by the Vermont Marble Company in 1882, and brought directly to Proctor to work in marble cutting. Word spread quickly, and soon the northern Italian was the dominant ethnic force in Barre, as well as in ancillary stone communities such as Northfield, South Ryegate and Hardwick. The greatest influx was in the years between 1899 and 1906, and by 1910, more than 14% of Barre's population was native to Italy.

Granite work not only attracted Italians to Vermont, but also brought skilled stoneworkers from Scotland who quickly found a home in the dominantly Scottish communities of Barnet and Ryegate. Those two towns were the only ones in Vermont settled directly from Scotland; Ryegate was settled by Scots in 1773 as a farming community under the auspices of the Scotch American Company of Farmers. Early inhabitants in neighboring Barnet were farmers from lowland western Scotland, brought there in 1774 by the United Company of Perth and Stirling. For 100 years no more Scots joined the pioneers who gradually became Presbyterian Yankees. Word of a need for good quarry workers reached Scotland and a second wave of Scots descended on the Green Mountains. The first of the new arrivals reached Barre in 1880. In 1881 and 1882, large numbers of Scots arrived in the granite quarries of Westerly, Rhode Island and Quincy, Massachusetts, and many soon migrated inland.

Speaking English, although in dialect strange to native ears, the Scots not only worked in the small quarries, but soon began to own them. At one time practically every granite quarry in northeastern Vermont was owned by a Scot. Early firms in Barre were Garrow and Rose (1881), Moss and Gordon, and Mortimer and McKenzie. By 1890, before the major influx of northern Italian stoneworkers, Barre's population was nearly 20% Scottish. For Washington County that represented 900 people, and there were an additional 170 in Caledonia, chiefly in South Ryegate, with some spillover into Groton.

Barre's population soared after 1880 with the Scots and later the Italians. From a small sleepy town of 2,100 in 1880, the population reached 8,450 in 1900 and 11,000 10 years later. In that year the population broke down as 32% native born, 38% foreign born, and 29% born of foreign parentage.

Granite Quarries

Barre today *is* Vermont granite, but that was not always the case. T. N. Dale reported in the 1907-1908 *Report of the Vermont State Geologist* that he visited "all the operative granite quarries and some of the more important granite prospects of the state—seventy nine in all—with a view to preparing a bulletin on Vermont granites. . . ." Without exception, all the quarries or prospects in the following list were within a mile or two of a railroad:

Barre	42 quarries	(all on Millstone Hill)
Woodbury	14 quarries	(6 on Robeson Mountain)
Hardwick	1 quarry	(on Buffalo Hill)
Newark	1 quarry	
Kirby	3 quarries	(all on Kirby Mountain)
Groton	1 quarry	
Ryegate	5 quarries	(all on Blue Mountain)
Topsham	2 quarries	(1 on Pine Mountain)
Derby	2 quarries	
Randolph	1 prospect	(adjoins Bethel)
Williamstown	3 quarries	(adjacent to Barre quarries)
Cabot	1 quarry	(north corner)
Calais	3 quarries	(in Adamant)
Dummerston	3 quarries	(all on Black Mountain)
Bethel	2 quarries	(on Christian Hill)
Rochester	1 quarry	(on Liberty Hill)
Windsor	2 quarries	(on Mt. Ascutney)

An abandoned Woodbury granite quarry sits atop Robeson Mountain. Stone from this quarry went by rail to Hardwick where it was finished.

The list totals 87 granite quarries, some not operating in 1907, and others simply small prospects from which a few stones had been removed. But the distribution of quarries is the distribution of granitic intrusions and the accessibility of railway transportation (Figures 6.1 and 6.2).

Like marble, there are differences in granite, although not to the extent that any stone removed from the ground, cut and polished, was at one time billed "marble." All granites are of igneous origin, and they are grouped into three major types—biotite granite, quartz monzonite granite, and hornblend augite granite. In appearance only, the biotite granites, such as those at Woodbury and Barre, are generally the "gray" or dark granites. This is because the mica, a mineral in all granites, is dark-colored. In the quartz monzonite granites, the mica usually is lighter in color, but sometimes can be dark-colored biotite. Mineralogically the primary characteristic of these granites is that "the soda-lime feldspar occurs in an unusual amount, nearly equaling or even exceeding that of the potash feldspars." Unfortunately, there is no really easy way to differentiate visually the biotite from the quartz monzonite granites, except that the former are usually darker and denser than the latter. Bethel granite (a white quartz monzonite granite) is coarse and absorbs water far more readily than the Barre granites. It also cleans better and stays white longer, thus it has been important for external building stone. The hornblend augite granite is distinctive. It is olive green in appearance and is technically a "syenite" rather than a granite. It occurs in Vermont only at Mt. Ascutney.

In the early years, granite production was insignificant compared to that of marble. In 1880, the first year for which statistics are available, the total value of Vermont granite sold was only $60,000. That compares with the $1.3 million for marble in the same year. The rise of the granite industry can be summarized in the following statistics:

Value of Granite Produced

1880	$	59,675
1890	$	610,963
1900	$	1,113,788
1907	$	2,693,886
1913	$	3,782,235
1916	$	2,560,579
1935	$	1,932,954
1945	$	10,805,607
1951	$	6,500,000
1962	$	7,500,000 (est.)

After 1950, data on the production of Vermont granite, marble and other stones is inadequate. The high figure reported for 1945 represents military contracts for war memorials. In 1983 the total value of all stone quarried in Vermont including granite, marble and slate, was $30.6 million. Granite was the most important.

Granite overtook marble as Vermont's major economically-important stone about 1913 or 1914, and has since maintained its preeminence. While little granite is used today for structural purposes, the industry produces memorial stones and also crushes stone. As early as 1916, 74% of Vermont granite was being sold for monuments, and only 26% for "building material." Were it not for the inevitable death, Vermont granite would be a depressed industry. Even so, there has been a large drop in granite workers from the 2,500 reported in 1916 to fewer than 900 employed today in *all* aspects of mineral extraction.

In 1980 there were less than 250 quarrymen in Washington County (which includes Barre). The golden age, if in fact there ever was one in Vermont granite quarrying, was in the early decades of the 20th century. The present industry, while profitable, is not the same as in that era when there were nearly 100 quarries in the state, and expert Italian craftsmen finished the rough-cut stone. Quarry Hill in Barre is pockmarked with old quarries. Only two still quarry the hard rock which has made Vermont famous. As of 1980 the only other quarrying was some small production from Bethel. Occasional stones still come from Woodbury, Derby, Dummerston and other places to replace structural granite needing replacement in buildings throughout the United States. The days are long gone when nearly every mass of granite in Vermont was being quarried.

A complete inventory of all granite quarries in Vermont in the *Report of the Vermont State Geologist* for 1909-1910 supplies an incredible mass of information on the industry at its maximum development—at least geographically. In the 1870s only two quarries were developed; in the 1880s that number increased to 12, only to decrease to five the following decade. Between 1900 and 1910, 21 new quarries were started. While there is little precise information beyond this point, the number of quarries probably expanded considerably until about 1920, only to decline significantly afterwards. This decline might be related to a 1910 comment by the state geologist that "this quarry is not worked at haying time."

It is hard to travel anywhere in the United States and not find Vermont granite. Probably every 20th century graveyard will have a few memorials, if not of Vermont granite, at least of granite which was polished and cut in the state. While stone from the quarries in Kirby, Hardwick, Ryegate, Topsham, Barre and Groton was used chiefly for monuments, other areas produced stone for many important buildings throughout the United

States. Granite from Derby can be seen in the Prison Ship Martyrs' Monument in Fort Green Park, Brooklyn, New York. This is possibly the highest granite shaft to be found in the country, 150 feet high, with a diameter of 18 feet at the base and 14 feet at the top. The quarries in Adamant in Calais chiefly produced monumental stone, but granite from the Old Lake Shore Quarry was used in the Soldiers' Memorial Building in Stowe. The Black Mountain quarries in Dummerston produced the stone used in the post office building, Troy, New York and the old Plaza Hotel in New York City. Because of its whiteness Bethel granite was very popular for imposing structures. The beautiful Union Station in Washington, D. C. is from stone quarried in Bethel, as are the state library and Connecticut Supreme Court buildings in Hartford, Connecticut and the Wisconsin State Capitol in Madison.

Woodbury too produced enormous tonnages of building stone. Woodbury granite can be found in the Pennsylvania State Capitol in Harrisburg, the Cook County Courthouse, Chicago, in the Kentucky State Capitol (home of 36 interior polished columns), and in the Carnegie Library in Syracuse, New York. Closer to home, the Soldiers' Monument in Manchester is of stone from Woodbury.

Large memorials made of Barre granite include the Joseph Smith Memorial in Bethel, Vermont, the Calhoun Monument in Lexington, Kentucky, the John D. Rockefeller Monument in Cleveland, Ohio, and, of all things, the Memorial to Persons Killed in the Flour Mill Explosion in Minneapolis, Minnesota. Except for the Vermont Statehouse, Barre granite was not used as much as some other Vermont granites for public buildings. This is because Barre granite is more massive and does not possess the "sheeting" which makes some other granites easier to split.

Slate

Marble, granite and slate are the stones for which Vermont is known. The third in the trilogy was less important historically in production and value, but has been economically important in those Vermont communities where it is a resource.

Slate is metamorphosed shale. It is dark in color, but the original sediments which were compressed into the shales often were colorful. That color shows in the slates we buy today for flagstones. Vermont slate generally has been described as "blue-green," although many Vermont slates are nearly black in color. Through a geologic accident, the red slates come entirely from New York, and crushed red New York slate has recently found an important market in tennis court surfacings. The Vermont slate industry once enjoyed considerable prosperity, with important markets in pool tables, blackboards, roofing slates, gravestones, school slates, window sills, and even "marbleized" slate for mantels.

A Colonel Alonson Allen often is credited with the first slate quarrying in Vermont, digging and splitting a bit of the rock from his back pasture in Fair Haven in 1839. In 1848, the first slate-roofed barn was built. It still stands a mile south of the Village of Fair Haven along Route 22A. The 1861 *Report of the Vermont State Geologist*, however, notes that as early as 1812, some slate was quarried in Guilford by the New England Slate Company. Very early slate quarrying in the United States took place about 1721 outside of Boston and as early as 1734 at Delta, Pennsylvania. All these early quarries produced roofing slates exclusively, the only real market for the material at the time.

The *Report* of 1861 describes three north-south slate belts in Vermont. The eastern belt ran from Waterford on the north to Guilford, cutting back and forth across the Connecticut River. A central belt included a zone from Lake Memphremagog south as far as Barnard, and a western belt included the towns of Sudbury, Hubbardton, Castleton, Fair Haven, Poultney and Wells. It was this last slate belt which was to become the most important of the Vermont slate areas (see Figure 6.1).

Slate in eastern Vermont never amounted to very much. The Waterford Slate Company began operations in the early 1850s. It produced some roofing slate, and even some tombstones which still can be seen in scattered cemeteries in northeastern Vermont. The Fairlee Slate Company worked a quarry in 1857, and the Howard Slate Company was active in North Thetford close to the Connecticut and Passumpsic Railroad about 1858. Slate from this area had been quarried as early as 1820.

The slates of eastern Vermont were generally rather poor. The stone was difficult to split, and often contained a large amount of iron in the form of iron pyrites. Those small brassy-yellow cubes common in the slates might be appealing to the eye, but soon rust when exposed to the atmosphere. A red or green stain appears initially on the surface of the square, but as the rusting proceeds, a small hole develops where the small pyrite crystal once found a nesting place.

The only area ever worked in the central slate zone was in Northfield, although some diggings occurred in East Montpelier. Quarrying in Northfield began before 1860 and lasted until the first World War. Several quarries operated intermittently over the years.

In 1860 the Northfield Slate Company employed 20 men and was producing 200 squares of roofing slates a month at an average selling price of $3.75 a square. (One square of slate is approximately 120 square feet; technically it is the amount of slate that would be required to roof 100 square feet with the slate so put down that there would be a three-inch overlap with each tile laid.)

In 1850, the future great slate-quarrying area of western Vermont was on a par with the other areas in the state. Production was small, with roofing slates predominant. School slates were an important product and some tombstones still were manufactured. Things began to happen in the 1850s which led to the significant expansion of the area, overshadowing developments elsewhere.

First came the Rutland and Washington Railroad, later the Rensselaer and Saratoga and finally the Delaware and Hudson. The railroad was welcomed enthusiastically by operators of marble quarries in the West Rutland area, and by the few fledgling slate operators in Fair Haven and Castleton. Regular service on the Rutland and Washington began in 1852. At this time two families from Wales arrived in Middle Granville, New York. The men skilled in working slate in the old country became active in the Penrhyn Slate Company which was the first slate company in Granville. They were followed soon by many skilled Welsh stoneworkers, who found ready employment in an expanding industry and provided the skilled labor necessary for expansion. As was the case with Barre granite, it was the combination of railroad transportation and a skilled labor force which led to growth of the industry in Fair Haven, Poultney, Pawlet, Wells and Castleton. As is true today in the slate areas of Pennsylvania, names such as Jones, Roberts, Thomas, Hughes, Lloyd, Williams, and Evans are indicative of this ethnic cohesion. More striking are the girls' first names of Megan and Gwen, or the boys, Llewllyn and even Gwillym. These small towns in western Vermont are one of the most concentrated areas of Welsh in the United States, and Green Mountain College in Poultney houses an important library collection of Welsh Americana.

By 1885, there were 72 firms working the slate belt and there were a considerably greater number of holes in the ground. A total of 29 slate companies were producing structural slate, 37 roofing slate, one slate pencils and five were engaged in producing marbleized slate. This was paint baked onto a slate slab to make it look like onyx. It was a popular product in the late 1800s for shelves, mantles, tabletops and clock cases. Structural slate was used for window sills, slabs, blackboards and flooring.

Pennsylvania always has ranked first in slate production but Vermont has been a consistent second, both in quantity and value of its product. Vermont average production from 1890-1900 was about 44% of the production of Pennsylvania. A prolonged strike in Wales during that period helped bolster U.S. prices, and the industry was remarkably prosperous.

By 1908, sales of Vermont slate amounted to about $2 million, only a little less than granite ($2.7 million), but considerably less than marble ($4.7 million). After this date the value of production gradually declined with competition not only from Pennsylvania, but from other materials as well. The data is as follows:

Year	Value of Slate Production
1910	$1,800,000
1916	$1,607,901 (63% roofing slate)
1921	$2,500,000 (approximate)
1945	$1,916,979 (includes New York)

Like other Vermont stone products recent data is a problem,

Piles of broken slate litter the Vermont slate belt as can be seen in this photograph of Wells. Below, West Pawlet clearly shows economic stagnation.

but now the tonnage of slate quarried exceeds that of marble, and the value of slate probably is about the same as granite. In 1981 slate for interior flooring alone was valued at $9.2 million. Other slate uses were less important.

It is dubious whether or not there will be much further expansion in the western Vermont slate belt. Roofing slate is still produced and rough slate for flagstones in nicely landscaped gardens is still available. But, because of the considerable weight involved, transportation charges seriously affect the retail market, and there seems little likelihood of the Vermont slate industry seeing any major boom. In the early 1980s there were still 17 companies engaged in either slate quarrying or milling in the western Vermont–eastern New York slate belt. Addresses show 11 in New York (all but one in Granville or Middle Granville), with the remainder in West Pawlet, Fair Haven and Poultney, Vermont.

New uses for an old product are illustrated by the Vermont Light Aggregate Corporation of Castleton. This division of Plasticrete Corporation quarries slate, crushes it, and expands it in a rotary kiln. The product is used as a replacement for sand and gravel in concrete blocks. Consequently the blocks are lighter and have better insulation qualities. A future use might involve the quarrying of the rock, and a reworking of the old broken piles of waste material for the aluminum content. Slate contains about 16% aluminum oxide (Al_2O_3). Bauxite, the present aluminum ore largely imported from Surinam and the Caribbean area, averages between 20% and 25% Al_2O_3 and being softer, easier, and cheaper to process is the major source of supply for American industry. This may change, and it is a possibility that at some time the slates of Pennsylvania, New York and Vermont may be valuable sources of this important raw material.

Talc, Asbestos and Soapstone

There was a previous explanation of serpentine, the ultramafic rock common along the eastern side of the Green Mountains. Alternating deposits of talc, asbestos and soapstone are strung like beads on a chain from the Canadian border to Windham County (Figures 6.1 and 6.2). Today asbestos is quarried or mined (both terms are used) only on Belvidere Mountain which sits astride the Lowell-Eden town line. Talc is mined (never quarried) in Johnson, Chester, West Windsor, Cavendish and other localities. Soapstone is quarried (not mined) presently in Chester and Newfane.

In 1845 Professor Adams, the state geologist, noted that "soapstone, so called on account of its greasy feel, is one of the softest minerals, being easily cut with a knife. It is a variety of talc...." Concerning its uses he says: "Besides its uses as a firestone lining for culinary furnaces and stoves, it takes a good polish and is an ornamental stone, although from its softness, liable to be defaced. It is used in the manufacture of some kinds of porcelain, to render the ware more transparent, and also for polishing, for removing grease spots from woolen or silk . . . etc." The good professor forgets to note its use in footwarmers, and of course could not foresee that today soapstone griddles would be a popular trade item featured in many Vermont roadside gift shops. He would be astonished to learn that the material now finds a use in marijuana paraphernalia. Laundry tubs, cutting boards, and even a lubricant (when reduced to a powder) were other uses of this unique rock which can be cut easily with a saw with only a bit more effort than that required to saw a pine two-by-four.

Until 1845, soapstone (or steatite) was quarried in Grafton, Bridgewater, Bethel and Rochester. Additional production was reported in 1861 in Marlboro, Roxbury, Warren, Waitsfield, Moretown, Waterbury, Stowe and other towns to the north. The 1861 *Report* makes the very valid point that: "beds are also found in Belvidere, Johnson, Eden, Lowell, Westfield, Jay and Troy, but we feel they are invariably associated with serpentine and occur in beds of limited extent." Unknowingly, the state geologist was talking of talc and asbestos deposits. There two are so closely related that the 19th century geologist had difficulty unraveling the complex mineralogy.

One company in Perkinsville still is quarrying and manufacturing soapstone articles. Other Vermont concerns are engaged in manufacturing stove panels and are finding a ready market because of the ability of the stone to heat quickly and then retain the heat for long periods of time. In fact, the 1861 *Report* concludes its discussion of soapstone with the following comment: "A 'Stone Franklin' stove, manufactured by the Tingley Brothers from the Weathersfield stone, now warms the room in which we are writing; and although it has been subjected to great heat—still is uninjured by crack or blemish, and we can believe that it will prove as durable as though it was made of iron."

The amount and value of soapstone quarried never has been too important. In 1916, Virginia was the leading soapstone state, and the total tonnage quarried in the United States was only 19,700 tons. Over the years there is little mention of the material. In 1920 the total value of soapstone *and* talc produced in Vermont was about $500,000, and in 1945 it was $841,000. The value of soapstone produced today is certainly well under $500,000, or less than 2% of the total value of Vermont mineral production. National statistics on soapstone do not even mention the state.

The combination of talc and soapstone in the reported figures is no accident as the two materials are closely related, both in their geology and in the areas in which they are quarried and mined. Talc gets no mention at all in the early geology reports. The emphasis is on soapstone because of its utilitarian value to the Vermont of the period. One of the first mentions of talc as a substance on its own merit was in 1908. Roxbury, Bridgewater, Lowell, Newfane, Rochester, East Granville, Chester, Moretown and Johnson are listed as talc localities. Mines were being operated at Moretown, East Granville, Johnson, Windham and Rochester, with Rochester, Johnson and Windham the most important. The mine at Johnson had been opened only recently. A Mr. Freeland Jewett, president of the Eastern Talc Company in Rochester reportedly commented: "There is no doubt but that the Vermont talc is the smoothest and softest of any produced in this country . . . The whole problem of producing talc in a profitable way is governed by two points; one of which is getting rid of impurities, and the other, having proper transportation facilities." Mineral-processing technology could eliminate the impurities, but once again, only railroad transportation could alleviate the shipping problem. One of the most ambitious railways in Vermont ran from the White River in Talcville just south of Rochester to the summit of the nearby hill where the talc was being mined. The mill itself was in Talcville at the foot of a precipitous incline. One of the major reasons for the development of the White River Railroad from Bethel to Rochester was the talc deposits close to the line.

In 1913, Vermont's talc production was worth $327,360 from the nearly 46,000 tons shipped. Both Virginia and New York produced considerably more in both tonnage and value. In a complete report of the industry in 1913 and 1914, the state geologist listed 24 towns in which commercial deposits were found. This 1913-1914 *Report of the Vermont State Geologist* (ninth in the series) contains detailed descriptions of each talc operation and is recommended reading for anyone wishing a more detailed discussion of the industry as it existed at the time.

By 1916 Vermont was producing 73,200 tons of pure talc annually, with a value of $501,000. Only New York was a more important producer. With uses as wide-ranging as a filler in bond paper, an ingredient in paint and varnish, and further use in the manufacturing of leather products, roofing materials, automobile tires, insecticides, talc crayons, and scented powder, the industry was doing well before the advent of synthetic chemical materials.

Small scattered mining operations were being consolidated gradually. The Eastern Talc Company of Rochester merged with the American Minerals Company (Johnson-1900) and the Magnesia Talc Company (Waterbury-Moretown-1900) to form the Eastern Magnesia Talc Company in 1924. This concern dominated the northern Vermont talc industry with its mines a few miles north of its mill in Johnson. Operations ceased in November 1983, but the mill was being reactivated under new ownership only two years later. Today the only talc production is centered in southern Vermont. Windsor Minerals, a relatively new concern, has mills in West Windsor and Ludlow and gets ore from scattered mines in the talc belt of Windsor County. Production comes from Chester, Windsor, Cavendish (Hammondsville) and other localities. Vermont Talc, a division of the Vermont Marble Company, has operations in Chester.

Recovery of pure talc runs about 20% of the ore mined and sent to the mills—a reasonably high recovery rate. The purity of the finished product is such that several major manufacturers of

Headframe of the Eastern Magnesia Talc Company mine in Johnson. The mine is no longer in existence, and the structure has been demolished.

talc powder get most of their raw material from Vermont. Vermont led the United States in talc production in 1983.

Because of its great utility to a pioneer society, interest first was concentrated on the soapstone found in the serpentine rocks of east central Vermont. Talc came next. Asbestos, the third mineral, evoked little interest or enthusiasm until after the turn of the century. No mention of asbestos fiber is found in the early reports of the state geologist. No commodity becomes a resource until a use is discovered for it, and in the case of bulky raw materials, until there is a way of getting the product out. The first real consideration of Vermont's asbestos deposits is in the 1909-1910 *Report of the Vermont State Geologist.* True chrysotile asbestos fiber apparently was discovered about 1893 on the southwest side of Belvidere Mountain by a French-Canadian lumberjack employed by Judge M.E. Tucker. Perhaps the Canadian was familiar with the asbestos of Thetford, Quebec. This asbestos is a northern continuation of the Vermont deposits. The discovery apparently set off some sort of mini-boom, because by 1906 there were four prominent asbestos properties in northern Vermont. One was in Lowell, with mineral rights owned by the same Judge Tucker, and another was on the Lowell-Westfield town line. On the south side of Belvidere Mountain, six companies had staked leases in the town of Eden. They included the New England Asbestos Company with a 198-year lease on 90 acres, the Brown Asbestos Company, the United States Asbestos Company, the Lamoille Asbestos Company, the Blake and Lewis Asbestos Company, and the Stearns and Farrington Asbestos Company. Although undocumented, it is conceivable that this asbestos rush, like the earlier gold rushes, may have been occasioned by the use of the material in brake linings of Henry Ford's tin lizzie, as well as the now-common uses in shingles, siding, roofing, cement, building board, paper, felt, and pipe coverings.

The last locale of intense asbestos speculation was on the northeast side of Belvidere Mountain in Lowell. A small mining community called Chrysotile was established there by the Lowell Lumber and Asbestos Company which had bought out the aforementioned Judge Tucker. In 1909 this company produced 2,100 pounds of asbestos fiber from its new mill with a value of about $200,000. Considerable optimism characterized the Lowell Lumber and Asbestos Company. There were even company pronouncements on the possibility of a railway up the Missisquoi Valley. The optimism apparently was unfounded. In 1910, the Lowell Lumber and Asbestos Company was the Chrysotile Asbestos Corporation, and there was no production, and certainly no railroad. Ensuing reports of the state grologist make no mention of asbestos in Vermont. Small production continued under various company names, but the diggings on Belvidere Mountain were unimportant in a national context. Tucked in a 1916 report on mineral resources by the U.S. Geological Survey is the following comment:

> The Vermont area contains very little spinning fiber, but it is now attracting much attention. No production has

recently been made. Although in the production of chrysotile asbestos Vermont cannot compete successfully with Canada, the material in Vermont should be regarded as a valuable reserve if the Canadian deposits were not available.

The Vermont Asbestos Corporation took over the old workings in 1930, invested some capital, and in that year apparently produced 83% of United States asbestos. Production amounted to 3,530 tons. Changing statistical measurements of production make a comparison of this figure to the 2,100 pounds of 1909 impossible, but apparently the industry was still alive, although woefully small compared to the production in Quebec. While the mines on Belvidere Mountain produce more than 90% of U.S. chrysotile asbestos today the amount is less than 10% of domestic requirements, and nearly all asbestos used in the country comes from the enormous deposits north of the Vermont border.

During World War II output from Belvidere Mountain increased significantly. In 1945, 150 men were employed and nearly 400,000 tons of asbestos-bearing rock were processed and at an average recovery rate of 6% about 24,000 tons of fiber were produced. The company shut down its old workings on the south face of the mountain and began production northeast of the original site. An aerial tramway was installed to bring the rock from high up on the mountainside to the mill.

Production continued to increase after the war, and in 1953 about 50,000 tons of fiber were shipped out, providing an important source of revenue for the struggling St. Johnsbury and Lamoille County Railroad.

During the 1960s production declined somewhat. The equipment was getting older and the richer ore body was being depleted. Faced with Environmental Protection Agency requests to control the amount of asbestos dust in the mill, the current owner, the Rubberoid Corporation, finally decided to sell the property. A closure would have had a disastrous effect upon the region. While only 200 workers were employed in 1973-1974, it was the only employment available. Loss of tax revenues to Lowell would have hurt. Tonnage would have been lost to the barely-surviving railroad. In an area already economically depressed a loss of 200 jobs could not possibly be absorbed into

The Vermont Asbestos Group mill and quarry on the flank of Belvidere Mountain in the town of Lowell.

existing industries. The situation worsened when no buyers were found for the property. In desperation, the workers bought the mine and its equipment. Two thousand shares were issued at a cost of $500 each, the selling price being $1 million. All shares were sold and the Vermont Asbestos Group became an employee-owned industry. The VAG flourished under local management. Emissions were cleaned up, production increased because of aggressive sales tactics, and by 1976 the U.S. Bureau of Mines reported that the value of Vermont asbestos production was about $7 million. The $500 shares were worth $2,200 in 1977 and after a sometimes bitter proxy fight the VAG was purchased by a local Morrisville businessman.

Since then Vermont's asbestos industry has had a checkered history. A new wallboard mill in Morrisville was supposed to use fibers from old tailings in manufacturing wall panels. The fibers had insufficient tensil strength and in 1982 the mill was leased to the Masonite Corporation.

Concerns about cancer have had a depressing effect on sales. About 200 employees are involved in the present operation, but 1981, 1982, 1983 and 1985 saw protracted layoffs and a sharp curtailment of production. The ore body now yields about 2.8% asbestos per ton but beneficiation will raise that to nearly 4% before milling and ensure reserves at least until about 1995. Production in 1980 was about 40,000 tons of fiber but it appears that the future of Vermont asbestos may be somewhat cloudy.

Building Stones and Lime

There are quite a few larger public and educational buildings in Vermont constructed of locally-quarried stone. The gray limestone campus of Middlebury College is striking as is the Redstone Campus of the University of Vermont. Other buildings include the Grand Isle County Courthouse in North Hero, the Vermont State Capitol, the headquarters buildings of the Vermont Marble Company in Proctor and the Old Stone House (Athenian Hall) in Brownington of which little is known.

Smaller homes of local stone sometimes can be found; there are a few of fieldstone construction, but glacially-rounded boulders usually were hard to work with, so these dwellings are rare. More common are structures of either limestone or gneiss (a metamorphosed granite) which were much easier to split and work by hand. Two areas of Vermont are unique because of their concentrations of stone houses. Both reflect the availability of stone suitable for that purpose.

The most concentrated cluster of stone houses is in Windsor County. These beautiful structures, constructed of local gneiss, were built between 1835 and 1845. There are about 75 of these buildings; 10 in Chester Depot along the main road north of the village and another 10 scattered throughout the rest of Chester. Eighteen are in Cavendish, largely along Routes 131 and 106. The remainder are chiefly in Reading, especially in South Reading, and some in Springfield. In addition to the homes, there are three churches and at least two schools showing similar construction. Most of the structures were built by the Clark Brothers of

Beautiful buildings of gneiss are found in a concentrated area in Windsor County. Above is the church in Reading; below, a private home in the same village. Other structures are common in Chester and Cavendish.

One of the regional concentrations of stone buildings in Vermont is in Grand Isle County. This is the library building on Isle La Motte, made of limestone from the Fisk Quarry. These limestones once were sold commercially as marble.

Chester Depot, and the gneiss used there was quarried on Mt. Flamstead.

Just north of Proctorsville on the Twenty-Mile Stream Road are two gneiss homes built by Zephaniah and David Ordway, two brothers who owned the local grist mill. The mill is now in ruins, but the old capstone of the front door, dated July 4, 1840, marks the spot of the Twenty-Mile Encampment of the Crown Point Military Road three miles north of the old mill. The geologic map in Chapter 4 (Figure 4.1) shows that this area of Vermont has a very complex geology. Metamorphism was considerable, and while granite does not lend itself to easy splitting, the metamorphosed gneiss is foliated and is much easier to work.

The other regional concentration of stone dwellings is in Grand Isle County although isolated limestone houses can be found throughout the Champlain Valley. There are at least 20 structures in Grand Isle County towns, many built of stone from the Fisk Quarry. The small library on Isle La Motte is a beautiful building, and the South Hero Inn of 1829 is one of the larger structures. Most were built between 1820 and 1840, allegedly by a builder from the north of England.

In the early reports of the Vermont state geologist there are few references to stone being used for building purposes. There is no mention of gneiss except long ago when it was confused with granite. Limestone, however, is a frequent topic although rarely noted as a building stone. This is because limestone is a very utilitarian material, and its uses for things other than structures was important. In the first *Annual Report of the State Geologist* (1845) it receives an equal treatment with marble, partly perhaps because even then the differences were unclear. While finely-pulverized agricultural limestone came into use after 1900, production in the 19th century mainly supplied the scattered blast furnaces with a flux (Chapter 5) and provided the many lime kilns with their raw material.

Lime kilns originally produced "lump lime"—pure nuggets of calcium carbonate. This material was called quicklime when it was crushed and was a very perishable commodity. One has to understand how lime kilns worked to understand them and their product.

Inside a typical kiln are three imaginary compartments, one at the top, one in the middle, and one at the bottom. They are not separated by any structure within the kiln itself, except that there must be a separation between the source of heat and the limestone above. The kiln is lined with refractory material throughout. The top compartment (called the hopper) is where crushed limestone is dumped, the middle compartment is the "shaft" where the limestone is "burned." It is narrower than the hopper and the charge of limestone easily falls into it from above. Below the shaft is the cooler where the burned lime falls. Iron doors called shears allow the burned lump lime to be removed.

Lump lime was crushed to a powder called quicklime, but sometimes the shipment from kiln to customer was in lumps depending on the individual order. The problem with the material was its high perishability because upon exposure to an atmosphere with any humidity it would harden and lose its bonding properties. The difficulty of keeping the product dry from producer to consumer was responsible for the many small kilns throughout the state. Most were on the limestones of the Champlain Valley, but other small kilns were in Plymouth, Cavendish, Weathersfield, Wilmington and other places where some form of limestone was found. Quicklime from Weathersfield was used in the Central Vermont Railroad tunnel in Burlington in 1850.

Hydrated lime began to replace quicklime about 1900. Hydrated (slaked) lime is a product in which the quicklime is treated to reduce its perishability so that production no longer had to be located close to the customer. In its manufacture, quicklime is fed into a hydrator where, under constant agitation, it is mixed with water. The end result is a packaged powder product capable of withstanding long-distance shipment without losing its property as a mortar and its other uses in the chemical, tanning or paper industries. The production of hydrated lime led to the closing of many small kilns which once dotted the state.

In 1916 Vermont lime production was worth more than $230,000. Another $68,000 should be added to this, representing quarried limestone for agricultural purposes, a use which was just beginning to become widespread. In 1916 too the Vermont Marble Company put into operation the most modern rotary kiln and hydrator in the country. Vermont ranked 19th in the United States in the tonnage of quicklime and hydrated lime produced (43,300 tons).

The year 1916 was the apex for Vermont's lime industry. Use and production was as follows:

Building (mortar and plaster)	77,741 tons
Chemicals	5,160 tons
Paper manufacturing	15,307 tons
Tanneries	6,407 tons
Agricultural	1,276 tons
Other uses	7,435 tons
	43,326 tons

Nine plants in 1916 produced 13,000 tons more lime than the 30 plants which had been operating as recently as 1913, a reflection of the less-perishable nature of hydrated lime. Excluding crushed agricultural limestone, 90% of production was

This old steel lime kiln is at the Huntley Quarry in Leicester Junction. It operated until about 1930 and is now rusting away. No old stone lime kilns exist in Vermont.

consumed outside of the state. Major users were the steel furnaces at Port Henry, New York and paper mills in Holyoke and North Adams, Massachusetts.

Lime output gradually declined during the 1920s and 1930s as major national producers easily could handle the small market which the state represented. In 1918 there were seven active operations and one inactive as reported by the Vermont state geologist:

> Missisquoi Lime Works Inc., Highgate Springs: Production began in 1888. Five woodburning kilns.
>
> Fonda Lime Kilns, Fonda Junction: Production began in 1846. Five kilns using soft coal. Capacity 18,000 tons annually.
>
> Swanton Lime Works, Swanton: Production began 1877. Five gas burning kilns and five wood burning. Annual capacity 15,000 tons.
>
> Champlain Valley Lime Corporation (of Massachusetts), Winooski: Production began in 1829. Three woodburning kilns. 3,000 tons but a considerable amount of crushed limestone for agriculture produced.
>
> Green Mountain Lime Co., New Haven Junction: Five wood and coal burning kilns. Annual capacity 20,000 tons.
>
> Brandon Lime and Marble Company, Leicester Junction: Two wood fired kilns (one still standing in 1985). Annual capacity 7,000 tons.
>
> Vermont Marble Company, West Rutland: One new rotary kiln. Burns marble. Annual production of hydrated lime 26,000 tons.
>
> Pownal Lime Company, Pownal: inactive, 1918.

As late as 1935 quicklime still was being manufactured at Swanton, Fonda Junction and New Haven, and hydrated lime was produced in Winooski by the Vermont Marble Company. The last plant to produce lime (in Colchester) closed in 1971.

The decline in lime production was accompanied by an increase in agricultural use of crushed limestone. As early as 1916 the following comment was made in the *Report of Mineral In-*

dustries in the United States published by the U.S. Geological Survey:

> ... the increase in the number of producing states points
> to a gradually broadening recognition of the value of lime
> in agriculture. A steadily increasing quantity of pulverized
> limestone is sold for this purpose at an average price of
> little more than $1.00 a ton.

While it was being recognized that limestone could help improve crop yields, Vermont farmers of the period were rather reluctant to try anything new. In 1929 only Maine was lower than Vermont regionally as regards agricultural use of limestone. On a pounds-per-acre basis, Massachusetts led with 92, Connecticut, 53, Rhode Island, 21, New Hampshire, 10.5, Vermont, eight and Maine, five. The value of limestone on acid soils is universally recognized now and the Swanton Lime Works and the Ground Products Division of the Vermont Marble Company are major local producers of this important product. In 1973 the Swanton Lime Works alone shipped more than 40,000 tons on the struggling St. Johnsbury and Lamoille County Railroad. In the early 1980s Vermont limestone production was valued at about $7 million.

Clay

Vermont's only other important non-metallic mineral resource was kaolin or china clay, not to be confused with famous "mud season" clay found throughout much of the state. Kaolin was something special and had its place in the development of Vermont industry. In 1845, the Vermont state geologist devoted a few paragraphs in his report to the subject of clay, but the word kaolin never appeared, possibly because it had not been invented yet. But 15 years later in the 1861 *Report* he devotes several pages to the topic. The word itself is derived from the Chinese word "kauling" which refers to a hill near Jauchu Fa in North China.

Clay is technically a kaolin clay when it is dominated by the mineral kaolinite ($Al_2 Si_2 O_5 OH_4$). Poorer grades are used in stoneware and pottery, and the finer materials in porcelain and fine china. Most Vermont kaolins come from the weathering of a mineral called feldspar. Many reports of kaolin extraction in Vermont are of dubious validity because there is no verification that the material is kaolin. It could be some less-valuable form of clay. The old reports made no distinction, calling all clay dug from the ground "kaolin."

The largest production of fine-quality kaolin clay came from beds in Monkton near Bristol. There in 1792 the Monkton Porcelain Earth first worked on clays reportedly similar to those of Bennington. Production from these clay beds continued uninterruptedly for 175 years. During the War of 1812 it was reported that the Monkton clays were used as whiteners for army belts, and completion of the Champlain Canal in 1823 provided an outlet for the product after it was hauled to Vergennes for transshipment to lake and canal boats. The material had many uses with its use in fine china being the most obvious and well-known. It was (and is) used in stove linings, paint and linoleum fillers, rubber tires and heels, roofing and even in Kaopectate! The last operator of the Monkton Porcelain Earth was the Vermont Kaolin Company which in 1955 built a modern mill alongside Route 7 and the Rutland Railway tracks in New Haven Junction. The company ceased operations about 1970, not because the clay beds were exhausted, but because high transportation costs and distance from markets made continuing production uneconomic. Paper companies were the largest consumers of kaolin in the 1960s but nearby producers could satisfy their needs. The modern mill now is owned by the Vermont Marble Company.

Mineral Industries Today

Throughout its history, most Vermont manufacturing was involved with the extraction and processing of raw materials. Vermont was a source of industrial raw materials for growing urban centers both in Canada and in southern New England. Wood and wood products were very important, and potash from wood ashes was Vermont's first export (See Chapter 11). Equally important were the various minerals, rocks, stones and mud extracted by various means from the bedrock hills or the flat valleys. As with wood, after 1850 the railroads too gave a significant boost to Vermont mineral industries, and minerals in various forms, along with people, were the state's most important exportable commodities for many years.

Today the mineral industries are relatively unimportant in the state's economy. By the optimistic calculations of the middle 1970s, the total employment in both the processing and direct extraction of minerals (mining, quarrying, and sand and gravel extraction) amounted to perhaps 4,000 workers, or 2% of the Vermont labor force of a little more than 195,000. (That compares with more than 16,000 people still working in agriculture.) The total payroll in 1972 included $7.2 million in extraction, $21.2 million in processing, and an additional $4.7 million in the sand and gravel business, for a grand total of $33.4 million. That same year skiers in Vermont spent some $52 million. Even if the indirect employment is added into the mix (workers on railroads which haul the stone, manufacturers of mining tools and equipment, companies which provide the power, etc.) there was a maximum of perhaps 2,700 more jobs attributable to the mineral industries with an additional payroll of $18.7 million. The grand total still equalled only out-of-pocket skier expenditures for the same year.

The industry seems to have stabilized since then. The 1980 Census of Population records 793 people who list "mining" as their major occupation. The Bureau of Mines reported that for 1981 there were approximately 1,200 workers in the Barre area engaged in all phases of the granite industry.

Another way of measuring the impact of the mineral industries is by their contribution to the Gross State Product, which is the total value of all goods and services produced. In 1982 (the most recent year that estimates are available) mining and construction—lumped together by statisticians—contributed $274 million to the grand total of $5.2 billion. Measured in this fashion, the combined industries were contributing about five percent to the state's economy and of the two, construction was far more important. In the same year, the travel (recreation) industry was estimated to have generated $760 million.

Copperas Hill, the quarries high on the mountainside in Dorset, the overgrown granite excavations in Kirby, and the piles of clay in Monkton are of the past. Yet in their day they contributed importantly to the growth of Vermont and provided employment in an era when there was little else available. Vermont granite and Vermont marble made the state well-known long before the tourist and recreation industries did. Even today Vermont granite and Vermont marble draw tourists to the state for the exhibits depicting the history and development of the industry. And for a few dollars a chunk of Vermont marble or granite (preferably polished) can be bought to adorn a mantle or bookshelf in far-off Westchester. The state's minerals played an important role in the development of a wilderness removed from the growing 19th century populations of southern New England, and as such they are of crucial importance in understanding Vermont's geography.

Weather Conditions

Most of us have a fascination for the weather, beginning early each morning when we turn on the radio to hear the local forecasts. I still can remember my father tapping his barometer and telling me, as I went off to school, that it might rain before I got home. He also told me something which I remember to this day—that a wind from the east brings rain or snow. He usually was right and now I know the reasons. Yet I still find the subject difficult at best and sometimes downright mysterious.

Weather (short term) and climate (long term) are the most variable of all factors that comprise our natural environment. No two days, weeks, months or years are the same—at least in New England. To be the local weatherman in the middle of the Sahara Desert would be paradise compared to being one in Vermont.

The following is from the diary of Lucius E. Chittenden, who may have copied it from notes made by Rufus C. Hovey of Brookfield, Vermont. It tells of weather conditions during 1816, a year celebrated as "1816 and Froze to Death."

March:	The fore part very hot and clear, and the snow went off with a great flood.
April:	Cold and cloudy.
May:	Cold and very backward. The 10th, the snow fell six or eight inches deep; and lay on forty or fifty hours.

May 29: Very cold, froze hard, trees not changed their winter color. Not one to fifty had any hay. Generally done planting corn. Grain sowed three weeks ago, not come up yet.

May 29: Very cold and wet, woods green, ground froze, apple trees not yet leaved.

June 6: The fifth very hot, the sixth very cold, and snowed all day long. The ground and other things began to freeze at one of the clock in the day time. Plum trees in full bloom. Black ash not leaved out yet.

June 8: Froze all day. Ground covered with snow all day. Ground froze five or six nights. All the trees on the high land, turned black.

June 11: The apple trees have wilted and the ground is froze.

June 28: The black ash begins to look green.

All sorts of tales involve Vermont weather. There are two seasons, winter and the Fourth of July. Legend has it that an old Vermont custom was to freeze grandpa during the long hard winter so he could wake up each spring full of vim, vigor, and vitality. The Blizzard of '88 gets more severe with each telling, but was a real climatic event for the time. More than 40 inches of snow fell over southern Vermont. (But a snow storm in January 1979 dropped an equal amount over the same area and hardly was mentioned in the Vermont newspapers.) Town-meeting day is the first Tuesday in March. It coincides with the melting snows and Vermont mud season, and it had been remarked that it was selected for that purpose. Few could get to the meetings.

As the most inland of New England states, weather and climate conditions in Vermont are much more like those in upper New York state and Montreal than they are like Boston, Hartford, Portland or coastal areas. The northeast storm in Vermont normally is less severe than elsewhere in New England. Hurricanes smash their way into Connecticut and Rhode Island, but usually lose their punch as they move north. Tornadoes are as rare in Vermont as they are in the whole region.

Weather records are fascinating for the arguments they provoke. Some of Vermont's are as follows:

Highest Recorded Vermont Temperature   Vernon   107°F
Lowest Recorded Vermont Temperature   Bloomfield   –50°F
    (New England Record)

Highest Annual Precipitation Recorded	Jacksonville	68"
Lowest Annual Precipitation Recorded	Cornwall	23"
Shortest Growing Season Ever Recorded	Bloomfield 59 days	

People love to talk about the weather, and it remains one of the few natural elements we have little control over. Once in a while clouds are seeded to produce a flood; dancers with tom-toms are hired to produce the impossible. Most Vermont ski-area owners have given up and installed snow-making machinery. Some farmers in the Champlain Valley are spending money in sprinkler-irrigation systems to make it rain when it is sunny and cloudless. (Between 1974 and 1982 the total amount of irrigated land in Vermont rose from 509 to 1,254 acres.)

The most important observable ingredients of weather and climate are temperature, moisture and winds. Pressure differences cause winds, but it is impossible to feel and see pressure. Moisture and winds are sensory experiences. Temperature is reflected in the daily and seasonal highs and lows, the length of the growing season, frosts, heating and cooling degree days and a host of other weather phenomena. Moisture takes the form of humidity when it is a gas in the atmosphere. At other times it is rain, snow, sleet, hail, fog, drizzle, freezing rain, and occasionally less common things like rime. All of these vary in Vermont both in time and in space and produce the complex climate of the state.

Temperatures

Most world climate classifications are based on average monthly temperatures and precipitation. All of Vermont falls into a climate called Humid Continental—Cool Summer. This is true of Maine and New Hampshire as well. Connecticut, Massachusetts and Rhode Island have Humid Continental—Warm Summer climates. The difference is only a matter of a few degrees and like any line on a map, central New England is really a zone of transition.

The difference is that all Humid Continental climates are defined as having an average temperature for the coldest month (usually January) of 32°F or below. The temperatures at the top of the scale are what distinguish the Cool Summer and Warm Summer varieties. Cool Summer means that the average temperature of the warmest month is below 72°F. The Warm Summer variety must have a July (normally the hottest month) temperature of 72°F or more. The difference is little. The July average temperature at Brattleboro is 70°F while the same figure for Hartford, Connecticut is 72°F. Probably no one could tell this difference except for reading about it, yet Vermont always seems to feel cooler, which is probably a response to the eye rather than the skin. Other Vermont July temperatures are: Burlington, 69°, Rutland, 70°, Bennington, 69°, Somerset, 64°, Newport, 68°, and Vernon (Vermont's hot spot), 72°. Outside the state, Springfield, Massachusetts registers 73°, Boston, 71°, Portland, 68°, Montreal, 70°, and Moscow, USSR, 66°.

The coolest summer termperatures are found at Somerset. Somerset is at an elevation of 2,080 feet and is one of the highest official stations in Vermont. Lake Placid, New York in the Adirondacks has a reading in July of 65°F, yet it is on the same latitude as Burlington. Lake Placid is more than 1,000 feet higher than Lake Champlain. The conclusion is obvious. Coolest New England summer terperatures are more related to *altitude* than they are to *latitude*. The highest temperature ever recorded on the summit of Mt. Mansfield is 80°.

The decrease in temperature as height increases is normal. The earth's surface itself is the primary radiator for the air above it, so as elevation increases, temperatures go down. The average temperature decrease in still air is about 3.5°F for every 1,000 feet in elevation. Mt. Mansfield then would tend annually to be about 14° cooler than Burlington some 4,000 feet below.

If the day happens to be windy, however, a different situation prevails. When air is moving up a hillside or mountainside as it does under windy conditions, the air is cooling by expansion, and this cooling is always at a rate of -5.5° for the same 1,000 feet. On a windy summer day then, if it is 85° in Burlington (certainly not uncommon) it is 22° cooler on the top of the mountain. No wonder people like to get up in elevation on a hot summer day. And no wonder Vermont had its era of Summit House hotels!

While summer temperature differences in New England and Vermont are related mainly to altitude (lower elevations warmer

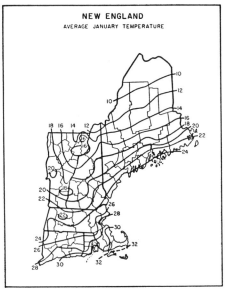

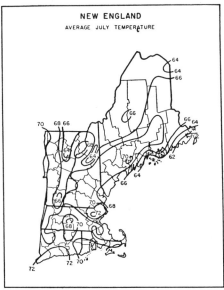

Figure 7.1. During the winter season, the effect of latitude is dominant in controlling temperature patterns. Altitude is important in summer. Throughout the year the influence of the Atlantic Ocean on coastal temperatures is pronounced. Source: *Climate and Man,* 1941 Yearbook of the U.S. Dept. of Agriculture.

and higher elevations cooler), in the winter season there are really extreme differences between northern and southern New England, so the effect of north or south location (latitude) is far greater during the winter (Figure 7.1). Some Vermont January temperature averages are: Chelsea, 15°, Northfield, 16°, Newport, 14°, Cornwall, 19° and Woodstock, Somerset, Burlington and St. Johnsbury, all 17°. Bennington and Brattleboro, in the winter banana belt, both have average temperatures of 22°. By contrast, Boston has 30°, Hartford, 28°, and New York City, 32°.

The effect of altitude in the winter is minor. The highest official station, Somerset, at more than 2,000 feet, has warmer temperatures (by only a few tenths of a degree to be sure) than Burlington on Lake Champlain.

To summarize, in the summer there is little difference in temperature between most of Vermont and other New England areas (Figure 7.1). If one goes *up* it does get cooler, but going north seldom involves much change. The winter is much different. Southern and coastal areas are milder, and northern and interior areas much colder.

Vermont temperature patterns are caused by three controls—altitude, of course, and latitude, or how far north or south a particular place is. A third factor is the effect of a large body of water. Water retains its summer warmth far longer than a land mass. This means that a location bordering a large body of water generally will be warmer during the winter than a place in the interior, or at least until the water freezes over. The reverse holds true during the summer when the water body exerts a cooling effect on temperatures. Cape Cod is considerably cooler in the summer than nearly any place in Vermont except for the summits of higher mountains. Lake Champlain is too small to have much marine effect, and indeed some of New England's hottest summer temperatures are found in the Champlain Valley. Within a mile or less of the lakeshore there are some temperature differences caused by the water, but the effect of the lake on regional climate is negligible.

Growing Seasons

One rule of thumb that gardeners employ in Vermont is not to plant tomatoes until after Memorial Day. That is a reasonably good rule. The length and warmth of the growing season is a critical temperature phenomenon. Since official weather records have been kept (this began in Burlington in the 1840s), the shortest growing season ever recorded in Vermont was at Bloomfield, June 20 to August 18, 1918. Struggling fields of oats and corn there had only 59 days between killing frosts. (Climatologists define the Subarctic as having a 90-day or less growing season.)

Scattered references, such as those found at the beginning of this chapter, are the only record of the weather in 1816. However, the entry does not mention frost (or snow) after June 11, and lack of comments during the summer suggest that things were reasonably normal after the middle of June. Since stories are embellished as the years pass, the infamous summer of 1816 may not have been too much different than many other recorded short growing-season years. In 1913, Burlington's growing season lasted only 96 days from June 12 to September 15. In 1918 Cavendish had a frost on June 21, and that summer had only an 82-day growing season. Brookfield is well over 1,000 feet high and normally would have a short growing season.

Most growing-season tables give average dates for the first and last killing frosts. Woe be unto the farmer who plans on the average. Better to use the shortest record as a guide, and even then things may change next year. Figure 7.2 is a map of the length of growing season, and the data below illustrates the situation at a few representative locations.

Average Date and Latest Date
of Last Spring Frost

	Average Date	Latest Date
Bennington	May 16	May 26
Burlington	May 4	June 12
Cornwall	May 8	June 11
Chelsea	June 1	June 29
Enosburg Falls	May 26	June 29
Rutland	May 16	June 20
St. Johnsbury	May 22	June 20

While average growing seasons do not mean much, they often reflect the climate. The longest growing season in Vermont is at Vernon (down in the southeast corner) with 166 days, and the shortest average at Somerset Reservoir (2,000 feet high) with 83. Almost three months' difference but only 50 miles separate the two.

The Champlain Valley area has one of the longest growing seasons. The season in Cornwall and Burlington is more than 150 days and Rutland's, on the southern edge, is 141 days long. Otherwise it is hard to make generalizations because topography is so important. Bennington's season is 136 days long and Newport's, along the northern border, is 135. Discounting high elevations, the shortest average growing seasons are in the smaller valleys. Woodstock's is 116 days, Chelsea, 111, Bloomfield, 113, Enosburg Falls, 115, Cavendish, 112 and Northfield, 127. For comparison, Hartford, Connecticut has 182 days, Chicago, 198, Buffalo, New York 180, and Philadelphia, 211. But areas of northern Michigan and Wisconsin have averages as low as 80 and 90 days, as do places in northern New Hampshire, New York and Maine.

Some of the shortest growing seasons are in small lowlands. These areas also record some of the coldest winter morning temperatures. This is because of a process called *air drainage.*

A much-photographed Vermont scene will be taken from the side of a ridge across a valley with the autumn foliage ablaze with color. It it is early morning, a favorite time with the sun low and casting distinct shadows, and if there is the inevitable white farmhouse with white wood smoke rising from the chimney, the photograph will capture a very common event. The smoke will spiral upwards to a certain point, but then level off as if stopped by a lid tightly clamped down over the valley. This is evidence of an air drainage inversion where there is colder air trapped in the bottom of the valley, and somewhat warmer air above. The warm rising smoke cools rapidly to the temperature of the colder air, and when it reaches the same temperature, it stops rising and flattens out at that elevation. The colder air trapped in the valley has drained down from the slopes on either side during the early morning hours.

Large valleys like the Champlain and the Connecticut will not

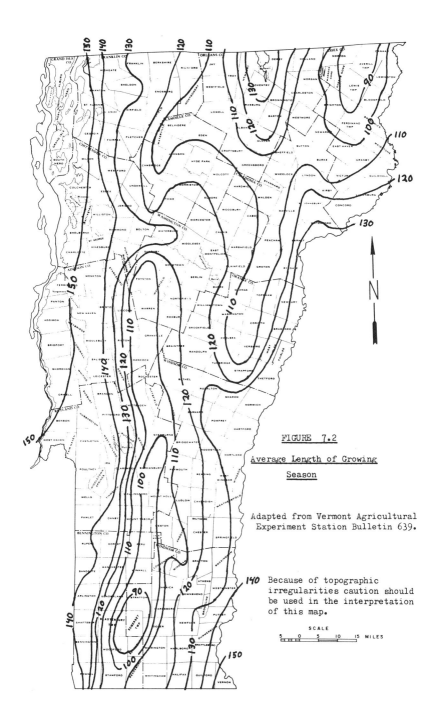

FIGURE 7.2

Average Length of Growing
Season

Adapted from Vermont Agricultural
Experiment Station Bulletin 639.

Because of topographic
irregularities caution should
be used in the interpretation
of this map.

SCALE

5 0   5   10   15 MILES

An inversion fog fills the Lamoille Valley beyond the two silos. Caused by cold air draining downslope, many lowlands have the same situation shown here. This is especially common in September and October. In the immediate foreground is a stone wall and a glacial till pasture. This photograph was taken in Cambridge. The farm buildings sit on top of an extensive kame terrace.

show this phenomenon; temperature inversions caused by air drainage are most common in smaller enclosed valleys. Growing seasons of far less than 90 days must be experienced in parts of Belvidere, Granby, Victory, Dover, Wardsboro and many other towns, but there is no official data to substantiate this.

If it is impossible to prove that many parts of Vermont have growing seasons typical of subarctic climates, it is equally impossible to prove that probably other parts of the state have a climate bordering on that of the French Riviera. While that may be stretching it a bit, there are certain to be some areas with average growing seasons longer than the 150-day situation in the Champlain Valley.

A fruit grower, for example, will select the site for an orchard with much more care than a dairy farmer will plan his hay field. Fruit (in Vermont almost entirely apples) is susceptible to frost and hail, but little can be done about hail which occurs only in the summer during random thunderstorms.

An orchard is placed where preferably two conditions are met, both relating to growing season characteristics. It is best to have a site which will be cool enough in the spring to delay the budding of the trees until the threat of severe frost has passed, and a site which also will allow a late harvest before frost occurs in the fall. In other words, a fruit grower needs the best of two worlds, and the distribution of Vermont orchards reflects the climate better than any maps. The shoreline of Lake Champlain and the hill slopes near Brattleboro and Putney are the major apple-growing regions of Vermont. For different reasons both represent the climatological optimum.

Surface water retains its summer heat well into September, and its winter chill well into June. This means that hill slopes adjacent to water bodies, especially if the wind tends to prevail off the water, tend to reflect the water's characteristics. Thus, the orchards along the Vermont shore of Lake Champlain, especially in Shoreham and in the Champlain Islands, have the desirable cool May temperatures and the equally desirable warm September temperatures.

The other apple-growing regions of Vermont usually are located on south-facing slopes, and while lacking the advantages of the Champlain region, they take advantage of southern slope, southern location and relative freedom from air drainage frost problems.

Precipitation

Vermont has a humid climate. That means that there is more precipitation than there is evaporation. Yet certain parts of the state can be very dry at times. Not many years ago farmers in Addison County hauled water for their stock, and today supplemental irrigation is becoming more common on corn and strawberry fields in the Champlain Lowland. Vermont's multi-million-dollar ski industry is based on snowfall, agriculture needs rain, and if there was not the West River, the Winooski, the Williams, the Clyde and the Lamoille, where would sewage be put?

In averages, Vermont is the driest of all the New England states (Figure 7.3). It is the most inland state so most moist air, if it had an Atlantic source, often is drier before it gets into eastern parts of the state. Similarly, air from the Gulf of Mexico or the Great Lakes usually has lost moisture before affecting western Vermont. Burlington with about 32 inches annual precipitation, is the same as Des Moines, Iowa. Probably about 80% or more of the moisture which in one form or another falls on the state comes from air masses coming from the west and south. But the big snows and big storms are caused by moist Atlantic air which once in a while gets to the Green Mountains, usually in the Nor'easter.

A map showing precipitation over the state will mirror the topography, and in fact it again is *altitude* which largely controls the amount and patterns (Figure 7.4). Air is like a sponge in that it has a considerable capacity to hold moisture in the form of water vapor (a gas). If a sponge which contains some water is squeezed, the water is forced out eventually. To do the same thing to air requires cooling it, because as air is cooled its capacity to hold water is reduced.

Therefore, to cause precipitation (rain, snow, hail, sleet) or forms of condensation (fog, dew, clouds) a mass of air must be cooled to a point at which the water vapor changes to a liquid or solid state (condensation). This is what happens to the outside of a cold beverage can on a muggy summer day.

One of the main ways of cooling air is by lifting it mechanically. Air is forced to rise (and therefore cool) as it ascends a mountain slope (Figure 7.5). If the air is cooled to the point where condensation takes place, then the moisture is released (orographic precipitation). This is why higher elevations always have more precipitation than lowlands.

While not a perfect correlation, the average precipitation totals for Vermont stations strikingly reflect altitude:

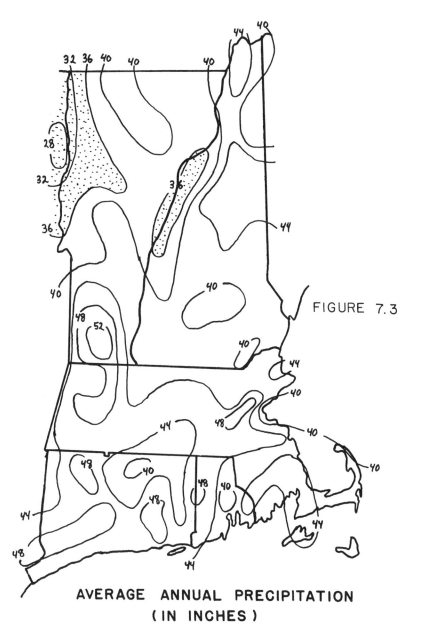

AVERAGE ANNUAL PRECIPITATION
(IN INCHES)

▨ LESS THAN 36"

SOURCE: NATIONAL WEATHER SERVICE

Town	Elevation (in feet)	Annual Average Precipitation (in inches)
Bellows Falls	300	34.8
Bennington	840	37.7
Bloomfield	930	37.7
Brattleboro	333	39.8
Burlington	350	32.3
Cavendish	800	38.1
Chelsea	1,070	35.8
Cornwall	504	31.9
E. Ryegate	443	32.4
Enosburg Falls	422	39.9
Garfield	1,300	38.7
Jacksonville	1,000	45.2
Mt. Mansfield	4,083	73.9
Newfane	450	46.2
Northfield	765	32.9
Rutland	610	36.0
St. Johnsbury	711	34.7
Somerset	2,080	51.6
So. Londonderry	1,000	37.3
Vernon	228	41.8
Wells	900	37.6
White River Jct.	490	33.8
Whitingham	1,450	45.7
Wilder	370	32.5
Wilmington	1,640	47.4
Woodstock	800	38.3

Several stations, including Newfane, Vernon, and Brattleboro, have higher precipitation and lower elevations. These three are located in southeastern Vermont and closest to the Atlantic Ocean. The higher totals for southeastern Vermont also can be seen by comparing the total precipitation of 45.2 inches for Jacksonville at an elevation of 1,000 feet with the 37.3 inches at Londonderry and the 35.8 inches at Chelsea, both 1,000-feet stations located farther north and further from a large moisture source.

Besides air which is forced up-slope and cooled, two other methods operate to raise and refrigerate large masses of air (Figure 7.5). One is common during the summer when local heating (as over a small pond, for example) will cause a column of air to rise and cool. Resulting convectional showers and thunderstorms often

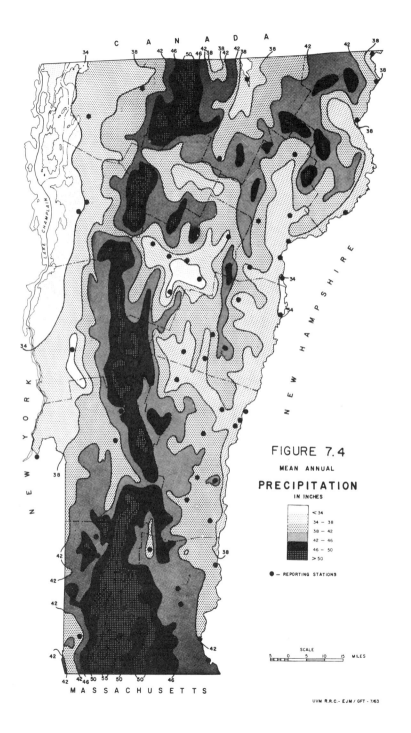

FIGURE 7.4

MEAN ANNUAL

PRECIPITATION

IN INCHES

	< 34
	34 — 38
	38 — 42
	42 — 46
	46 — 50
	> 50

● — REPORTING STATIONS

SCALE

5 0 5 10 15 MILES

UVM R.R.C.- EJM / GFT - 7/63

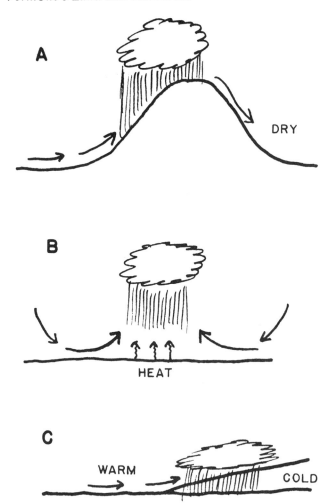

Figure 7.5. *Causes of Precipitation.* A. *Orographic* uplift is when air is forced over a mountain with attendant cooling, condensation and precipitation. The lee side or "rain shadow" is drier. B. *Convectional* uplift occurs when there is a local source of heat causing warm air to rise and cool. This often produces local convectional showers and thunderstorms. It is a summertime phenomenon. C. *Cyclonic, or Frontal,* uplift happens when warm and cold air masses collide. The warmer air is lighter and is forced aloft where it cools. Clouds are extensive. This type of precipitation occurs all year long with the passage of warm and cold fronts associated with cyclonic storms.

produce heavy localized rainfall.

Finally, when a cold mass of air meets a warm air mass, the warmer air, being lighter, rises over the colder air. This again produces cooling and often precipitation and is common throughout the year. Most precipitation in Vermont occurs because air is being lifted up mountainsides throughout the year and frontal activity happens every season. But during the warm season only, when convectional showers are added to the mix, total amounts of precipitation are higher. For example, Burlington receives a total of 2.0 inches of precipitation in January, and 3.9 inches in July. Bennington has 2.5 inches in January and 4.7 inches during the hottest month. The only Vermont locations which do not show a pronounced difference between winter and summer precipitation amounts are in the south and southeast. Brattleboro's totals for both January and July are 3.5 inches and Somerset receives 4.7 inches in both months.

The large amounts of precipitation in southern Vermont during the winter are translated into heavy snowfall and usually there is more snow in the southern Green Mountains than in the northern areas. Brattleboro itself, relatively warmer and down in the Connecticut valley, gets more than 80 inches of snow annually. Burlington receives about 78 inches. Higher elevation areas receive more. Chelsea gets about 100 inches and Somerset 106 inches. Lowest snowfall totals are in the Champlain Valley (Burlington is the second-lowest snowfall station in Vermont), and highest amounts are on the Green Mountain summits, especially in southern parts of the state. Mt. Mansfield averages 150 inches and Killington on occasion can receive up to 200 inches of snow in a typical ski season. That may not seem like much when compared to the 500-inch totals on the Cascade Mountains of Washington and Oregon, but it is sufficient white gold to maintain a flourishing winter recreation business.

Fog and Clouds

The air being pushed up the sides of Vermont's green hills provides the moisture responsible for the greater snowfall and rainfall amounts at higher elevations. As condensation occurs at

The reason why highlands receive more precipitation than lower elevations is illustrated here. As moist air ascends Killington Peak it is cooled, and at a certain variable temperature the moisture condenses and clouds form. This is called "orographic" precipitation.

various altitudes, depending on the moisture content of the air and its temperature, clouds form. Sometimes the flat bases of the puffy white cumulus clouds are below the level of the highest peaks, but more commonly they are far above. It is an unusual day that does not see a line of clouds along the crest of the Green Mountains. Those clouds always indicate that air is rising and cooling.

Fog is nothing but a low cloud. Expected at higher elevations, the picturesque early-morning mist over many lowlands is sometimes a surprise. Many valleys in the state can have heavy fog, most common in fall and spring. These valley fogs are caused by cooling associated with air drainage.

As the cold air fills up the valley, and if its temperature of condensation is right, fog will form as the moisture condenses.

Today there is an interest in alternate sources of energy. Those who watch Vermont weather and understand its characteristics sometimes regard with amusement attempts at promoting solar energy. While the amount of solar energy which falls annually on Egypt is enough to power every machine in the world, the amount of solar energy which falls on Vermont is about the smallest amount in the United States. Not only because Vermont is small, but because it is one of the cloudiest places on the North American continent. Records of sunlight, cloud cover and solar radiation are taken only at Burlington and they do indeed paint a gloomy picture. Southern parts of the state are better, but northern Vermont has an atrocious degree of cloudiness. (See discussion of solar energy in Chapter 9.)

The reasons for this cloud cover are two-fold. One is the great frequency of clouds in mountain areas caused by air moving up-slope and condensing. The other is the unfortunate fact that Vermont sits astride the major cyclonic storm tracks crossing the continent. Practically all miserable weather that develops in the central United States passes across the state on its journey to the North Atlantic. Not only do these storms bring clouds and precipitation; they also bring rapid changes in temperature, with alternating outbursts of polar air one day and tropical air the next.

Storms and General Circulation

Weather patterns move across the middle latitudes (and the United States) generally from west to east because of the circulation pattern of the atmosphere. The prevailing wind for most places in Vermont is westerly and southerly, although souther-ly surface winds are more common because most valleys have a north-south orientation.

One of the clearest expressions of prevailing winds is the pattern of acid rainfall over the northeastern United States. Figure 7.6 clearly shows a southwesterly flow of air spreading higher acidity from source regions in Pennsylvania and the Midwest. This acidity has been identified as at least one factor affecting fishing-water quality and vegetation in Vermont and New York.

Winds from due west generally tend to be dry and moderate

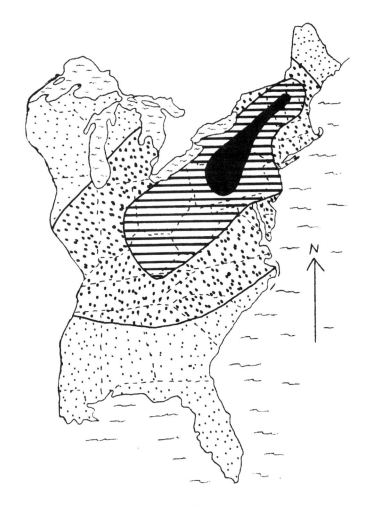

Figure 7.6

Rainfall Acidity

■	Acidity greater than 4.2 pH
☰	Acidity 4.4 - 4.2 pH
⦂	Acitity 4.7 - 4.4 pH
⦂	Acidity 5.6 - 4.7 pH

Average rainfall pH 5.7

Source: Likens, *Chemical and Engineering News,* Nov. 22, 1976.
Note: The lower the number, the higher is the acidity.

in temperature. Winds from the northwest are dry also, but can be extremely cold and blustery during the winter. Air coming from the southwest and south is normally rather mild and humid and is responsible for much of the rain and snowfall over the state. Northwest winds are usually Continental Polar in origin; they originate over central Canada and usually bring dry and cool, or cold, conditions depending on the season. On the other hand, winds from the south originate over the Gulf of Mexico and South Atlantic and are warmer and wetter. They have a Maritime Tropical source.

If this is not enough, there is another mass of air waiting to pounce which can produce true misery. This is air normally over the stormy North Atlantic ocean. It is cold and wet (Maritime Polar), and is associated with a northeast flow responsible for heavy winter snowfall. Most wet Atlantic air comes in on northeast storms which usually do not affect western Vermont as they do the rest of the state. These storms normally travel up the coast, keeping offshore, and when they get to the vicinity of Long Island begin to pump air into northern New England. Major winter snowstorms invariably are caused by northeast winds coming off the Atlantic. Because the Green Mountains intercept much of the moisture, the Champlain Valley remains relatively snow free in comparison to other parts of the state.

Cyclonic storms form along the boundaries of Polar and Tropical air. These storms, or areas of low pressure, have cold fronts and warm fronts, a counterclockwise air movement and clouds, rain and snow. Since the average meeting zone of Tropical and Polar air is over northern New England, storms cross Vermont with remarkable persistence throughout the year (Figure 7.7).

Like its landforms and geology, Vermont has a complex weather and climate. The only real generalization possible is that if the immediate weather is disappointing it is bound to change in a few hours. Air masses and storm paths from all parts of the country converge on the state bringing remarkable weather changes in a short period of time. The existence of the Taconics, the Green Mountains, the Adirondacks, the hill areas of eastern Vermont, the Champlain Valley, and Lake Champlain combine to produce a mixture which discourages an easy summary.

Lowlands generally are drier and warmer than highlands, but

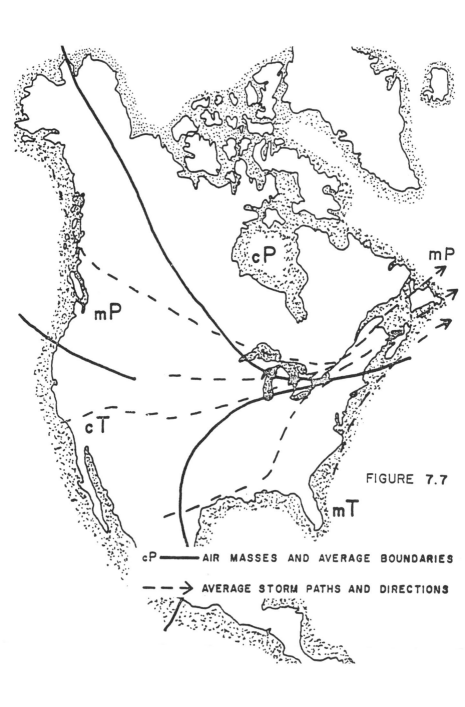

cP ────── AIR MASSES AND AVERAGE BOUNDARIES

── ─ ➝ AVERAGE STORM PATHS AND DIRECTIONS

FIGURE 7.7

some of the coldest minimum winter temperatures and shortest growing seasons are in small valleys. Regionally, southern Vermont is wetter than the rest of the state and northwestern Vermont is one of the driest areas in all of New England.

In addition, the climate is changing, but no one really knows just what this means. Long-term changes are examined in Chapter 10 and it is reasonably well-understood that since about 1000 A.D. there has been a long-term cooling trend. It is less clear what has been happening to precipitation, although it is more humid today than it was 800 years ago.

Most climatologists think that the last 20 years have seen a short-term cooling trend in the Northern Hemisphere, compared to a warming trend during the 1920s, '30s, and '40s. If it does exist, this trend is confusing because with the artificial addition of carbon dioxide to the atmosphere through industrial and automotive pollution, it should get warmer today, not cooler. It is now supposed to be getting wetter too, but there is precious little data to document such changes.

Eight places in Vermont which record climatological data were selected at random to try and discern any measurable trends. Until 1940, the total average January temperature for Burlington, Cavendish, Chelsea, Cornwall, Newport, Rutland, St. Johnsbury and Woodstock was 18.32°F. The warmest place was Cornwall, with 20.2°, the coldest Chelsea at 15.8°. From 1940-1976, the overall average was 17.11°, or more than a degree cooler. Rutland was high with 20.6° and Newport low at 14.7°. It seems then that at least winter temperatures are getting a little colder.

Summer temperatures? For the same comparative years, the pre-1940 July temperatures for these stations was 68.23°, and 68.49° in the more recent time span studied. Summers are a shade warmer, while winters perhaps a degree cooler. Equally inconclusive are average annual precipitation calculations. Until 1940 the stations totaled a yearly average of 36.11 inches, and since then, 36.46 inches.

So perhaps it is getting a little cooler and a little wetter, but it is hardly dramatic and if anything, this data is rather tenuous and inconclusive.

Such is Vermont's weather. Of all elements in the environment, it probably has a greater bearing on our day-to-day activities than anything else. Snow shovels sprout like weeds in November, and patio furniture is common in April. It influences our choice of clothing and footwear, and it certainly promotes different kinds of seasonal recreation activity.

Precipitation in all its forms is an integral part of weather. And throughout Vermont's history, the waters on the land have had an important role in transportation, recreation, providing drinking water, generating power and, in too great amounts, floods.

The next two chapters look at two aspects of the water resource. The first discusses what happens when there's too much water as well as the floods which often result. The other chapter discusses how water, transformed into energy, produced the means for Vermont to develop an industrial economy, and how it supplies electricity to a growing population today.

Floods and Flood Control

A small body of water called Long Pond once occupied a few acres in the southern part of Glover just north of the Greensboro town line. There, at an elevation of 1,280 feet, it was the source of the Barton River which drained northward through Glover and eventually into Lake Memphremagog.

Glover, just barely settled by 1810, had a normal need for water power for the mills serving the small community. The townsfolk had built a small dam on the Barton River just upstream to form Mud Pond, in which water for power was impounded. Mud Pond never amounted to much, and during the fall when the water was low it was all but dry most of the time. The people of Glover wondered how they could get more water into Mud Pond to get more power. Perhaps if they enlarged the outlet of Long Pond the flow of water would be increased and Mud Pond would be full forever?

On June 6, 1810, most of the able-bodied men of Glover (some 60 in all) set out with a variety of picks, shovels and hoes to see what could be done about helping Mother Nature a bit. The outlet of Long Pond was a bed of hard gravel which was attacked with gusto. Delightedly, the onlookers saw more and more water draining across the gravel as the picks dug deeper and deeper. Suddenly a shovel thrust into the gravel penetrated into a bed of soft sand. With the force of all of Long Pond behind it, the water quickly ate deeper into the now-exposed soft underpinnings of the natural dam and away went Long Pond as the workers scrambled for safety from the rushing waters. While they watched, Long Pond quickly emptied itself and a wall of water rushed downstream uprooting trees, boulders, demolishing Mud Pond, and on the way, most of Glover itself. Cutting a path nearly 600 feet wide and from 30 to 60 feet deep, the tor-

177

rent swept downstream. Long Pond was empty in a little over an hour, Glover was well nigh gone a half hour later, and the surge of water reached Newport on Lake Memphremagog, about 25 miles away, in six hours.

Today a stone marker is found next to a grassy depression along Route 12, commemorating Runaway Pond, sometimes called Dry Pond locally. The explanatory marker was emplaced in 1910, the 100th anniversary of what may have been Vermont's first major flood, and probably the only flood in Vermont caused by human hands. While the 1927 flood was *the* Vermont flood, innumerable other floods must have occurred repeatedly throughout the state's history. Town histories invariably refer to "freshets" which washed out this or that grist mill, or removed the produce from this or that valley. A "violent freshet" swept away four grist mills, four saw mills, one woolen factory, one carding machine and several other buildings in Poultney in July 1811. Enough water to qualify for the term "flood" before 1927 occurred in 1771, 1811, 1839, 1850, 1869 and 1895.

A flood is a simple phenomenon. Anytime the channel of a stream is too small to carry the water available, the water must go over the banks. Floodplains have been caused by repeated flooding and are places on which flooding is normal and to be expected (see Chapter 2). The fact that there has been development of villages, farms, shopping centers and subdivisions on floodplains does not mean that there no longer will be floods. The cause of the excess water is simple. It can come from rapid snowmelt or from precipitation. Many variables will influence the amount of runoff including the type of vegetation, the slope of the ground, whether the soil is frozen, or even the types of flood-control structures in existence.

The 1927 Flood

On November 1, 1927, a small cyclonic storm was approaching Vermont from the west and on the evening of November 2 gentle rain began to fall across all of the state to the Canadian border. The rain began in the west and gradually spread east, but no significant amounts fell. Towards midnight on November 2 the rain began to peter out and it looked like November 3 might be a bit cloudy and wet, but would not interrupt the daily routine of the citizens.

But also on November 1 a weak storm was working its way up the Atlantic coast with northeast and east winds north of it bringing moist air onshore and spreading light precipitation along the Middle Atlantic coast. New York received some rain from this system on November 2. The moist easterly flow of air began to reach into southern Vermont early in the morning of November 3 just as the rain from the western storm was beginning to taper off. Traveling at a ground speed of 30 to 40 miles per hour it was a blustery, wet beginning for a day in Brattleboro. Flowing inland across southern New Hampshire, the Atlantic air met no major highlands in its path until it began ascending the southern Green Mountains. This initial lift, with consequent cooling, was enough to squeeze some moisture out of this wet air and it began to rain steadily during the morning of November 3.

Under normal conditions, this event never would have become particularly noteworthy, and November 3, 1927 would have gone into the record books as a typical wet, gloomy Vermont day. But several seemingly unrelated events conspired to produce the state's greatest natural calamity.

Out in the North Atlantic was a cell of cold high-pressure air. With no weather maps no one really knew it was there, but because of what happened it must have been there. This mass of cold air, unusual for the area, settled over the region south of Greenland and Iceland and did not move towards Europe as it should have. This effectively stopped the coastal storm in its tracks and it deviated from its normal path someplace off Cape Cod, all the time continuing to pump the relatively warm, moist air into Vermont. The western storm also stopped moving, and a thick mass of cold air behind its frontal system settled over western Vermont and the whole Champlain Valley. While no one was paying attention to temperatures on November 3, the noon temperature at Burlington was 15° colder than at Brattleboro.

Something else was important. October 1927 had been an unusually wet month. The Weather Bureau observer in Northfield had recorded 5.64 inches of rain for the month, compared to an average for October of 2.48 inches. Streams were unusually full for this time of the year and the ground was nearly saturated. Additional moisture would be hard to absorb.

As the wet air from the Atlantic began to ascend the Green Mountains, it also encountered the cold air which had piled up over western Vermont. Up and up it went, with attendant cooling, condensation and precipitation. Incredible amounts of rain began to pour down as the storm systems stayed in the same place through all of November 3 and well into November 4. Streams, already full from the wet October, could not handle the runoff. The saturated ground could hold no more. Before the last drop fell late on November 4, 84 Vermont residents were dead, and property damage was estimated at $25 million. Damage was particularly severe in the Winooski basin because more people and valuable property were located there. Only western Vermont along Lake Champlain escaped devastation. The Lamoille River was half-way up to the second floor in the Village of Cambridge. The soldier's monument in the village today has a line on it marking the height of the floodwaters.

Bolton led the unhappy list of deaths in towns with 26, followed by Waterbury with seven. In the Winooski Valley alone there were 55 deaths attributable to the storm and flood. Lives were lost in such scattered places as Royalton and Sharon (White River), Wolcott (Lamoille River), Coventry (Black River in the north), Troy (upper Missisquoi) and Bennington.

One of the unique things about the 1927 flood is that the maximum rainfall fell over Vermont, and most damage occurred in the state. Of the 69 New England towns with some damage from the resulting flood 41, or 60%, were in Vermont. As reported by the American Red Cross, 30,390 people suffered flood losses, of whom 18,880 were residents of Vermont. A total of 407 buildings were completely destroyed, 300 of which (74%) were in Vermont. Partially-damaged structures totalled 1,578, of which 1,247 were in the state.

By the time it was over, Somerset, at 2,000 feet elevation in the southern Green Mountains, had measured 9.65 inches of rain (Figure 8.1). Along the Green Mountain summit as much as 15 inches may have fallen. At Northfield, it worked out to one-half

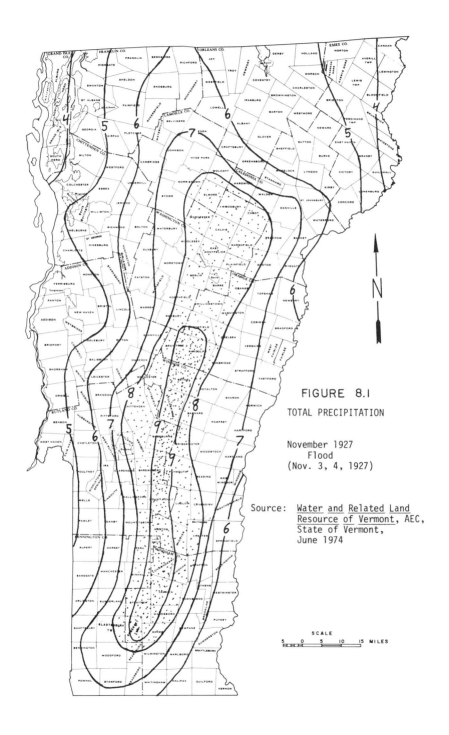

FIGURE 8.1

TOTAL PRECIPITATION

November 1927
Flood
(Nov. 3, 4, 1927)

Source: <u>Water and Related Land Resource of Vermont</u>, AEC, State of Vermont, June 1974

SCALE

5   0   5   10   15 MILES

inch per hour for nine hours. Downstream at Hartford, Connecticut on November 6 the crest passed at a height of 29.0 feet, surpassed only by the floods of 1854, 1936, 1938 and 1955. Depending on where you were, the last drops fell late in the afternoon of November 4, and that was generally in northeastern Vermont as the storm began to move west in the general circulation.

Gaysville was obliterated. The Dog River ran wild and the Ward Lumber Company in Moretown, the village's economic base, went downstream. In Proctor, trains of the Rutland Railroad were nearly underwater as Otter Creek rushed over Sunderland Falls. The West River received the West River Railroad for ever. On the Connecticut River, downtown Bellows Falls became an island. Damage to assorted structures and the new New England Power Co. dam then under construction was over $1.2 million alone. New water level records were established up and down the valley.

For us the most important result of the 1927 flood is the flood-control measures initiated through the first bit of federal largesse that Vermont ever accepted. While Governor John Weeks repeatedly turned down offers of help from Washington, the temptation for flood-control dams was too strong. With a population clamoring for structures to prevent a repetition of the disaster, Vermont in 1933 accepted its first federal aid under the administration of Governor Stanley C. Wilson.

Flood control will be discussed later in this chapter. But reflect on the unique combination of circumstances which caused the deluge. There has been no repeat of the peculiar combination of weather events that caused the flood, but there is no assurance that it cannot happen again. The remarkable thing about weather is that there is no pattern that we can discern. No two days are alike, and certainly no two winters. Under the right circumstances, and at the right time, Vermont will experience another 1927 flood, and because of development patterns in the state it will be worse than before, at least with respect to property damage. If $25 million in 1927 was equated with 1980 dollars, the total would be nearly $300 million.

The 1927 flood is classed as a Precipitation Flood since a prolonged drenching rainfall was its cause. The rain falling steadily and heavily quickly overloaded the already-full streams and it

East State Street in Montpelier on November 4, 1927 before the floodwaters had receded. (Photo from the Vermont Historical Society.)

After it finally stopped raining on November 4, 1927, State Street in Barre was part of Stevens Branch. One result of the flood was the construction of the East Barre flood-control dam in the 1930s. (Photo from the Vermont Historical Society.)

was impossible for normal drainage to cope. Contributing to the severity of the flood was the fact that in 1927 far more of Vermont watersheds were in farmland than now. Runoff from cleared land is considerably greater than from a forested watershed. A North Carolina study of a clear-cut area allowed to grow back showed an increase in runoff of 14 inches the first year after cutting, falling to eight inches the fifth year and six inches the 10th year. After 35 years, the runoff was estimated to be about one inch more than if the land had been kept in forest initially. As more of Vermont grows back to timber and clear-cutting is discouraged, flood runoff will be reduced materially, rendering less likely a repetition of the tragic events of November 3 and 4, 1927.

Snowmelt and Precipitation Floods

The most common flooding experienced throughout Vermont is the annual meadowland innundations which occur every spring. Some years are worse than others, but no year goes by without some bottomlands being flooded by the runoff from melting snow. When ice dams (or ice jams) develop at narrower points in the valley, upstream areas often can have severe flooding and the National Guard is called out with dynamite, backhoes and other equipment to dislodge the packed ice. Rarely do the annual spring floods cause much damage, and often their greatest negative effect is to so saturate the floodplains that spring plowing is delayed. There are usually a few wet basements, some inconvenience to residents, but rarely is there loss of life or significant property damage.

Yet the worst flood in the history of New England was the tragic submersion of March 1936. While Vermont's damage was less than that experienced nine years before, it was still a major Vermont flood. What happened downstream in southern New England and New Hampshire was catastrophic. While all was quiet in the Winooski and Lamoille valleys, in the southern Green Mountains streams rose to more than 16 feet of their normal levels and considerable damage was done. Vernon Dam barely held, and if it had gone Greenfield, Massachusetts would have

Two pictures, taken a week apart in late March 1976, of normal meadow-land flooding in the Lamoille Valley outside of Cambridge Village.

been washed off the map. At the height of the flood, water was pouring over the lip of the dam to a depth of 11 feet, some two feet higher than the 1927 flood. On March 21, the flood crest passed Hartford at a height of more than 37 feet—a record which may never be broken. Rainfall associated with the storm systems ranged up to eight inches in western Massachusetts and southern Vermont, and six and one-half inches at Pinkham Notch in New Hampshire's White Mountains.

The rainfall total over southern Vermont was a little less than that in the 1927 disaster, but this time the rain was falling on a land mantled with white. Combining the rainfall with the water already on the surface in the form of snow produced a total amount of water available for runoff of more than 30 inches in the White Mountains and more than 16 inches in parts of southern Vermont. Most of this water did indeed run off, and downstream ice jams like the one at Holyoke, Massachusetts compounded the problem. Here for the first time was a large amount of precipitation combined with a lot of snow on the ground. What might have been a normal Snowmelt Flood developed into the worst flood disaster in New England. Since 1936 this combination has not happened again, but who is to say that it will not? As a direct result of the 1936 flood, the U.S. Army Corps of Engineers began its extensive flood-control program in the Connecticut River Valley.

Sometimes it is suggested that heavy rain falling onto a thick snowpack will not result in flooding because the snow will act as a gigantic sponge. Perhaps this would be true in February, but later in the year, as the weather warms, the snow compacts and has little excess capacity left to absorb more water. This is what happened in 1936 and probably can happen again. That it has not happened has been fortunate, and while flood-control works may help next time, Vermont probably will experience another flood of the magnitude of those of 1927 and 1936.

Summertime floods are not uncommon and they invariably are Precipitation Floods. They usually accompany a cloudburst associated with rapidly rising moist air as in a thunderstorm. Since the rain usually starts with little warning and continues as a constant deluge, streams rise very quickly and flooding is brief and local damage often is severe. Such flash floods happened

Waters of the West River rage against the bridge in South Londonderry during the June 1973 flood. (Photo courtesy of Bill Best.)

West River floodwaters finally cover the South Londonderry bridge during the June 1973 flood. (Photo courtesy of Bill Best.)

over parts of southern Vermont in 1973 and 1976, with valley areas from Ludlow south chiefly affected. The rain usually stops as suddenly as it started and after their brief rampage the rivers return quickly to their normal channels. Army Corps of Engineers' flood-control dams on the Black River and the West River materially helped to control flooding downstream on those rivers, but did little to help communities upstream and on the tributaries. Whetstone Brook washed out the major bridge through Wardsboro and several vacation homes ended up some hundreds of yards downstream. Severe flooding occurred in parts of Jamaica both years. The rainfall pattern, while from a different cause than the 1927 disaster, was remarkably similar in its geographic distribution.

More recently, severe localized flooding also affected a narrow east-west zone in northern Vermont on June 6-7, 1984. A slow-moving warm front stagnated from St. Albans to Wells River, and severe showers produced up to seven inches of concentrated precipitation. The Wrightsville Dam held back floodwaters which otherwise would have damaged Montpelier, but there was significant damage upstream on the North Branch, especially in Worcester. Damage estimates reached $16 million and much of the area was declared a federal disaster area.

Flood Control

The 1927 Legislature appropriated more than $8 million to repair the ravages of the 1927 flood, and urged measures be taken that would not cause a repetition of the damage. After much study, the War Department recommended several sites for flood-control dams. The state chose three locations, all in the Winooski Basin, as appropriate places. Construction on the East Barre Dam, the Wrightsville Dam and the Little River Dam began in 1934 by the Civilian Conservation Corps under the supervision of the Corps of Engineers. The attitude of the state was certainly to protect its people and not to worry about anyone living downstream in Connecticut or Massachusetts. The Little River Dam is the only one with much water (Waterbury Reservoir) behind it. The other basins normally are empty.

These structures were designed and located to protect Vermont property and people. Most flood-control structures built in more recent years have had as their goal the protection of downstream Connecticut Valley areas, and their construction was related directly to the 1936 flood which did so much damage outside of the state (Figure 8.2). The largest flood-control dams in Vermont (the Ball Mountain and Townshend Dams on the West River, the North Springfield Dam on the Black, the North Hartland Dam on the Ottauquechee and the Union Village Dam on the Ompompanoosic) are all on important Connecticut River tributaries. They were built during the 1950s and are owned and operated by the Corps of Engineers. Other flood-control structures in Vermont are under the jurisdiction of the Vermont Department of Water Resources. The large dams on the Connecticut River are power-generating facilities (Chapter 9). New England Electric built, owns, and operates these dams. The Wilder Dam north of White River Junction has some storage capacity but was not designed as a flood control structure. Interestingly, the Vermont communities which lost taxable land with the development of the Corps of Engineers' projects are reimbursed for that tax loss by several sources: Massachusetts contributes 50%, Connecticut, 40% and Vermont, 10%.

Attempting to control floods by dams is the best structural approach to the problem of floods. Leaving an empty basin behind the structure provides room for the excess water to be stored until it can be released gradually.

The other common way to control floods is by building dikes or levees along the streams and around the built-up areas on floodplains. There are no such structures in Vermont, but they are common in Connecticut and Massachusetts from Northfield, Massachusetts south. Building a dike is like fixing the leaking roof with a pail to catch the drops which come through the ceiling. The carpet stays dry, but the roof still leaks. This is why upstream dams actually are much better than downstream dikes. Dikes attack the problem where it occurs rather than getting at the source of the difficulty. They rarely are high enough for the unexpected, and where they exist, the river itself has problems depositing its sediment.

Dikes then are not a long-term solution to too much water.

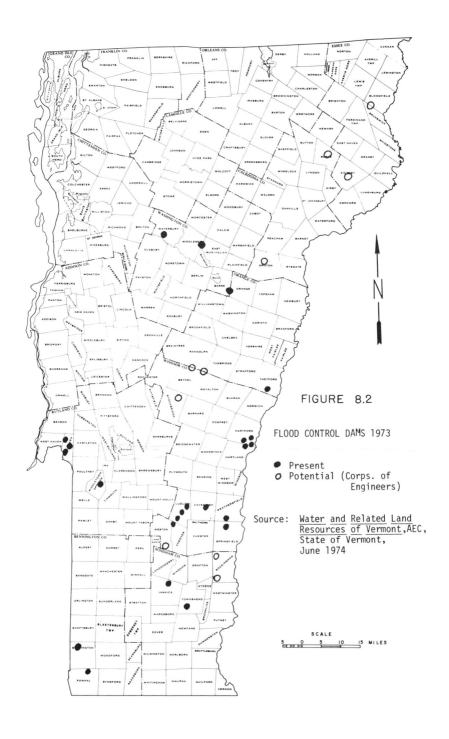

FIGURE 8.2

FLOOD CONTROL DAMS 1973

● Present
○ Potential (Corps. of
    Engineers)

Source: Water and Related Land
         Resources of Vermont, AEC,
         State of Vermont,
         June 1974

SCALE
5   0   5   10   15 MILES

Route 100 in Wardsboro after the July 1976 flood. (Photo by Jonathan Meeks.)

But at the same time, there are thousands of people who, without the foggiest notion of streams, weather, soils, or floodplains, have bought land, built homes and invested their life savings in a plot of land in central Connecticut which never should have been built upon in the first place. Dikes represent the immediate response to the immediate problem, and the major dike-raising epoch in New England occurred shortly after the 1936 floods.

No dikes have been built in New England since about 1940, and probably no more will be. The Army Corps of Engineers always has urged upstream control rather than downstream, and the 1970 *Report of the Connecticut River Basin Commission* emphasized the need for more upstream flood-control dams to control downstream Connecticut River flooding.

In that report several sites in Vermont were recommended for dams to control Connecticut River water levels. The year of the report (1970) coincided with a cresting of environmental activism in Vermont.

Victory and Gaysville became rallying points for some of the first focused environmental activity in the state. The Corps of Engineers had recommended that these were the two best sites for additional flood-control dams. The proposed dam on the Moose River (a tributary to the Passumpsic) in Victory would have destroyed a large bog if a flood occurred. The dam at Gaysville in the upper Ottauquechee would have caused a scenic valley to be flooded. Few people would have had to be relocated, and the two sites suggested were probably the only two places in Vermont where flood-control dams would have a minimal impact.

Both the Victory Dam and Gaysville Dam projects are dead for now. Environmental groups were successful in opposing their construction, and now Victory Bog is a waterfowl management area. In an all-New England view, the two dams might have alleviated eventual suffering in Massachusetts and Connecticut, but in a Vermont view, they would take irreplaceable land largely to benefit people outside the state. The question of flood-control dams in Vermont and New Hampshire to benefit downstream areas certainly will come up again.

As surprising as it may seem, the realization that the best way of stopping damaging floods is not to be in the way of the water has appeared only rather recently. A river may spill over its banks every spring, but if no one is inconvenienced, and there is no damage, it hardly deserves to be called a flood. It may seem to some like closing the barn door after the cows have escaped, but further development in flood-prone areas is beginning to stop. While this still does not solve the problem for people still living on floodplains, it means that in future years flood-damage assessments will be proportionally less than if development in flood areas continues unchecked.

Keeping development out of flood areas requires legal zoning, and today many Vermont communities have enacted regulations for this. Most valleys in the state have been surveyed by the Corps of Engineers for the Department of Housing and Urban Development and the Vermont Department of Water Resources. Areas that will be flooded have been identified and mapped, and it is a simple matter for local planning commissions to transfer those lines to their own official zoning maps. Regulations require

Victory Bog was once proposed by the Corps of Engineers as a site for a flood-control dam. It became a rallying cry for a growing Vermont environmental movement during the 1960s. Today it is a wildlife management area.

A clear water line on the trees shows the height of water impounded during the July 1976 flood behind the Ball Mountain Dam in Jamaica.

Future flood heights measured agains a home on the Winooski River flood-plain south of Essex Junction. (Corps of Engineers photograph.)

that in an area delineated as a flood-hazard area, any future structures on the land must be graded to a height above the 100-year flood, or the height that theoretically would be reached by the maximum flood of the century.

The 1927 flood was a hundred-year flood, cresting at Essex Junction on the lower Winooski at 51.4 feet above normal stream level. The 1936 flood crested there at 23.5 feet and was not a hundred-year flood. How long one must wait for the next great flood is unknown. The Corps of Engineers defines that flood as one cresting at 40.5 feet. If that is not horrible enough to con-template, the theoretical maximum flood stage on the lower Winooski will be at 62 feet or more than 10 feet higher than the 1927 flood. For structures already in defined flood-hazard areas of the hundred-year flood, owners can qualify for federally-sub-sidized flood insurance once the land is zoned as a floodplain. In Vermont the 1985 rate was 25 cents for every $100 valuation. Therefore, a $50,000 home could be insured for $125 annually.

Lakeshore Flooding

On April 5, 1976, Lake Champlain rose to an almost unprece-dented 101.7 feet above sea level, and in May 1983 stood at an-other high 101.3 feet. These represent the second- and fourth-highest water levels ever recorded, the maximum being the 101.8 feet of March 30, 1903. In 1903 there were few cottages around the lake, farmland ran down to the lakeshore in Grand Isle County, and little note was taken of the high water. In 1976 va-cation homes crowded much of the shore, docks extended into the water, trucked-in sand provided some man-made beaches, many lawns were landscaped carefully, ferries plied back and forth across the lake, and marinas and other commercial develop-ments were common.

Owners of shore property sandbagged their homes and watch-ed in horror as the causeway to Isle La Motte was almost de-stroyed by waves pushed by strong northwest winds. On the Richelieu River Canadian property owners saw their vacation re-treats from Montreal virtually under water. A clamor arose in the valley for some mechanism to control Lake Champlain. Compounding the issue is the fact that the lake drains north, and any control structures would have to be built in Canada.

It is hard to determine precisely what has been responsible for the recent lakeshore innundations, but there appears to be two probable factors. One involves higher precipitation (and run-off) in the basin, the other certain modifications to the Chambly Canal.

Judged at least by climatological data recorded by the National Weather Service in Burlington, precipitation appears to be increasing. In the 50-year period 1875-1925, the average was 32.57 inches, for the 50 years between 1925 and 1975 it was 33.13 inches. In the short period from 1975 through 1983 precipitation averaged a whopping 37.35 inches with a record 50.16 inches in 1983.

Total yearly precipitation, however, is less significant than that during the winter season. Winter precipitation is runoff which often flows into Lake Champlain creating the high spring water levels. Taking only 10-year average figures for winter (November-April) precipitation, and the average high water levels for the same 10-year periods, striking correlation appears.

For example, the period from 1957 through 1966 had an average winter precipitation total of 11.66 inches and an average maximum water level of Lake Champlain of 98.61 feet. This was a period in which many lakeshore homes were constructed. The following 10 years (1967-1976) produced a 10-year average of 15.16 inches and a maximum lake level average of 100.31 feet.

Between 1976 and 1984, winter precipitation at Burlington averaged 14.89 inches and the maximum lake level average was 99.76 feet. The lake rose above 100 feet in five of those years. While period averages are a crude method of analysis, there is certainly a suggestion that precipitation trends, especially those of the winter season, do have a bearing on the behavior of Lake Champlain. Unfortunately, there is no way in which specific precipitation amounts can be used to predict the behavior of the lake because there are a variety of variables such as the groundwater level, depth of snow and its compaction, and amount of surface runoff on various types of vegetation areas, among other factors. Yet overall, there is a rough correlation between more rain and snowfall and higher levels in Lake Champlain.

The Burlington lakeshore was innundated when Lake Champlain reached its second-highest level of 101.7 feet in April 1976. Below, the lakeshore on a typical late spring day.

One of the most important points in all of this is that a great deal of development of Lake Champlain's shoreline happened during a period in which the lake levels tended to be lower than normal. Thus when the lake began to behave in a more "normal" fashion, many new property owners were surprised and upset at shoreline erosion of nicely-landscaped gardens and wet-to-over-flowing basements.

Yet even long-term residents have told me that they have been surprised by the recent high waters which now appear to be the norm rather than the exception. Studies have shown also that shoreline erosion is now more of a problem than ever before.

Although it's difficult to prove, what may be involved is a little less space available through which the lake must drain.

Paralleling the Richelieu River in Quebec is the Chambly Canal, which was constructed mostly between 1835 and 1843. The canal, with a 6 foot draft, made it possible for small ships to navigate between the St. Lawrence River and Lake Champlain. The canal was never too important, although it did help in the 1870s when Burlington was a major sawmilling center.

With the rise of pleasure-boat activity on Lake Champlain, Canadian authorities began a systematic program of canal improvements in the 1960s. This involved reconstruction of locks, dredging where appropriate, and strengthening the wall of the canal where the waters of the Richelieu had eroded foundations. The end result of this was to enlarge the area of the canal slightly thus slightly narrowing the river in several places. This, in effect, constricted the outlet of Lake Champlain and thus made it impossible for the lake to drain in its normal fashion. Combined with the higher basin precipitation, these changes may in part explain the recent high water levels and lakeshore flooding.

The average Lake Champlain water level is given usually as 95 feet for the year. During the fall it is usually a little below that but has never fallen lower than 93 feet. Minimum levels are in October and maximum levels normally at the end of April at around 99 feet. The proposal to regulate the level is pushed most vocally by Canadian interests, where during the 1976 lakeshore flooding more than $3.4 million in damages were claimed. This compares to $2.6 million in Vermont and $1.4 million in New York State. The International Joint Commission has endorsed

Cottage on Keeler Bay in South Hero. It was a small island in Lake Champlain in early April 1976.

the concept of water-level regulation. The general idea is to build a structure which will allow the lake to act as a gigantic flood-control basin, lowering the water during the winter season to allow it to fill during the spring runoff, but to a height which would not endanger shore property. The idea sounds fine in principle but worry is expressed by Vermont and New York officials over the effect that water control might have on fish, wildlife and botanical habitats.

The disadvantages of too much water are obvious. Still, without the flow of streams, Vermont never would have developed a 19th century industrial economy, nor would the state have had the highest percentage of national hydroelectric use at one time. The basement full of water is pumped out using electricity, in many cases generated from water. The following chapter looks at water and other sources of electricity.

Electrical Energy

Historically, Vermont depended upon its own resources to supply its power needs. Wood and water provided the energy needed on the frontier. But as transportation improved, wood was replaced first by anthracite and then bituminous coal. With technological advances, waterpower was replaced by far more convenient and transportable electricity. Over the years, petroleum and gas replaced wood, and electrical energy produced from sources undreamed of came to dominate the state's electrical-energy production.

Since 1973 and the well-known Arab oil embargo, the national energy situation has been clouded at best. Power plants converted to oil or natural gas in the 1960s were converted back to burn coal a decade later. The popularity of nuclear-generating facilities grew rapidly during the 1970s, accompanied by many cries of protest from environmental groups. Consumers cut back on their consumption of electricity, making it nearly impossible for utility planners to project future demands.

Vermont, at the end of the energy "pipeline", was (and is) particularly susceptible to national energy policies, and attempts are continuing to make the state less dependent upon external sources of power.

On October 1, 1930, President Hoover pushed a button to start turning the waterwheels of New England's largest single hydroelectric development, at that time the fourth largest in the country. This power came from Comerford Dam, the first development of the Fifteen-Mile Falls stretch of the upper Connecticut River. New England was becoming electrified, but a third of the towns in Vermont were still without electricity and about half of all New England's manufacturing plants were being run with mechanical energy (belts, wheels and pulleys).

Not including self-supplied industrial production, Vermont in 1930 had a generating capacity of about 180 megawatts, 91% of which was from waterpower. The entire year saw a total production of 480 million kilowatt-hours of which the state, with more than 75 of its towns without electricity, exported 178 million kilowatt-hours, or about 37% of its electrical generation. There were 82,000 domestic customers that year, by far the lowest total in New England. Sixty-three percent of all Vermont homes were electrified, but only 13% of the farms, compared to more than 45% in both Maine and New Hampshire. Vermont, with its scattered rural and predominantly agricultural population, continued to lag behind the rest of New England in securing electric power through the 1930s. The Rural Electrification Administration Act of 1935 had a greater impact on Vermont than on any other New England state.

The first commercial production of electricity in Vermont was in 1886 when a small boiler engine was connected to six streetlights in Montpelier. In the same year the first hydroelectric plant was built on the Winooski, with power generated for Burlington. Green Mountain Power Company, the state's second-largest utility, got its start in 1891, with the Vergennes Electric Company and its hydroelectric plant on Otter Creek probably the second hydroelectric facility to be built in Vermont. The village of Barton followed in 1894 with a small plant, and the plant on the Winooski in Essex Junction was built in 1902.

Electric Energy Sources

Nearly every stream in Vermont has at one time or another been harnessed to provide power. The technology was simple, and almost common sense. If someone washed a frying pan (or spider) in a current of water, the force of the stream flow would

The largest hydroelectric facilities on the Connecticut River are the Moore and Comerford developments on the upper Fifteen-Mile Falls section of the river. This is the 140 Mw Comerford station in Barnet. Power from Quebec destined for New England consumers is delivered here for transmission throughout the region.

require strength to hold the implement. Could not that obvious power be harnessed? The first use of a stream's power was the undershot wheel. Natural rapids in the stream would be used here, the waterwheel having paddles which moved in a clockwise direction as viewed from the opposite bank. The mill would be built next to the rapids, and the wheel usually would stick out at right angles to the old building, turning so its paddles would be moved by the normal flow. Naturally, the speed of the water would affect the speed of the wheel. Slow in the fall, rapid in the in the spring, something that had to be planned on. The under-shot wheel, probably the most common in Vermont, was about 30% efficient. In other words, 70% of the force of the water was being wasted, and improvements were necessary.

The overshot wheel came next, and was about 75% efficient. But a mill with an overshot wheel required more work, including a dam to hold back the water in a mill pond. The principle was using the weight of the water as it either flowed over the top of the dam, or more commonly in a small spillway, to drive the wheel. In this case the wheel did not have flat paddles, but rather buckets. Water flowing over the dam would drop into the buckets, and the wheel would revolve in a counterclockwise direction, the weight of the water rather than the speed of the stream flow determining the amount of power produced. Because this method required a millpond, or reservoir above the site of the mill, the power was not liable to as much seasonal fluctuation as with the undershot wheel. Nonetheless, as with all water-generation of energy, the reservoir would be allowed to fill as appropriate, then the water released as necessary. The same principle applies to modern hydroelectric plants. Today, as in 1800, Vermont hydroelectric plants develop their maximum power output when water is high, and generate much less in the fall and winter when stream flow is at a minimum. Unfortunately, northern New England's peak electrical demand is still in the winter. Any utility dependent upon water-generation of electric energy in Vermont is required to purchase additional megawatts from other sources.

Electrical generation is measured in two ways. Most common is the installed capacity of a plant, expressed in kilowatt-hours or megawatts. This is the maximum amount of electricity capable of being generated in a twenty-four hour period. The Vermont Yankee nuclear plant has a capacity of 540,000 kwh, or as it often is expressed, 540 Mw. The small hydropower plant on the Lamoille River in Fairfax has a capacity of 2,000 kwh, or 2 Mw. Plants do not produce at capacity because demand drops considerably between 9:00 PM and 5:00 AM.

A kilowatt is 1,000 watts, or the amount of electricity consumed by a 100-watt bulb burning 10 hours. Kilowatt hours (kwh) are kilowatts (1,000 watts) multiplied by the number of hours of use. If the light burned for an entire month (about 720 hours), electrical consumption would be 72 kwh. In 1984, the average residential customer of Green Mountain Power Corporation consumed 752 kwh a month, or 9,022 kwh a year.

In 1979 CVPS, the state's largest electric utility, announced that its expected demand for 1992 would be 644 megawatts.

From all sources in 1979 the company could secure only 437 Mw. The Vermont Public Service Board has estimated that electric-power consumption will increase at a rate of 2.1% per year through the year 2000 even if use per household and use per employee remains at 1980 levels.

This estimate may prove to be conservative. Between 1979 and 1984, electricity sales by Central Vermont Public Service Corporation went from 1,175,497 Mwh to 1,511,528 Mwh, an increase of over 28%, or an annual growth in electricity consumption of 5.7% a year. Vermont's second largest utility, Green Mountain Power Corporation, for the same period, saw an annual growth in sales of 7.7%. Most growth in both cases came from commercial and industrial users. Residential consumption has lagged.

While statistics will show that Vermont annually produces more power than it consumes, the whole matter is quite complex because of utility ownership of facilities, economics, and transmission capabilities. Using Central Vermont Public Service Corporation as an example, in 1981 the company secured its power for eventual resale to its customers from the following sources:

Source	Amount %	Location (%)		Cost/kwh	
Nuclear	46	Vermont Yankee	80	2.8	cents
		Maine Yankee	9		
		Connecticut Yankee	8		
		Yankee Rowe	3		
Hydro	30	Power Authority, N.Y.	58	1.0	cents
		Company Plants (Vt.)	29		
		Hydro Quebec	12		
		Other	1		
Coal	14	Merrimack, N.H.	57	3.5	cents
		Ontario Hydro	43		
Oil	10	New England Pool	65	7.0	cents
		New Brunswick	15		
	100%	Other	20		

Source: 1982 Annual Report, Central Vermont Public Service Corporation.

Taking the entire state and the 26 private and public utilities providing power in 1980, the sources of electricity were as follows: nuclear, 33.2%, hydroelectric, 34.4%, oil, 17.0%, coal, 13.4%, and the remainder an unclassifiable mix of 1.8%. For many years Vermont's lowest-cost power has been 150 Mw from the New York Power Authority plants on the St. Lawrence and Niagara Rivers. That energy, costing 1.0 cents per kwh in the early 1980s, was largely lost upon the expiration of the Vermont-New York contract in 1985, although the power loss will be phased out gradually over a period of time.

Projections by the Vermont Public Service Board suggest that by 1990 Vermont's electric energy mix may be about 53.2% nuclear, 32.7% hydro (mainly through importation of Quebec power), 9.3% coal, 3.5% wood, and the remainder from gas and oil, 1.4%. Those estimates hinge upon the completion of the Seabrook, New Hampshire nuclear plant.

In the mid-1980s, the heavy reliance upon low-cost nuclear and hydroelectric sources provided Vermont residential customers with the lowest-cost electricity in New England (for 750 kwh a month). Only Maine had somewhat lower cost at other usage levels.

Implicit in all of the above is that the sources of electricity for Vermont are widespread and what is produced within the state has little bearing upon what is consumed. As an example of this situation, Vermont utilities are entitled to only 55% of the electricity from the Vermont Yankee nuclear plant in Vernon because in-state utilities own only 55% of the plant. In a similar fashion, the six New England Power Company dams on the Connecticut River contain a total of 27 individual generating units. Contractually, Vermont is not entitled to any of the power produced by the dams, yet six of the generating units, representing about 60 Mw, are located in the state. This is 60 Mw of hydroelectric energy which is "exported." The same is true with the 5.0 Mw Searsburg Station and the 45 Mw Harriman Station in Whitingham, both on the Deerfield River and also owned by the New England Power Company. This totals 110 Mw of hydroelectric power leaving Vermont for consumption elsewhere.

The result of this is that the state actually consumes only 38% of the electric power produced within its borders, and has to get

62% of its electricity elsewhere. Until recently, most of the hydro came from PASNY plants, which was Vermont's lowest-cost power. In the mid 1980s nuclear power from Vernon was costing just under 3.0 cents per kwh.

Hydropower

Using water to generate electricity requires an initial high capital investment in dams, generators and turbines. Operating costs are low after that, the resource is renewable immediately and the supply permanent and seasonally dependable. Hydroelectricity is clean energy; no smoke, soot, or radiation accompany production. Fish ladders and elevators make it possible for hydrodams not to impede spawning fish.

There is more electric gold in Vermont's streams, but utilizing all of it is impossible. In a complete survey of the nation's hydroelectric potential that was made in the 1960s, only 25.8% of U.S. waterpower was developed. In Vermont 35% was developed (Table 9.1).

TABLE 9.1

Hydroelectric Energy, 1963			
Area	*Developed Mw*	*Undeveloped Mw*	*% Developed*
United States	40,214	115,948	25.8
New England	1,249	3,128	28.5
Maine	350	1,786	16.0
New Hampshire	396	571	41.0
Vermont	185	345	34.9
Massachusetts	182	248	42.3
Rhode Island	2	-	100.0
Connecticut	133	178	42.8

Source: Statistical Abstract of the United States, 1966.

Like any resource, those sites most economic to develop are used first. As more of the potential resource is utilized the costs rise. While it seems that Vermont may have about 345 Mw of potential hydroelectricity to develop, in actual fact it is much less, but how much less depends upon development costs.

The map of hydroelectric and reservoir storage dams (Figure 9.1) shows Vermont pockmarked with these facilities. Most are very small plants. Total hydropower production in Vermont in 1977 was about 885 million kilowatt-hours from an installed capacity of 193 Mw, distributed among approximately 70 operating stations, including 60 Mw on the Connecticut River alone (which should not be counted). In that same year, the Vermont Yankee nuclear plant at Vernon produced 3,538 million kilowatt-hours of electrical energy. Producing less than 20% of Vermont's electric energy needs, the share of hydro probably will remain constant. With few economic sites left, development will be costly, and the amount of power produced in each case rather small.

Excluding the Connecticut and Deerfield Rivers projects, owned by the New England Power Company, there are 47 working hydro plants in Vermont. The largest is the Green Mountain Power Corporation dam at Essex Junction with a rating of 7.6 Mw. Vermont's other plants are equally insignificant. Central Vermont Public Service Company has three powerhouses on the Lamoille River in Milton, their combined capacity amounting to 14 Mw. The Chittenden Reservoir development in Rutland County is 3.6 Mw, and Sugar Hill, above Lake Dunmore, 2.2 Mw. Other major dams, at least by Vermont standards, include the Green Mountain Power Corporation plants at Moretown, 3.2 Mw, Marshfield, 5.0 Mw, and the Little River Dam in Waterbury, used also for flood control, 5.5 Mw. Newport has a 5.6 Mw hydroplant, and Swanton has a 4.6 Mw installation at Highgate Falls on the Missisquoi. As small as it may seem, if the Winooski River is harnessed between Burlington and Winooski with a new plant, the 12 Mw production may become the largest Vermont hydroelectric-generating facility.*

By contrast, developments on the Connecticut and Deerfield Rivers by the New England Electric Power Company are impres-

---

*In 1985 there were discussions concerning the development of a 24 Mw hydro facility in Sheldon Springs.

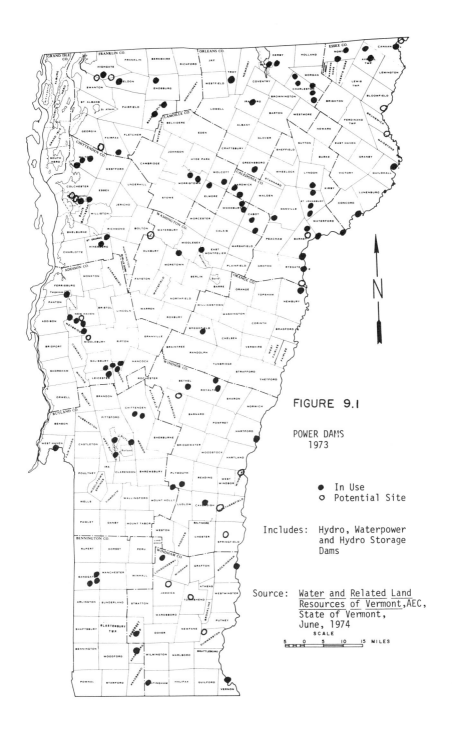

FIGURE 9.1

POWER DAMS
1973

● In Use
○ Potential Site

Includes: Hydro, Waterpower
and Hydro Storage
Dams

Source: Water and Related Land
Resources of Vermont, AEC,
State of Vermont,
June, 1974

SCALE

5 0 5 10 15 MILES

sive. The Deerfield River in Searsburg and Whitingham produces 50 Mw for customers outside Vermont. The six dams on the Connecticut produce as follows:

Vernon (1908-1909)	24.2 Mw	2 of 10 generators in Vermont (8.4 Mw)
Bellows Falls (1928)	40.8 Mw	all three generators in Vermont
Wilder (1950)	32.4 Mw	1 of 2 generators in Vermont (16.2 Mw)
McIndoe Falls (1930)	10.5 Mw	no generators in Vermont
Comerford Dam (1930)	140.4 Mw	no generators in Vermont
Moore Dam (1956)	140.4 Mw	no generators in Vermont
TOTAL	388.9 Mw	Six Vermont generators (65.4 Mw)

The entire Connecticut River flowing between Vermont and New Hampshire is producing nearly 150 Mw less than the single nuclear reactor at Vernon. But the power dams have a great impact on the Vermont communities in which they are located. The tax revenues generated by these and other hydro facilities in 1980 amounted to more than 25% of the tax revenues for Lunenburg, Concord, Waterford, Barnet, Hartford, (Wilder), Rockingham, Bellows Falls, and Vernon along the Connecticut River. Similarly, Readsboro, Searsburg and Whitingham enjoy similar tax benefits from the New England Power Company plants on the Deerfield River. Elsewhere in Vermont, towns like Chittenden, Milton, Goshen, Moretown, and Weybridge benefit in the same fashion from hydroelectric plants.

Because of their attractiveness, especially from an environmental standpoint, all the waterfalls in Vermont are being examined closely to see if they can be developed. Many abandoned power dams are being reconsidered. Some will generate again, but possibly at a higher cost than the utilization of nuclear sources already built or under construction. In the late 1970s, the citizens of Bristol were looking again with interest at the old Bartlett

Completed in 1909, the Vernon hydroelectric plant and dam is the oldest on the Connecticut River. In the foreground is the new fish ladder allowing the upstream migration of Atlantic salmon.

Vernon Dam on the left was the first hydroelectric facility built on the Connecticut River. Just upstream is the Vermont Yankee nuclear plant which uses the reservoir for cooling water and steam generation. This plant has one of the best safety and operational records of any nuclear plant in the United States.

Falls Dam on the New Haven River (1.4 Mw potential), which had generated electricity from 1892 to about 1950. Farther north, the village of Swanton, already with lower-than-average electric rates, was considering enlarging its dam on the Missisquoi, while Enosburg Falls citizens, who share the river, wanted to enlarge their present plant. Enlargements of existing generating stations at both Morrisville and Hardwick along the Lamoille River were being discussed. On the Dog River in Northfield, two old plants were being looked at carefully, and on the Black River in Ludlow, an old dam was being considered as a possible source of energy. In Bridgewater on the Ottauquechee, people were talking about the old dam at the woolen mill, and downstream in Hartford others were looking at two old dams in that town. The citizens of Springfield wanted to dam up the Black River north of town, flood some land in Cavendish, and divorce themselves from the private utility serving their area. The residents of Cavendish were not overly happy about this proposal.

In Bradford, 1.5 Mw is being generated now from a small dam on the Waits River, and 2.2 Mw is coming from a new plant in East Barnet. Other hydro proposals and dreams have involved having the Corps of Engineers turn flood-control dams at Jamaica, Townshend, North Springfield, Hartland, and Union Village (Thetford) into multiple-purpose dams to provide power development in addition to flood-control and recreation facilities. While flood control and power development are basically incompatible uses of the same water (flood control means no water behind the dam, power development means a full reservoir), it was estimated that the Ball Mountain Dam in Jamaica would be able to generate between 10 and 15 Mw. The Wrightsville flood-control dam north of Montpelier was having a small hydro plant installed in 1985, and consideration was being given to a dam in East Georgia on the Lamoille River. In the same year the old Bolton Falls Dam on the Winooski was being reactivated (potential 7.5 Mw).

Notwithstanding its appeal, it does not appear as though all the potential 345 Mw of hydrogold can be developed. The Connecticut River is fully utilized as are most other larger streams. As the remaining sites are marginal at best, they can be developed only at considerable cost.

The largest hydroelectric plant in Vermont is the 45 Mw Harriman Station on the Deerfield River. Owned by New England Electric, none of this power is consumed in the state. It is located about a mile north of the Massachusetts border, and water comes through a tunnel from Harriman Reservoir. The surge tower is the structure on the hillside above the plant.

The small 2 Mw hydroelectric plant at Fairfax Falls on the Lamoile River.

According to the Vermont Public Service Board, which for several years has been making a detailed inventory of potential sites, there are precious few places left to develop economically. Excluding the enlargement of existing facilities like the Boise Cascade Company dam in Sheldon Springs, there are only six facilities which exceed 10 Mw of power capacity. Four are the flood-control dams at North Hartland, Wrightsville, Townshend and Jamaica (Ball Mountain). The other two were on the Lamoille River in Fairfax and the Chance Mill site on the Winooski. Projections indicate very high costs for development. The small 1.5 Mw facility in Bradford was constructed recently at a cost of about $4.5 million. The Public Service Board also has estimated that the *maximum* addition to in-state hydroelectric development will be somewhere between 30 and 60 Mw of power.

Another problem with the use of streams for hydroelectricity is that it conflicts with the use of that water for the disposal of domestic and industrial waste. Balancing the amount of water with the amount of sewage is a critical factor, and therefore the Vermont Department of Water Resources has been trying to develop assimilative-capacity figures for most Vermont streams which service waste-treatment plants. Simply stated, a given amount of water is necessary to handle a given amount of waste without a deterioration in water quality and a negative effect upon fish populations. Since municipal wastes must utilize oxygen in the decomposition process, even after passing through primary- and secondary-treatment plants, the allocation is expressed in pounds of ultimate oxygen demand (UOD).

The flow of Vermont streams varies greatly with seasons. The flow is minimal during the winter when power needs are the greatest. As the flow of water decreases, hydroplants have to store the water behind the dams for release when the peak power demands occur in the early morning and evening hours. As all plants along a river do this, the flow becomes a mere trickle at certain times, often below the assimilative capacity of the river to handle the wastes from the treatment plants. Therefore, the ill-defined assimilative capacity of a stream puts a limitation on further hydroelectric-power production of that body of water.

With limited possibilities for any great hydroelectric expansion other, more imaginative, ideas to tap streams come to the fore.

One is the on again-off again proposal for pump-storage plants. Massachusetts has two of these plants.

In 1966 and 1967, the Vermont Electric Power Company (VELCO) commissioned a Michigan firm to conduct studies for a 400 Mw to 1200 Mw pump-storage plant. Nine sites were identified within an 80-mile radius of Burlington, seven in Addison County alone. The most highly-regarded site was in West Salisbury, just south of Middlebury. Opposition surfaced immediately with groups such as the Society for the Preservation of Rural Ferrisburg and the Abbey Pond Watershed Protective Association voicing strenuous opposition. The citizens of Salisbury were up in arms at the thought that Salisbury Swamp would become a lake for an electric plant. The Addison County Regional Planning and Development Commission went on record as opposing pump-storage plants. The plan soon came to naught but the sites haven't been forgotten.

The idea behind such a plant is simple, but very expensive to implement. A depression at some height above a water body is designated as a reservoir, and necessary dams and embankments are built to provide the outlines of a pond. During late night and early morning hours when electrical demand is low, the installed hydroplants utilize their energy to pump the water up to the hilltop pond. The water is released during the daytime to a newly-constructed plant at the bottom of the hill, which in turn generates power. The Bear Swamp project at Rowe, Massachusetts (625 Mw capacity) is an excellent example of the principle. It works, it makes sense, and it is the maximum use of water, a renewable resource. On the other hand, it might cause a pristine mountainside pond or marsh to become an artificial reservoir, and it is a very expensive piece of engineering. In an energy-starved area such as New England, many of whose residents have reservations about nuclear energy, it might be a viable alternative.

Totaling all the potential local waterpower sites discussed in the early 1980s produces a figure of about 60 Mw of power, still far short of the maximum estimated 345 Mw of power potential of Vermont's waters. This megawattage is expensive, every watt gained through public hearings and innumerable impact statements at additional cost. While power developments do not have to go through Act 250 hearings (Chapter 12), the Public Service

The Bear Swamp pump-storage electric development on the Deerfield River in Rowe, Massachusetts. In the 1960s Addison County, Vermont, was studied as a possible site for a similar type facility.

Board and other agencies must assure themselves that the development will not have any major adverse effects.

Another alternative for hydropower for Vermont is to use power generated elsewhere. The first thoughts towards securing Quebec energy surfaced in the late 1960s, but it was not until escalating nuclear costs, costly nuclear-plant shutdowns, and the loss of New York power that serious plans emerged in 1983 and 1984.

To tap the vast hydro potential of Quebec's Churchill Falls and La Grande projects requires transmission links with existing

New England networks. One line will cross Essex County, tying in with existing facilities on the Connecticut River. Vermont will be entitled initially to 69 Mw of the 690 Mw of power to be carried. The other connection is through Highgate north of St. Albans. This link had the potential to supply 200 Mw of power in 1986. Both sources will supply electricity at a cost based upon a certain percentage of prevailing fossil-fuel plants in the New England region. These costs were estimated at from 3.3 to 4.0 cents per kwh in 1985; more expensive than New York power or power from the Vermont Yankee nuclear plant, but less expensive than new in-state hydro facilities and less expensive than power from Burlington's new wood-burning facility.

Traditionally, nearly all in-state electrical generation has been from many small hydro plants. But as consumption began to rise with the population growth of more than 14% in the 1960s, Vermont power companies began to look for additional energy supplies. Non-hydro sources include nuclear energy, coal, gas, oil, wood, and even wind and solar power.

Coal, Oil, Natural Gas

Coal, oil, and gas never have been significant in Vermont, although the Moran municipal plant in the City of Burlington has used a combination of these to produce up to 58 Mw of power. Low-cost Champlain water transportation helps. In 1977, the Moran Generating Plant burned 40% coal, 38% natural gas and 22% oil to achieve a 51.4 Mw production. Since then, one boiler has been converted to wood chips and use of both oil and natural gas curtailed severely. With the opening of Burlington's new McNeil wood-burning plant, the old Moran station shut down.

Coal is America's most abundant conventional fuel resource, and even with costly air-quality restrictions, it can be used economically in comparison to other energy sources. Even shipping coal to Vermont and burning it in a local coal-fired plant could produce electricity at a lower cost than wood, oil, or natural gas. Nuclear energy would be slightly less expensive, according to 1980 figures. But because of the public impression of coal as a dirty fuel, and the hearing process involved in receiving a permit for a new generating facility, the utilities are reluctant to consider coal as a potential fuel. A good example of the problem is the rejection by the Maine Public Utilities Commission of a 568 Mw coal-fired plant on the Maine coast. Burlington's new 50 Mw wood-burning facility would possibly be more economic as a coal-burning plant, even with expensive transportation of the fuel into the area, but public sentiment is a powerful force in utility planning.

One of the basic laws of electrical generation from conventional fuels is that it is nearly always less expensive to burn the fuel at its source, whether it be coal, oil, wood, or natural gas, and then transport the energy as electricity to the consumer. A ton of coal can move through a transmission grid at a much lower cost than it can move by rail or barge. This is the primary reason why Vermont's two largest private utilities have invested largely in plants outside Vermont where the fuel is closer to its source, or where it could be delivered at a low cost. Vermont obtains power from Ontario power plants on the shore of Lake Ontario burning United States coal from the Pennsylvania and West Virginia coal fields. The situation is similar to getting power from a coal-fired plant on the Maine coast.

What makes sense is more coal-burning plants in the coal regions, Vermont utility investments in them, and the electricity moving through new higher kv transmission lines to the Vermont customer. But this may mean more acid rain and outcries from citizens seeing transmission lines obstructing their views of nature.

In the *Burlington Free Press* on August 16, 1979, a headline read: "Exxon Begins Search for Oil in Highgate." Dreams of oil and natural gas in the sedimentary rocks of the Champlain Lowlands have brought about surges of optimism over many years that Vermont would become an energy producer. The most recent enthusiasm was stimulated by a well drilled to a depth of 12,400 feet by Shell Canada just a few miles north of the Quebec boundary.

The Champlain Valley is what geologists refer to as a "sedimentary basin"—an area known to contain oil and natural gas. The American Gas Association maps the area as a "potential" source region. In 1957 Mrs. Lawrence Bellrose of Swanton re-

An oil drilling platform rises near a dairy farm in St. Albans Town.

ported that "We had a new well drilled 650 feet deep and hooked the water into the house. After you drew it from the tap it looked and tasted like Alka-Seltzer. One day a fuse blew out in the cellar and a strange hissing noise was coming from the water storage tank. My husband went down to the cellar to see what was wrong. He struck a match and the room lit up with a ball of fire." Poor Mr. Bellrose had struck natural gas, and his and similar experiences ushered in Vermont's mini oil boom.

Since 1957 Vermont has seen the Maquam Oil and Gas Development Corporation, the Peter Henderson Oil Company, the Vermont Gas and Minerals Corporation, the Cambrian Corporation and the Dexter Mining Corporation come and go. The Cambrian Corporation, still in existence, persuaded Petrofina Inc. to hire the Falcon Seaboard Drilling Company of Tulsa to drill a well in South Alburg. That enterprise drilled down a little more than 5,000 feet before quitting. Wells were drilled to a depth of 3,500 feet on Grand Isle and 4,900 feet in St. Albans in 1956.

They also drilled at several other places in northwestern Vermont. In 1984 the Columbia Gas Transmission Corporation drilled an exploratory well in Fairfield just east of St. Albans. The well was planned to go 10,500 feet deep but the company, after drilling through hard Vermont schist, gave up at half that distance.

Unquestionably there is oil and natural gas but it is uncertain if they exist in commercial quantities. A couple of old drilling platforms stick up among the trees waiting for someone to drill deeper. There are signs along the shoreline of Cutler Pond in Highgate warning the hiker not to light a match or smoke. The Alburg Mineral Springs probably got much of its popularity from the sulfur waters common to the Champlain Islands.

In 1979 there was some discussion of an oil refinery at Lunenburg. The great Montreal-Portland oil pipeline was to be tapped there. Lancaster, New Hampshire may get a refinery, and eastern Canada might get less oil. Vermont does have a lot of oil under its soil, but it moves swiftly in a pipeline and probably never will be tapped. Natural gas may develop into something, petroleum probably less, but curiously enough, the state sits on top of two rather scarce resources. Their existence probably will make little difference in the total Vermont energy picture.

Nuclear Energy

With native natural energy sources rather skimpy, Vermont utilities have been concentrating on other possible energy sources to meet consumers' needs. In the 1960s the choice was made to go the nuclear route; a proven technology was available, and relatively low-cost energy could be provided for an area at the end of the energy pipeline.

In following what appeared to be the only economic alternative, Central Vermont Public Service Corporation and the Green Mountain Power Company announced in August 1966 that the General Electric Company had contracted to build a 540 Mw nuclear-power plant at Vernon at a cost of $88 million. It was scheduled for completion in the fall of 1970.

The Vernon site was no accident. Cooling water was available from the Connecticut River and the location was within low-cost transmission distance to large population centers. The original site, however, was to have been on Lake Champlain near Burlington. That proposal led to activity by an environmental group called the Lake Champlain Committee which strongly opposed construction of the plant on the lake.

The Vernon site also met with stiff opposition. The Conservation Society of Southern Vermont organized and produced testimony from a learned Ph.D. that yearly deaths from radiation emissions at the plant would approach 32,000. Notwithstanding this opposition, construction continued and the plant was finished on schedule. By 1972 it had yet to generate any electricity because of the activities of the Natural Resources Defense Council and the New England Coalition on Nuclear Pollution. Additional problems relating to thermal pollution of the Connecticut River also delayed the start-up date.

The Vernon generator is a boiling-water type. The heat from the reactor changes the water to steam, which in turn powers the turbines. The steam then is condensed to water and returns to the reactor. The water serves two functions—in the form of steam it provides the energy to the turbines, while in its liquid state it cools the reactor. To do this requires an intake of water at a rate of 780 cubic feet per second. Vermont Yankee had signed a contract agreeing to obey all Vermont regulations relating to water use as long as the Vermont regulations were consistent with the Atomic Energy Commission guidelines. But formal protests by both Massachusetts (downstream) and New Hampshire (which owns the river), requested the Vermont Water Resources Board to order the plant to discharge lower-temperature waters into the river.

Responding to the Massachusetts and New Hampshire protests as well as heated opposition from several environmental groups, the board ruled that Vermont Yankee could not raise the temperature of the Connecticut River *at all* when the base temperature of the water was 70°F or more, and could raise the temperature in a "mixing zone" of three acres only 10°F when the river water is less than 35°F. This meant the addition of 11 cooling towers at a cost of $6.5 million, plus a share of the plant's output to run the 150 horsepower fans installed in each tower. Large amounts of steam and mist are added now to the Vernon atmosphere.

The first kilowatt of energy was ground out of the Vermont Yankee turbines in 1973, only two-and-a-half years behind schedule. The plant had been completed on time, but add-ons and increasingly stringent safeguards delayed initial operation. Costs skyrocketed with the delays. What was contracted as a $88 million facility in 1966 was estimated to cost $120 million only three years later. By the end of September 1970, the plant was costing $125 million, and reached $191 million in March of 1972. In March 1973, the whole installation was appraised for $251 million.

Until quite recently, nuclear energy had been the lowest-cost source of electricity for an area like Vermont. In fact, the relatively lower cost of electricity in the state (compared to many areas of the northeast) is largely the result of a heavy reliance on nuclear and hydroelectric sources. While cost estimates of various types of electrical generating plants often are questionable, a report presented to the Vermont Public Service Board in January 1977 explored the possible economics of nuclear, wood, oil-fired, and coal plants. Taking into account all necessary environmental add-on features (like stack scrubbers for a coal plant) and thinking of mid-1980 dollars and a privately-financed operation, the results were as follows for 50 Mw of electrical generation at 85% of capacity:

Type of Fuel	Average Annual Cost Mills/kwh for 30 Years		
Wood	High	50.2	Low 47.8
Nuclear	High	45.8	Low 40.8
Oil	Average Yearly:		53.6
Coal	Average Eastern/Western		49.8

These 1977 estimates took into account the initial construction costs, operating costs and fuel costs for a 30-year period (the estimated life of a plant). As such they were probably the best available for the period. Analysts considered a local wood-burning plant feeding into VELCO transmission lines and nuclear, oil, or coal plants anyplace in the New England region.

Even more recently, nuclear estimates appeared very attractive. As late as March 1980, the Burlington Electric Department estimated that for an electric plant operating at 85% of capacity and money costing 7%, the 10-year present worth of power and energy costs would be: nuclear, $180 million; coal, $192 million, and wood, $209 million. Fuel costs, as of 1986 in mills per kilowatt-hour would amount to: nuclear, 9.50; coal, 24.94, and wood, 30.06, annually. The estimates are contained in the "Certificate of Public Good" accompanying BED's application for its 50 Mw wood chip plant.

During the 1970s such estimates led Vermont power companies into purchasing small shares of ownership in several New England nuclear plants, both planned and under construction. Through such arrangements, electric companies are entitled to a share of a plant's output in proportion to their ownership. As an example, Central Vermont Public Service Corporation would be entitled to 36.6 Mw of the 2,300 Mw of Seabrook I and II in New Hampshire, and 20 Mw from Millstone III in Massachusetts.

Nuclear costs have risen sharply since 1980, far exceeding earlier estimates. While power from installed facilities remains reasonable in price (3.0 cents per kwh from Vermont Yankee in 1984), the cost of power from the new plants will be considerably higher than imported hydroelectricity from Quebec. In mid-1984 eventual Seabrook power was estimated to cost anywhere from 14.0 to 25.0 cents per kwh when Seabrook I begins operation in 1987.

Wood

When environmental concerns with Vermont Yankee were at a peak in 1973 the first serious thoughts were given to using wood as a source of electrical energy in a commercial plant. In that year Green Mountain Power Company prepared a study and applied for federal funding to convert a small plant in Milton to burn green hardwood chips. At the time nothing came of the work, but Burlington now has a 50 Mw wood chip plant. The pioneer 1973 study, done by William

Beardsley, developed some tentative cost figures for such an installation producing 50 Mw of power:

Fuel Type	Construction Costs/kwh	Power Production/Mills per kwh
Nuclear	$400	12 - 22
Wood	280	20
Solar	900 - 2,950	60
Wind	372 - 500	20
Gas Turbine	100	16 - 30

While construction costs for a nuclear facility were estimated to be higher than a comparable wood plant, operating costs were considered to be somewhat less. Thus in the early 1970s the two types of plants were considered to be competitive in providing power. The Vermont Public Service Board, however, remained skeptical and commissioned Allen J. Schultz to prepare a report on the matter. In 1977 Schultz wrote: "The average annual cost for 50,000 kilowatts of power and associated energy at high capacity factor delivered to the Vermont transmission grid is more expensive from an investor financed 50 Mw wood-burning generating plant constructed in Vermont, than from a large nuclear power plant installed in New England." This mirrored the thinking of power planners of the mid-1970s that nuclear energy would remain competitive.

Nonetheless, the Burlington Electric Department pushed ahead with plans for an $80 million 50 Mw wood chip plant. The application was approved by the Vermont Public Service Board in 1981 and the plant was completed in the spring of 1984. In January 1985 it was costing 7.9 cents per kilowatt-hour to produce the power; considerably higher than earlier estimates. Furthermore, in the words of Timothy Cronin, BED spokesman, as reported in the March 27, 1984 *Burlington Free Press:* "The assumptions used when the...facility was planned have changed." Demand has not increased as fast as expected, so BED found itself with a considerable excess of surplus expensive power to dispose of. The 1985 cost was comparable to oil-fired power that year, and higher than coal, installed nuclear or potential Quebec hydroelectricity.

As the Burlington plant was being planned, and throughout

the hearing process which preceded the granting of a permit, there was a great deal of discussion as to the economic viability of the plant and the potential environmental impact that it would have in its hinterland.

In the early 1980s most wood-burning electric plants were located in Washington and Oregon and were using waste wood from sawmills. In Vermont, a plant burning green wood chips was a first-of-a-kind situation, but the Burlington Electric Department had experimented for two years with green wood chips in one boiler of its Moran Generating Plant and had decided that the project was feasible, at least technically.

Green wood chips with an average moisture content between 35 and 40% can burn. But the average heating value is only about 5,000 Btu per pound, as compared to more than 13,000 Btu for low-sulfur western coal. This means that the tonnages of raw material for a wood chip plant are extremely high. In the Burlington case the facility consumes about 200,000 cords (500,000 tons) of wood a year, or 550 cords a day.

What this means is that the most critical costs associated with the plant involve location with respect to raw material, the transportation of the raw material to the plant, and the cost and availability of the wood supply. Once the fuel supply is in place, generation costs are the same whether it be natural gas, oil or coal. Hence the reason why the production costs are greater than estimated is because of raw material supply and transportation.

Ideally, it was planned that the fuel would come from the large annual poor growth (rough and rotten) in Vermont's forests, growth which is crowding out growing sawtimber and hindering regeneration. In 1973 Beardsley pointed out that there was enough surplus wood growing annually in a 24-mile radius to fuel a 50 Mw plant. In 1977 the Wood Energy Institute in Waitsfield estimated that fuel could be supplied by the rough and rotten wood growing in a 50-mile radius of the plant (using Morrisville as an example).

In 1985 the Burlington Electric Department was receiving raw material from Canada as well as from Essex County, Vermont, far beyond a 50-mile radius of supply. In 1973 it was estimated that the wood would cost $10.50 per ton, delivered. In 1977 the estimate was $15, and in 1985 the supply of wood chips was costing more than $20.

There are three reasons for this extension of the supply area and the greater than estimated costs. First, harvesting the rough and rotten or surplus growth is more expensive than predicted because it involves selective cutting. This is much more expensive than clear cutting. Furthermore, as most Vermont forest-land ownership is in small private parcels (Chapter 11), many landowners are unwilling to have a wood harvest because the large machinery required to do the job economically often causes considerable environmental damage. Foresters may urge selective thinning of woodlots to improve forest stands, but many new owners of property are adverse to any tampering with their forest land. The economics of wood chip use were based originally upon controlled experiments on public lands in Duxbury and Victory.

Secondly, wood simply costs more. In 1980 the Vermont State Energy Office estimated that 650,000 cords of wood were being used as fuel in Vermont homes, and 15% of the state's total energy needs were being met by burning wood. During the winter of 1978-1979 the U.S. Department of Agriculture reported that 43% of Vermont homes were using wood and that at least 55,000 people were being kept warm exclusively through the burning of wood. In 1969 wood was selling at a statewide average price of $38.71 a cord. In 1979 it was $58.01 and in 1983, $97.52. Variations showed the highest prices to be in the Burlington area, the lowest in the northeast.

Finally, it was anticipated originally that all wood for the plant would be delivered by truck, increasing flexibility and lowering transportation and handling costs. However, it was thought that highway congestion in the vicinity of the plant would be so excessive that the Vermont Public Service Board in granting the construction permit specified that 75% of the wood chips would have to be transported by rail. A rail-staging area is located in Swanton now, and Swanton is concerned with the impact of truck traffic on the community. And since Swanton is some 40 miles from Burlington, the "50-mile radius" has become academic. The Burlington Electric Department has had to invest approximately $1 million in 20 specially-built freight cars which operate in shuttle service between Swanton and Burlington, often creating significant traffic congestion at the "Five

Corners" in Essex Junction.

When a 50 Mw wood chip electric plant first was discussed, it generally was agreed that its most logical site would be in some community closer to a source of wood than Burlington. Morrisville, Richmond and Waterbury were mentioned. Fuel costs would have been lower, but the City of Burlington was determinded that the plant would be located within the city—in the midst of Vermont's greatest population concentration. Defying logic, the plant is sited now in the floodplain of the Winooski River with the City of Winooski downwind of the high stack. And Burlington residents have complained of watering eyes and other ailments caused by smoldering wood chip storage piles.

A wood-burning electric plant appears to have problems, both in terms of possible environmental impact and in terms of cost of supply. On the other hand, wood is a renewable resource and if only surplus growth of poor-quality trees is used, there could be a positive impact on the quality of Vermont's forests (Chapter 11). No one knows what will happen in 30 years. Eight cents per kilowatt-hour looks expensive for the moment but may be very attractive in the future. The plant contributes about $10 million a year to the regional economy; it employs 40 people full time and up to 400 others part time in wood supply and transportation.

Solar, Wind, and Trash Power

Beyond conventional hydroelectric power and less-conventional nuclear- and wood-generated power come the favorite topics of the 1980s. All three of these power sources are high-cost in a commercial sense using present technologies, but each, locally and individually, may be important sometime. Refuse, if it is compacted into cubes with all glass and metal first removed, can yield about 6,000 Btu a pound. The problem is that Vermont does not have enough trash to use it for power. The refuse collected from 90,000 people, delivered to a single processing site, would fuel a small 5 Mw generating plant. Nevertheless, in 1985, plans were being made for the construction of a small plant in Rutland.

Wind and solar energy have some possibilities. In 1941 the famous Putnam Wind Generator atop Grandpa's Knob in Rutland County was the first commercial wind-generating station in the United States. A 117 foot-high windmill was erected there. A turbine with two 87-foot blades was installed on top of the mast. The generator was capable of producing one-and-a-quarter megawatts. In 70 mph gales, one-and-a-half megawatts were cranked out once or twice. Starting March 3, 1945, and for 23 days thereafter, the wind generator fed power into the Central Vermont Public Service Company system. During that period the winds allowed the machine to operate 143 hours, 25 minutes (26% of capacity) with a total production of 61,780 kwh. Early on the morning of March 26 one of the blades broke loose and tumbled 750 feet down the mountainside. It had worked, but with a wartime shortage of materials the generator never was repaired, and Grandpa's Knob now serves as a repeater station for Vermont Educational Television. At the time that the plant ceased operating, CVPS estimated that rebuilding, or installation of additional similar wind generators, would cost $191 per kilowatt finally transmitted. Lincoln Ridge was examined as another site, but the company concluded that any costs above $125 per kilowatt-hour were uneconomic. Thus ended commercial electric energy from a wind-driven plant.

Grandpa's Knob showed that it could be done. Today it is common to see small windmill generators in many places in Vermont supplying small amounts of power to homes usually some distance from a highway or power line. As late as 1950 there still were 50,000 windmills providing electricity on the prairies of the Middle West and Great Plains. These small turbines play a real role in providing power to places where it would be expensive to string conventional electric service. They are welcomed by the power companies, but the commercial generation of electric power from wind is still a while off. NASA is engaged in this research, as well as private companies such as Boeing and Grumman.

At an average wind speed of 10 mph a small home wind generator can produce about 700 kwh over a month's time. The trouble again is cost. The 1976 cost was more than $10,000; no small sum when repairs as well as routine servicing are necessary.

A month's supply of electricity (750 kwh) in Montpelier in 1978 was $32.62. At that rate it would be more than 25 years before the cost was amortized. Commercial plants are not cheap, and at the moment we don't know how efficient or economic they might be. One authority said in 1974 that windmills could compete with natural gas at $1.20 per hundred cubic feet. The 1984 price of natural gas in Vermont was less than two-thirds that. In 1973, Beardsley figured that the construction costs of a commercial wind-generating plant would be between $372 and $700 per kilowatt-hour produced, compared to $400 for the Vermont Yankee nuclear plant.

Not only are larger wind-generating machines expensive, there is also a question about where they should be placed. Highest average wind speeds occur with increasing altitude, so the summit of the Green Mountains is a logical place.

In 1980, the Green Mountain Power Company proposed placing an experimental three Mw wind generator along the same Lincoln Ridge looked at 30 years ago. Outcries by residents of Lincoln sank the proposal, but Green Mountain Power Company may move the site a few hundred yards into the town of Warren, whose residents are enthusiastic about a wind-generating facility. Such are the frustrations of utilities when it comes to innovative forms of electrical generation.

The amount of solar energy which strikes the earth's surface each year is incredible. Enough sunlight hits Egypt to power every machine in the world. Even in Vermont, the amount of solar energy over 36 square miles (one Vermont town) is equivalent to nearly half of New England's annual electric requirements.

But there are two fundamental problems. One is the facilities necessary to trap a large amount of solar energy, the other is how the power can be stored during periods of minimal sunshine. The first is no major concern, although construction of a large solar-energy concentrator is expensive, estimated in 1973 to cost anywhere between $900 and $2,950 per kilowatt-hour installed capacity.

Cloudiness is a formidable problem. Vermont is one of the cloudiest areas in the United States, and only five first-order National Weather Service stations in the conterminous U.S. have more cloudy days than Burlington's 199. They are Portland,

Eugene and Salem, Oregon; Seattle, Washington; and Binghamton, New York. In New England, only Mt. Washington and Caribou, Maine are cloudier.

As with small wind generators, small solar collectors will continue to help individual homeowners with their energy bills. But solar energy supplying a large generating facility in Vermont is certainly a long way off. Given the high degree of cloudiness over the region, along with low winter temperatures, it is unlikely that solar energy, whether commercial or home-installed collectors, will do much in the immediate future to satisfy the state's growing energy needs.

Energy in Retrospect

The two largest private utilities in Vermont have planned on augmenting much of their future power requirements with nuclear generation elsewhere in New England. Both have an interest in developing more local hydropower and securing more hydroelectricity from Canada. The state's third-largest utility, the publicly-owned Burlington Electric Company, has constructed a wood-burning facility. No utility is making plans to generate commercial amounts of power from the wind or from the sun very seriously. Most of Vermont's electrical energy in the immediate future is to come from nuclear and hydro sources, and while nuclear costs have escalated enormously, Vermont's electrical-energy costs still remain below regional averages. In 1984 the average Vermont residential cost of electricity was the lowest in New England except for Maine, and commercial and industrial rates were the lowest in the region.

Vermont's 26 electric utilities face an uncertain future. Energy costs have fluctuated widely in recent years; nuclear plants have been shelved or shut down for long periods of time. Public Service Commissions have been increasingly critical of rate requests. The public, faced with rising electric bills, has been more vocal. The power question was put into perspective by Governor Richard Snelling in August 1981. As quoted in the *Burlington*

Steam rises from the controversial McNeil wood chip plant in the Burlington Intervale.

Free Press (August 13, 1981), the governor said:

> If they simply take polls, what they will find is that people want electricity. They want it cheap, but they do not want nuclear plants; they do not want coal plants; and they do not want dependency on OPEC; and they don't want transmission lines.

Vegetation

A book which deals with Vermont's natural-resource base must be concerned with the forests of the state because they played an enormously important role in history, providing shelter, fuel and exportable products. Even today nearly 3,700 Vermonters are employed in various types of wood-related industries. There have been at least two recent and widely-available books which deal with the character of vegetation in the state. *The Nature of Vermont* by Charles Johnson and *A Guide to New England's Landscape* by Neil Jorgenson are excellent and detailed treatments on the subject. They both are highly recommended to those interested in the subject.

Some years ago Interstate 89 was built between Montpelier and Burlington following, for the most part, the winding course of the Winooski River as it cuts through the Green Mountains. Modern engineering dictated that the road be as straight as possible with smooth and gentle curves capable of handling high-speed traffic. One of the results of construction was relocation of old Route 2, as its winding course constantly interfered with the straightaway standards of the new highway.

Sections of the old highway have been forgotten now by highway crews. Pigweed pushes up between slabs of concrete, and

Separated by 20 years, two views of the same hillside in Hancock show brush taking over old hill pasture. More boulders have come to the surface, the stone wall of 1955 now is hidden, and a snow fence has given way to a nicely painted rail fence containing horses. Is this a picture of a changing Vermont?

small elders have established themselves. What was the main east-west highway in northern Vermont a few years ago is returning to brush and in 50 years the works of man as represented by these concrete slabs, highway fence posts, and asphalt shoulders will be impossible to find.

Climax Vegetation

If one were to stand back and watch nature at work for a few hundred years, one probably would see the complex vegetation of Vermont revert to what nature intended it to be. Northern hardwoods comprised mainly of birch, beech, and maple, would predominate. Our forests today are not always the northern hardwoods because human modifications of the vegetation landscape have been continuous since the first tree was felled.

There always is a problem in assuming that the northern hardwoods are the climax (natural vegetation) for most of Vermont because there are differences in soil and climate from place to place, and the natural vegetation is going to reflect these differences. In fact, there are really four primary natural-vegetation zones. One is represented by northern hardwoods, common below 2,000 feet except in northeastern Vermont. In the central Champlain Valley, an oak and hickory forest might be the climax. Above 2,000 feet and in the northeast, spruce and fir probably would dominate. Above 4,000 feet scattered spots on Mt. Mansfield, Camels Hump and Killington Peak exhibit fragile alpine tundra.

Accounts of early settlers and land surveyors who commonly used trees for boundary lines are one source of information on what the early forests may have been like. In northern Vermont the most common trees noted in the surveyors' reports were beech. They probably comprised about 40% of the trees in the old forests of Chittenden County. That compares with perhaps five percent today. Beech even may have accounted for 13% of the trees in the forests of the northeast, today dominated by spruce and fir. The following data on pre-settlement forests was derived by Thomas G. Siccama in a Master of Science thesis at the University of Vermont.

TABLE 10.1

Composition of Pre-Settlement and Present Forests (%)

Tree Species	Northern Vermont Pre-Settlement	Chittenden County Pre-Settlement	Chittenden County Present
Beech	30.4	40.4	4.7
Maple	15.4	15.8	23.8
Spruce	16.4	5.6	1.9
Birch	11.0	5.1	16.2
Hemlock	10.8	7.3	11.0
Pine	1.2	6.3	12.0
Oak	.6	2.8	5.6
TOTALS	91.2	83.3	75.1
Other Species	8.8	16.7	24.9

Besides changes in the proportion of individual species, one clear observation is that present forests appear more diverse than pre-settlement ones. This is because people planted shade or ornamental trees many years ago. These different species now have propagated themselves in the surrounding forests. In addition, certain trees were preserved because of their beauty or utilitarian value, and thus were able to regenerate themselves.

Vegetation Patterns

It is hard to generalize the present forest cover because of human modifications and the complex topography and climate of the state. There is not too much change from north to south, except for the persistence of the spruce and fir forest of the northeast and some similarities between the Connecticut and Champlain Valleys. As can be expected, there are important changes related to altitude.

Except for the highest tundra elevations, there are 24 common tree species found throughout Vermont. Certain species will dominate in certain areas, but there is no way of mapping that clearly. These common species include:

Deciduous	Coniferous
Beech	Balsam Fir
Yellow Birch	Tamarack
Paper Birch (White Birch)	Black Spruce
Gray Birch	Red Spruce
White Ash	White Pine
Black Ash	Canada Yew
Hop hornbeam ("Hardhack")	
Bigtooth Aspen Quaking Aspen ("popple")	
Black Cherry	
Northern Red Oak	
Black Willow	
Basswood	
American Elm	
Red Maple	
Sugar Maple	
Silver Maple	

Another 28 species occur widely in scattered localities. Black, scarlet, burr, pin and white oaks are found in the Champlain Valley, in narrow zones along the southwest border with New York, and along the Connecticut River as far north as Newbury. Shagbark hickory, bitternut hickory and mockernut hickory have a distribution that tends to parallel that of the oaks. Not surprising when the two species have an affinity for the same sort of warmer, drier environment. Representatives of the walnut family include the black walnut, restricted to a small area in south central Addison County, and the butternut, widespread except in Essex and Orleans Counties. Butternuts were one of the most useful trees to the early settlers, not for their weak wood, but because the nuts yielded a dark stain when boiled that was useful as a dye. Indians used to boil the nuts and the oil that floated to the top was used as a butter—hence the name. The boiled sap yielded a very sweet syrup, the crushed nuts once were used to poison fish, and the bark yielded drugs. This is an example of a tree which probably is more widespread today than in the past because it had an important use and was preserved when others were cut.

Logging roads penetrate the spruce and fir forests of Essex County. Nearly all land in the unincorporated townships is owned by large lumber companies but is open to the public for recreational use.

Many logging roads are closed each spring during mud season. "Mud Season" is affectionately known as Vermont's fifth season.

Rock elm and slippery elm are found in Vermont, but are far less important than the American elm. Sassafras trees occur in the Connecticut Valley in the southeast, and in the southwest corner of Bennington County where mulberry trees also are found. Red pine is scattered in every county except Bennington and the western half of Windham. Pitch pine occurs along the Connecticut River as far north as Barnet, and is located also in parts of Franklin, Grand Isle, Chittenden and Addison Counties. Franklin, Chittenden, and Addison Counties also have small stands of jack pine which, like many pines prefers the well-drained sandy soils found in certain parts of these areas. Cotton-wood, like so many other species, occurs in the Champlain Valley near the lake from Shoreham to the Canadian border, and also along the Connecticut River in the southeast. White spruce is found with black and red spruce over much of northern Vermont, but is absent south of a line from Bradford to Burlington, although it is common above 3,000 feet on the southern Green Mountains. Flowering dogwood, one of the most beautiful small trees in New England, is rare in Vermont. It does occur in a small area in Castleton and Fair Haven, in the southwestern third of Bennington County, and in a narrow zone along the Connecticut River as far north as Dummerston. The cedars and junipers are represented by red cedar, northern white cedar, and common juniper (often called dwarf juniper), and are scattered widely.

Other species have minor representation. Sycamore is found along Lake Champlain between Burlington and Orwell, and in the southeast and southwest corners. There are two patches of box elders, one along Lake Champlain in Chittenden County and north including the town of South Hero, the other roughly along Route 7 in the southern part of Addison County and the northern part of Bennington County. Yellow poplar is found in three scattered areas, but since poplar (aspen) is a universal tree in Vermont it should be regarded with its relatives. The same is true of sweet birch; it joins its close relative the yellow birch, which is the most common birch in Vermont. Hackberry, like cotton-wood and other trees, is restricted to the border of Lake Champlain and along the Connecticut River in the southeast.

Altitude is a primary control over the common trees which grow in the state. This is as true today as it was in 1800 when the land was first cleared and settled. Chittenden County encompasses both the lowest elevation in Vermont (Lake Champlain, 95 feet) as well as the highest, Mt. Mansfield, 4,393 feet. The following table, adapted from the thesis by Thomas Siccama, shows species distribution by altitude for Chittenden County in 1800.

TABLE 10.2

Forest Composition, 1800 (%)				
	Below 500'	*1000-1500'*	*2000-2500'*	*3000'+*
Beech	31.3	55.7	24.0	- - -
Maple	16.3	14.0	8.0	- - -
Birch	4.9	6.1	18.0	- - -
Hemlock	10.4	4.9	- - -	- - -
Oak	5.1	.3	- - -	- - -
Pine	12.0	.3	- - -	- - -
Spruce	.7	11.3	46.0	85.7
Fir	- - -	- - -	4.0	14.3
TOTALS	80.7	92.6	100.0	100.0

Beech is very common with its wide range of tolerance for various moisture and temperature conditions. Among the other hardwoods, maples tend to thrive at lower elevations while birch tends to be associated with greater altitudes. Spruce and fir dominate to the exclusion of all else closer to the mountain summits. Oak and pine are associated with the warmer, sandy-soil areas of the Champlain Lowland, and it was the high incidence of pine which initially gave rise to the important lumber industry of Burlington.

With more land being cleared after 1800, farming pushed upwards to close to the 2,000 foot elevation throughout much of Vermont. The original forests were destroyed almost completely below that elevation, the only parts left often being along property boundary lines where stone walls snake across the old upland pastures. The last land to be cleared was usually the highest elevation, and it also was that land that often was the first abandoned.

Thus, many old upland areas have been growing back for more than 100 years and in places appear to be reverting to a climax condition, although considerably different than their original state.

When farmland is abandoned, a general sequence of vegetative change sets in which, if left undisturbed, gradually will see the area changed back to its original state. The following plant-succession sequence should be expected over much of the state below 2,500 feet in elevation and excludes the northeast.* Local site situations will produce something different.

Stage	Duration (years)	Average Elapsed Time (years)
Bare Field	1	1
Weedy plants (forbes), including pigweed and mustard. Some grasses.	1–2	2½
Grasses dominate, some weeds.	3–5	5½
Woody shrubs, brambles, raspberries.	8–12	12½
Small trees, including gray birch, hop hornbeam (ironwood), alders, poplar, white cedar, some white pine, hemlock.	30–40	36
Subclimax, mainly white pine, some birch, spruce and fir in northeast.	100–150	average 140 years but possible after 75
Northern hardwood climax	permanent	possible after 125 years

Throughout Vermont, these various stages often can be seen. What is most distinctive, at least from the air, is the subclimax of white pine, usually with spruce and fir and birch mixed in. In

---

*Information on plant succession was provided by Dr. Hubert Vogelman of the University of Vermont botany department.

Abandoned farmland shows up as patches of sub-climax white pine in this view near Greensboro.

the fall of the year a clear patchwork of rectangles, squares and innumerable odd-shaped pieces of land show green in contrast to the yellows of the old fence lines. These white-pine patches represent fields abandoned many years ago, and to an experienced eye, the height of the trees is a good indicator of the date of final abandonment.

While different figures are used, the 1870s probably saw the maximum amount of cleared land in Vermont, and the 1880 Census recorded that of the *total area of the state*, 55.4% was "improved farmland." The definition of improved farmland then in use was reasonably liberal, but it at least serves as an indication. Unfortunately, no material exists which can provide objective data on cleared land prior to 1850. Land-use data was not reported until the 1850 Census, so that the amount of land that was cleared or semi-cleared for sheep farming can only be guessed at. It was probably less than that in the 1870s because only 43.9%

of the land was improved by 1850 and it is unlikely that much land had reverted to non-farm uses. (See Chapter 11 for a discussion of exactly how much Vermont land actually was cleared.)

As the land has gone back to forest it has not become the same forest which existed in the early 1800s. Rather it has become more diverse, with many more species of trees. Table 10.3 shows the recent forest composition of Chittenden County. The material is adapted from Thomas Siccama.

TABLE 10.3

Chittenden County Forest Composition, 1962 (%)					
Species	*Below 500'*	*1000-1500'*	*1500-2000'*	*2000-2500'*	*3000'+*
Beech	3.5	11.5	11.8	5.9	- - -
Maple	17.9	40.7	41.3	45.9	- - -
Birch	13.3	17.6	23.2	45.9	19.0
Hemlock	13.8	9.7	2.8	- - -	- - -
Oak	9.5	1.9	4.9	- - -	- - -
Pine	18.0	1.9	1.5	- - -	- - -
Spruce	- - -	6.2	8.0	1.8	12.2
Fir	- - -	- - -	- - -	- - -	68.8
TOTALS	79.0	89.5	93.5	99.5	100.0

Several obversations can be made from a comparison of this with pre-settlement forests (Table 10.2). Perhaps most noticeable is the wide distribution of maple and birch hardwoods at the expense of the beech. While it is tempting to read a climate change into this, the actual answer involves the reproduction characteristics of individual species. Beech will regenerate given more time, but is slower in coming back than either of the other two major hardwoods.

Other changes involve the much-lower density of spruce at higher elevations, probably attributable to logging operations for this species in preference to fir. Also, the preponderance of hardwoods above 1,500 feet suggests that large areas of land at that elevation may have reverted to the climax, although with a different composition than the earlier forests. The increase in spruce

Limestone and white cedar provide a unique Vermont landscape through much of Grand Isle County.

and pine in the 1,000–2,000 feet zone, and especially pine at lower elevations, also illustrates the subclimax pattern. In another 50 years the spruce and pine forests of that elevation probably will disappear if left undisturbed.

Local site conditions for specific species cannot be seen by looking at tables. Hemlock, for example, is a persistent tree at lower elevations, but at those elevations prefers steep slopes along the sides of ravines and in other areas which do not receive much sunlight.

The pine and oak forests of the Champlain Valley associate closely with sandy delta deposits, but the incidence of northern white cedar (arborvitae) over large areas, especially in Grand Isle County and near Lake Champlain, is very striking to anyone familiar with the area. Its distribution corresponds almost exactly with the areas of limestone in the valley since it prefers a soil reasonably high in calcium carbonate ($CaCO_3$), or a soil with a high pH factor. Nearly all the split-rail fences in Vermont are of native northern white cedar and are especially common in non-glacial till areas of Grand Isle County.

In certain small areas, mainly in Addison County, patches of oak and hickory forest are fairly common. At one time probably far more extensive, these trees may represent a relic stand, a plant association left over from a past era. All indications from these forests suggest that somewhat warmer and drier conditions prevailed in parts of Vermont than is presently the case. Adding further proof to this observation is the evidence gleaned through bog-pollen analysis.

Pollen Analysis and Past Climates

Lakes are temporary items on the landscape; all will disappear through the combined effects of siltation from streams draining into them, and from vegetation encroachment from the sides. When the lake or pond closes over with vegetation it becomes a quaking bog. There are between 30 and 40 of them in Vermont. Bogs provide us with an opportunity of deducing what the past vegetation was in the vicinity of the ancient lake. Over thousands of years, trees and shrubs growing around the sides of the old lake constantly shed their pollen onto the water where it gradually sank to the bottom. Over many years layer upon layer of pollen accumulated. By taking a core sample and examining the material under a microscope, a record of the vegetation sequence is provided. This has been done at many localities in Vermont, and a picture is emerging gradually of what has happened to Vermont's vegetation and climate since the last retreat of the great ice sheets.

The record of pollen begins about 10,000 B.C. when spruce and fir pollen began to accumulate in the floor of lakes peripheral to the melting ice. A cold, moist climate prevailed, to be expected in a periglacial environment. A little above the spruce and fir zone is more pine pollen, suggesting a moderation of the climate, and then we find the first hemlock, followed and mixed with maple, suggesting more warming. About 1,000 B.C. oak, pine and hickory become common, suggesting a considerably warmer, and for the first time, drier condition. The oak and hickory forests of Addison County probably are left over from this period, and all the evidence points to a maximum warming trend.

This is substantiated elsewhere by Viking records of the coast of North America and Greenland and was apparently a world-wide phenomenon, certainly in the Northern Hemisphere at least. Since then there has been a gradual cooling trend with somewhat more moisture. In the Champlain Valley the record shows maple, birch and spruce pollen above the oak, pine and hickory. The overall trend appears to be continuing today, but our climate record is too short to make many educated guesses as to when the next ice sheet will be upon us. To confuse things further, while there appears to be a long-term trend towards colder and wetter conditions, shorter cycles of warming and cooling are superimposed on that trend.

Other unique evidence supports the contention of a past warm climate maximum. In addition to the relic oak and hickory stands, other relic plant populations are common in Vermont. In North Troy there are some three acres of great laurel growing wild. The species is similar to the well-known rhododendron of southern New England and again is probably left over from a previous warmer period. The black gum trees, common in Colchester Bog and in a bog in Vernon, are yet another relic.

Trees tell us much about Vermont's past climate and land use. The wholesale tree-cutting of the 19th century was related to farm enlargement, fuel and shelter, and industrial needs. While more of the state was left in forest than is generally supposed, wood was a terribly important ingredient in the economy, and its importance is growing again. The following chapter considers the wood resource, how it has been used in the past, and what is happening to it today.

Wood Industries

Until recently, Vermont's economy was based almost entirely on agriculture and on farm-related industries. The major exceptions to this were industries involved with raw-material extraction and processing, mainly stone (Chapter 6), and wood. The first patent issued by the U.S. Patent Office (1790) was to a Vermonter for an improved method of potash manufacturing. An historic-site sign marking this event is next to the highway in Pittsford.

When the first serious settlement of parts of the state began in the 1760s 95% of Vermont was forested. There are records of open intervales up and down the Connecticut Valley, and there may have been some natural oak openings in the Champlain Valley, but otherwise the first settlers had to clear a patch of land. The first logs went into shelter. Everyone initially lived in log cabins similar to the Hyde Log Cabin preserved as a museum in Grand Isle. A small clearing was needed to grow foodstuffs to maintain the family, and trees had to be cleared to let in the sunlight so woodland pasture could be used for grazing by the family's few animals. Wood was the raw material at hand, although stones were heaved laboriously to the sides of the small openings. It was only logical that wood and products related to wood would become the first export of the frontier to be exchanged for needed manufactured items.

Potash

With no real way of moving out bulky logs, especially in areas away from a large river or Lake Champlain, the settler was forced to produce a commodity from wood that was both light and reasonably valuable. In such a way did potash, and later pearlash, become the first Vermont export commodity, and the first generator of external capital.

Someone surely answered the following advertisement that appeared in an 1816 issue of the *Vermont Journal* (of Windsor). "The subscriber will pay 14 shillings per hundredweight in cash for well drilled SALTS OF LYE or 18 shillings per hundred, 1/4 part money and the remainder in goods for any quantity delivered to his store in Windsor. He hath on hand a quantity of shoeleather of good quality." From Windsor the potash was loaded onto one of the shallow 60-foot flat boats that went down the Connecticut River. Its eventual destination may have been England.

Why was potash so valuable? Potash (or potassium carbonate) was used in the manufacture of glass and soap, and was essential in its soap form to cleansing and processing raw wool. England's woolen industry, vital to its 18th-century economy, had a great demand for potash for use in "fulling," or the wool-cleaning operations in its mills. With its own forests virtually exhausted, England turned to Russia and the American colonies as the sources for what was a vital raw material of the time. In 1770, $290,000 worth of potash was exported from the colonies and the quantity exported increased steadily. England did everything possible to foster potash production, even to providing how-to manuals for its production.

Potash was hard to make and required a great deal of labor, but it could be manufactured with simple technology from an abundant raw material. Hardwoods were burned (softwoods had too much resin) and the ashes then leached. Commonly, the ashes were placed in a wooden box with narrow spaces between the boards, and water poured over them. The operation often was repeated several times, each leaching process resulting in a more-concentrated solution of lye. The lye then was boiled in large iron kettles (which sometimes turn up in local antique shops as "sap-boiling" kettles), and after the water evaporated, the remaining white salts were scraped from the inside of the pot and packaged in wooden kegs or other suitable containers. About 40 pounds of potash could be produced from the burning, leaching and boiling of the ash from a large elm tree, and was worth about $3 in the colonial era.

The earliest settlers exported the commodity piecemeal in small quantities, but as oxen were acquired and rudimentary roads connected the interior settlements to water, 500-pound loads went out of the remote clearings, worth perhaps as much as $50. Refinements in the manufacturing process resulted in the production of pearlash which was used in producing baking soda. Farmers who did not manufacture potash sold their ashes; hearth ashes were favored especially because they were very fine in size. Until a method was developed in the 1850s to manufacture potash from salt, the industry was an important part of Vermont's early economy, and many acres of trees undoubtedly were burned for that purpose. As late as 1840, 718 tons of potash were produced in Vermont, with Washington County the leader with 150 tons.

Prior to the opening of the Champlain Canal (connecting Lake Champlain to the Hudson River), potash, and later lumber from western Vermont, went north. To the east, the earliest canal in the United States (begun in 1791) bypassed Bellows Falls and oriented the traffic of eastern Vermont southward. In 1791 the sandy site of Burlington was covered by pine forests and the population of 330 found themselves sitting on an important softwood resource because earlier royal decrees had reserved all "white and other pine trees" for the masts of the Royal Navy ships. In 1786 Ira Allen constructed the first sawmill at the lower falls of the Winooski.

The Early Lumber Industry

In 1794, Stephen Mallet, for whom Mallet's Bay in Colchester is named, sent the first log raft of Vermont white pine north to Quebec, and began a traffic that lasted many years. During the same period, small sawmills were becoming established on available water-power sites. These mills primarily served their immediate areas. The larger mills at Burlington–Winooski, and at Bellows Falls and Brattleboro were there for an entirely different reason—to provide a commodity that was in increasingly short supply elsewhere.

It was common practice in Vermont to construct log rafts during the winter on the river and lake ice, and with the spring melt the current would take the prized lumber in the right direction. In western Vermont the northward traffic lasted only until about 1820. In eastern Vermont, log rafts, and the inevitable logjams, rode on the Connecticut and White Rivers until around 1900. The great pulp and paper industry of Holyoke, Massachusetts got its start from Vermont and New Hampshire pulpwood. This initial dependency continued for many years.

The northward flow of wood traffic from western Vermont ceased abruptly for two reasons. One was the opening of the Champlain Canal through Whitehall, New York in 1823; the other was politics. In 1807, Congress passed the Jefferson Embargo, which prohibited trade with western Vermont's major customer, Canada. Vermonters generally ignored the ban and smuggling was rife, with Canadian trade flourishing for 10 years after its prohibition. Not only was wood moving north into Canada, but a wide variety of other products including bar iron, wrought nails, potash, meat, maple sugar and flax were involved. Vermont was receiving salt, liquor, textiles, tea, coffee, chocolate, and hardware in return. In 1808, the first year of the embargo, lumber worth $400,000 was in Burlington awaiting shipment north. Smuggling on the lake flourished for a few years as Vermonters persisted in selling to their traditional market.

The War of 1812 put a temporary crimp to water smuggling on Lake Champlain, and most items went overland. Wood, however, was a bit too bulky to move in the quantities required, and thus a reorientation of trade to the south became necessary for this product. Some wood went north after the War of 1812, but the days of the great log rafts were over. Even the completion of the Chambly Canal (1843), bypassing the rapids of the Richelieu River, made little difference to the new southward trade direction of the Champlain Valley.

The completion of the Champlain Canal, however, had a profound effect on industry. While earlier northward traffic generally consisted of rough logs to be milled later in Canada, the Champlain Canal fostered local sawmilling, and the shipment of boards on boats to southern markets. Its construction reduced the cost of shipment of goods (including lumber) from about $30 to $10 a ton. Goods that formerly took 25 days to ship now took only 10. On the Connecticut River the rate for canal boats going south from Windsor was still an expensive $32 a ton and the shipping time was 25 days. These differentials created by the opening of the canal led to Burlington's growth and a significant expansion of its trade hinterland. Until 1850 Burlington and other lakeshore towns in the Champlain Valley attracted trade from as far as Woodstock, Derby Line, St. Johnsbury, and even Bradford on the Connecticut River itself.

With the trade advantages of western Vermont over the eastern part of the state, the forest resources of the former could not contribute to prosperity forever. By the early 1840s, accessible stands of wood in the Champlain Valley were few and far between. Traffic in lumber declined.

Vermont always had exported timber, but in 1835 the state joined the eastern United States in importing timber from the Ottawa valley of Canada. Railroads were interested in this trade immediately, and the Champlain and St. Lawrence Railroad Company (in Canada) assigned 20 cars for hauling timber between Laprairie and St. Johns, bypassing the rapids of the Richelieu River. Beginning in 1843, when the Chambly Canal opened, canal transportation overtook the railroad in importance, and the great years of the canal were linked closely with the later movement of timber to Lake Champlain and Burlington. Around 1875, rough timber was replaced by finished lumber, which date coincided with Burlington's decline as a major sawmill center.

American railways accomplished several things when they

finally reached into Vermont in 1849 and 1850. They made the canals of an earlier era obsolete (although the Champlain Canal did not reach its maximum tonnage until 1899, to decline after that). They also stimulated a great deal of forest-cutting for fuel before the days of anthracite, and later bituminous coal, and they replaced the canal as a quick and inexpensive method of exporting Vermont wood. But like the canal boats, the railways could afford only to ship out lumber, not logs, so Vermont began producing dressed, rather than rough, lumber.

The wood-burning locomotives had insatiable demands for fuel, and wood remained an important locomotive fuel in Vermont well into the 1880s. Fuel depots were located conveniently along the railways, and the sale of wood became a big business in parts of the state and certainly stimulated local industry as well as further cutting into the forests. Wood which had been valueless before now was worth $5 a cord along the railroad. The New Hampshire Board of Agriculture reported that in 1883, the railroads focusing on Concord annually consumed 70,000 cords of wood. With the densest forests of the 1880s capable of producing 50 cords per acre, there was an annual cut just for that market of more than 1,400 acres.

Although the first shipment of coal arrived in Burlington in 1851, wood remained a primary fuel for many years. Steamboats on the lake did not begin using coal until about 1858, and by 1880 but 70,000 tons of coal were being brought into the region, mainly by water. In 1882, 725 barges of coal arrived in Burlington, most loaded at Hoboken, New Jersey from the anthracite mines near Scranton, Pennsylvania. By 1893 nearly all coal shipped into Burlington came by rail.

The construction of the Champlain Canal, the need for wood in the initial years of the railroad era, the necessity of shipping milled lumber rather than rough logs, all led to a resurgence of the lumber industry in Vermont. With its good rail connections to the south and its history in sawmilling, it was only natural that Burlington would be able to capitalize on a new trade. By 1856 mills were beginning to turn out dressed lumber and the city's new role as an important sawmilling center lasted into the 1890s. In 1867, Burlington was the fourth leading lumber port in the nation. Peak production was reached in 1873 when 170 million board feet of lumber was produced, employing 760 men. At the time, the total sawlog cut in Vermont was more than 300 million board feet. The industry had come a long way from 20 million board feet produced in 1856. Burlington now ranked third in sawlog production in the country, following Chicago and Albany, and maintained this position into the 1880s.

Cleared Land

With its large demand for wood, Burlington relied mainly on the resources of Canada, but Vermont's forests were hacked away also because of the large nearby market. By 1880, all the accessible white pine in Vermont was reportedly exhausted. Chittenden County in 1880 was only 20% forested, the lowest percent in the whole state. By all accounts, the 1870s saw the maximum amount of cleared land in Vermont, but the estimates vary. It has been suggested that 80% of the entire state was cleared, but that is highly unlikely. In fact, one of the *Special Reports* of the 1880 Census, "Report on the Forests of North America", contains a map which shows Vermont generally well-covered with trees, and contains a good estimate of forest cover still amounting to 39.2% of the state's area. Conversely, this means that 60.8% was cleared if there are only two categories of land use. Using the material on agricultural land in the 1880 Census, and accepting the definition of improved and unimproved farmland in that source, 55.4% of the area of Vermont was improved. The amount of actual "cleared" land probably lies somewhere between those two figures. Curiously, Vermont's major era of land clearing was not associated so much with an expansion of farming as it was with satisfying the demands of an important lumber industry and the fuel requirements of a growing industrial base.

Thanks to modern satellite photography it now is possible to calculate accurately the vegetative cover of Vermont. In 1980 only 16.8% of the state's area was open non-forested land. Urban areas accounted for .7%, and 82.5% of Vermont was forested (56.4% hardwood, 15.4% coniferous and 10.7% mixed).

Sawmills and Lumber

By the early 1900s, Vermont's forest resource was in marginal condition, and it was not until into the 1920s that regrowth had put about half of the state's acreage back into trees. The Commissioner of Forestry established in 1928 that 64% of the state's area was forested. The wholesale clearing had left its mark and a resource which had been important in early economic development was in poor shape. There was enough wood to satisfy local needs, but little to ship outside. Pulp and paper mills, once dependent upon a local resource, looked elsewhere for their supplies, and Burlington, once the queen of lumber cities, looked to other industries to maintain its economic base.

By 1930 the 658 permanent sawmills reported for Vermont in 1900 had shrunk to 545. In 1977 there were 105, and by 1984, only 99 commercial mills. Through 1930 the decrease reflected a decreased resource upon which to draw. The lower numbers since then are a reflection of economies of scale with larger mills and flexible truck transportation of rough logs.

The history of sawmilling is reflected in Figure 11.1 made from data furnished by William Gove, Wood Utilization Forester for the State of Vermont. Peak production was in 1889 with 375 million board feet of lumber sawed; the low point (not shown on the graph), was 1922 with only 96 million board feet. Another increase in production took place during World War II and shortly thereafter with an important market for pine boxes. Since then production has been erratic, with an all-time recent high of 233 million board feet in 1984 and a low of 175 million board feet in 1970. Some recent higher-production years have been related to demands of the pine and hardwood furniture industries.

For many years softwoods (conifers) were more important than hardwoods for sawlogs. In 1910 softwoods accounted for nearly 70% of the sawlog harvest. Figure 11.1 shows that throughout the 1950s softwood cut was more important than hardwoods, a trend that appears to be redeveloping today. Softwoods are the primary wood for home and building construction, while hardwoods traditionally have been used for more expensive purposes such as veneer logs, flooring and fine furniture. While the

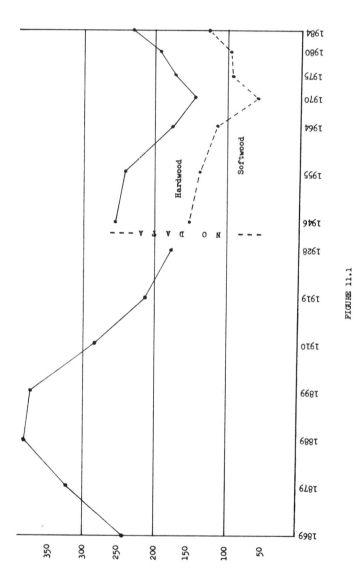

FIGURE 11.1

VERMONT SAWLOG PRODUCTION: 1869 – 1984

Millions of Board Feet

This large sawmill, at least by Vermont standards, is in West Wardsboro.

major markets increasingly demand softwoods, Vermont has its abundant supplies of northern hardwoods.

The present cut is about 56% softwood. As more sub-climax pine and spruce forest comes in (Chapter 10) the number of softwoods should increase, but cutting may increase as well. In the seven-year period 1963 to 1970, the net volume of standing sawtimber declined 11% for hardwoods, but increased 22% for softwoods. More recently there has been a sharp reversal of this trend. Between 1973 and 1983 hardwoods increased 30% while softwoods increased by only 10%. In 1983 the state's forests comprised 8,502 million board feet of hardwood sawtimber (64%) and 5,082 million board feet of softwood sawtimber (34%). Sugar maple is by far the most common hardwood species, while spruce is the most common softwood.

The Forest Resource

Vermont is more than 82% forested, and as more land reverts to non-farm uses that figure will increase slightly. In comparison, Maine is 90% forested, New Hampshire, 89%, and both Connecticut and Massachusetts are about 70%. Nearly all of Vermont's forestland is classed as "commercial" forestland; that is, land that is producing, or capable of producing, a certain volume of timber and that is not withdrawn from timber utilization by statute or administrative regulation. The few small wilderness-designated areas cut into the commercial forestland to some degree, but at least 75% of Vermont is commercial timberland.

According to the U.S. Forest Service, between 1973 and 1983 annual growth of sawtimber was about 250 million board feet; that is, wood suitable for that use was increasing by that much annually. It also means that when annual cutting exceeds that figure, unless there is good management, there are potential renewable resource problems. In Maine, the leading lumber and pulpwood state in New England, 1970 saw a cut of 1,299 million board feet, which at that time was 75% of annual growth. Vermont's 1984 cut of 233 million board feet was below current annual growth but indicates a need for good management practices.

Although the 1984 sawlog cut was the highest in recent years (Figure 11.1), future growth of the industry may be slower, and actual cutting may decline. There are three reasons for this. One is the composition of the forests, with hardwoods greatly outnumbering softwoods. Another is the ownership of forestland, there being thousands of small owners rather than large acreages owned by companies, the state, or the nation. Finally, the escalating costs of timberland are great, and as taxes rise with value, it precludes many timber firms from acquiring timber-producing property.

While the first problem has already been mentioned, the ownership situation is a can of worms because the attitude of small woodlot owners towards cutting of their trees varies greatly. As late as 1948, farmers owned 49% of Vermont's commercial forestland. Today they own less than 20%. Farm use is generally a good use since these owners look upon their land as a money-making investment. This is not always the case with a new class of owners buying up old farmland. These "NIPF" (Non-Industrial Private Forest) owners are often a mystery. They include retirees, corporate executives, high school and college teachers, and people from a host of other vocations. In 1950 this class of ownership stood at 29%; today it is almost 60%. Many of these people regard their woodland as a social rather than economic asset.

So almost two-thirds of Vermont's forest is in the hands of a group who may or may not allow harvests of their timberland. In recent years such programs as "encouraged management" have been made available, and the Vermont Department of Forests, Parks and Recreation is optimistic that NIPF owners will welcome good management and selective cutting on small woodlands. The problem of the cost of selecting individual trees for harvest in a particular woodlot remains, however. The end result of all this may involve some commercial forest acreage being withdrawn from that available for logging. For contrast, Maine, the most important timber state in New England, has only 49% of its forest land under small private ownership.

About a quarter of Vermont's commercial forestland is in state or national forests or is owned by large companies. These include International Paper Company, Atlas Plywood, and Champion International (formerly St. Regis). The latter is the largest private landowner in the state with over 225,000 acres—mainly in Essex County and nearby areas in northeastern Vermont. Along with some smaller commercial forests, these are the best-managed timberlands in Vermont.

Wood-using industries need an assured supply of raw material and, preferably, control of the land which grows the raw material. Yet acquisition of timberland is becoming very expensive. A study done in 1974 on the valuation of Vermont forests found that the average price for timberland increased from $163 per acre in 1968 to $402 in 1974, an increase of more than 146%.

Frank H. Armstrong's 1974 analysis clearly showed that regionally, southern Vermont had the highest-value forestland, and lowest prices prevailed in the northeast. Towns close to larger ski areas and urban places had, as expected, considerably higher-priced forestland than those farther away. Towns with significant out-of-state land ownership such as West Windsor, Manchester and Arlington had unusually high values. The price of timberland, therefore, bears a direct relationship to the increasing acreage of this resource concentrated in smaller parcels owned by private individuals, usually non-farm in orientation.

Statewide property taxes now average approximately $4 an acre for woodland. As the annual average growth on Vermont timberland is about 50 board feet of sawtimber per acre per year, and the current average price for wood is approximately $60 per thousand board feet, the marketable annual growth in dollars is only $2 per acre per year! That is often less than the taxes and forces the owner to cut in excess of growth if the forest is to be an economic investment.

The situation of a 2,000 acre commercial forest illustrates the low profitability of wood harvesting. In 1980, sawtimber cutting produced a gross income of $2.26 an acre. From that was subtracted the management expenses (67 cents per acre) and taxes (83 cents per acre), resulting in a net profit of 76 cents an acre, or a return of six-tenths percent per year per acre.

Given some of the uncertainties of the land ownership situation and high land costs, future expansion in the use of Vermont's forest resource may be slower than in recent years. On the other hand, sawtimber cut may increase because of demands of local wood-using industries and a devaluation of the dollar which presently encourages most Vermont retail lumber dealers to sell Canadian wood.

The Wood Industry

Wood and wood processing are vital to the Vermont economy. In 1980 there were 50,600 workers employed in manufacturing plants in the state. While there are 18 categories of manufacturing, three—lumber and wood manufacturing, furniture and fixtures, and paper—are tied directly to a wood resource, either domestic or imported. Total employment in these three categories was 9,050, or 18% of the Vermont manufacturing work force. Furthermore, 400 manufacturing plants scattered throughout the state (about 38% of all plants) were employing these people.

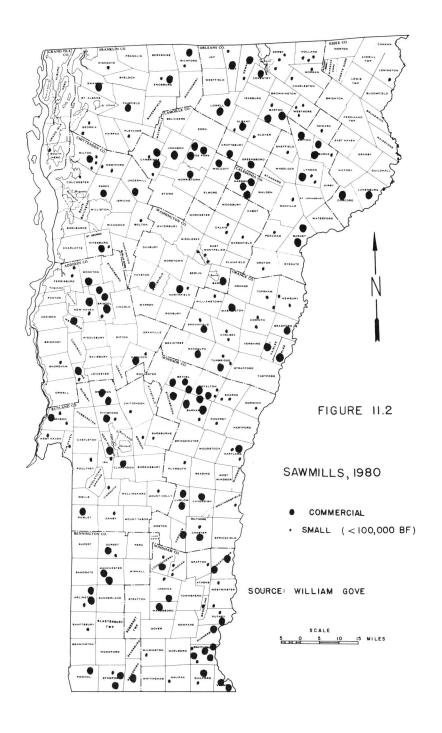

FIGURE II.2

SAWMILLS, 1980

● COMMERCIAL

· SMALL (< 100,000 BF)

SOURCE: WILLIAM GOVE

SCALE

5 0 5 10 15 MILES

The highest employment (3,700) was in the category of lumber and wood. This represents the loggers in the woods, the workers in the sawmills, bowl mills, pallet works, bobbin mills, golf tee factories, shingle mills, clapboard mills, toothpick plants, clothespin factories, etc. This category is divided into primary and secondary plants; primary plants (sawmills) produce the rough boards and lumber, and secondary plants convert that into innumerable articles from cutting boards to bowls to tabletops. Primary-wood industries are widely scattered (Figure 11.2), and

TABLE 11.1

Sawlog Production:1928–1984
(in %, by species)

Hardwoods	1928	1976	1984
Ash	2.7	3.5	4.3
Poplar	.4	1.0	2.6
Basswood	2.3	.6	.4
Beech	9.3	5.8	3.5
White birch	18.5	4.8	3.1
Yellow birch		6.8	5.0
Elm	.3	.4	.4
Hard maple (Sugar/Red)	26.8	17.4	14.9
Soft maple (Silver)		3.9	3.0
Oak	.8	4.9	5.1
Other	.1	1.7	1.3
TOTAL HARDWOODS	61.2	50.3	43.7
Softwoods			
Hemlock	9.8	10.0	10.9
White pine	7.7	26.8	24.5
Red pine	- -	.6	1.2
Spruce and Fir	21.2	10.4	18.7
Cedar	- -	1.8	.9
Tamarack	- -	- -	.2
TOTAL SOFTWOODS	38.8	49.7	56.3

Source: Industrial Survey of Vermont (1928) William G. Gove (1976 and 1984).

reflect the desirability of being close to the source of raw material. Logs have a low value by weight, and it is advantageous for saw-mills to locate close to where the logging is being done to reduce the cost of initial transportation. Finished sawlogs (lumber) have a higher value and therefore can better bear the transportation costs from the sawmill to often more distant secondary plants.

Nearly all wood cut in Vermont sawmills is homegrown. In 1984 only 39 million board feet were imported, and of that total, New Hampshire supplied more than half. Fifty million board feet were shipped out of the state. A substantial amount of sawtimber from Essex County is processed in northern New Hampshire. Vermont sawlog production by species is shown in Table 11.1. There is a trend towards more softwoods, with white pine, spruce and hard maple predominant.

The geographic pattern of sawlog cutting in 1984 is shown in

TABLE 11.2

Sawlog Cut, Board Feet Per Square Mile, 1984

County	Total Cut per square mile	% Hardwood	% Softwood
Addison	11,938	68.9	31.1
Bennington	23,911	88.3	11.7
Caledonia	46,034	22.4	77.6
Chittenden	11,322	43.7	56.3
Essex	33,609	46.0	54.0
Franklin	13,335	24.2	75.8
Grand Isle	- -	- -	- -
Lamoille	35,323	45.4	54.6
Orange	20,477	33.0	67.0
Orleans	23,996	49.5	50.5
Rutland	29,050	66.2	33.8
Washington	21,734	27.2	72.8
Windham	30,545	30.4	69.6
Windsor	25,038	36.9	63.1
STATE	25,150	43.7	56.3

Source: Calculated from *Vermont Forest Resource Cut Summary, 1984* compiled by William G. Gove, Vermont Dept. of Forests, Parks and Recreation.

Table 11.2. In the table, the cut has been reduced to a per-square-mile basis so that the unequal size of counties is not a bias. Caledonia, followed by Lamoille and Essex, are most important.

Most wood processing in Vermont is lumber from sawtimber. Of the total wood of all types cut in the state (including pulpwood), two-thirds ends up as rough lumber which may undergo further processing in secondary plants. The only other major use of sawtimber is for veneer logs in which thin sheets are peeled from logs for eventual use in paneling and furniture manufacturing. Six percent of the state's wood harvest goes into veneer logs, all hardwoods from sawtimber trees. Veneer mills are located in Rutland, Newport and Bradford. Sawlogs and veneer logs account for nearly all sawtimber production. Cordwood represents most of the remaining wood harvest.

Pulp and Paper

Two-thirds or more of Vermont's annual wood harvest is sawtimber, measured in millions of board feet. The remainder, recently increasing, is wood sold by the cord. In 1982 almost 90% of the cordwood produced was sold as pulpwood; the remainder as woodchips for use as pulpwood, chips for particle board manufacturing, and a small amount sold as boltwood. This does not include the substantial amount of green wood chips needed for industrial and utility fuel, the large amount of sawmill residue used for that purpose, or wood used for residential heating.*

*In 1981 a survey of fuel wood consumption was taken in Vermont. In that year 103,347 cords were used for industrial fuel; 23,044 cords for electrical generation in Burlington's Moran Generating Station; 25,000 for commercial establishments, and a whopping 508,699 cords for residential use. This represents 660,090 cords which is not reflected in the official harvest figures which for 1981 was reported as 255,592 cords. That is the figure used in Figure 11.3.

In that year too, 88% of Vermont homes were burning some wood, and 41% depended on wood as the primary source of heat. Over half (54%) of wood users cut their own fuel wood.

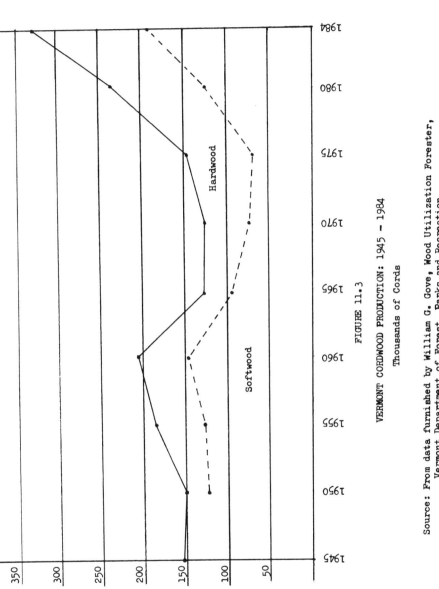

FIGURE 11.3

VERMONT CORDWOOD PRODUCTION: 1945 – 1984

Thousands of Cords

Source: From data furnished by William G. Gove, Wood Utilization Forester,
Vermont Department of Forest, Parks and Recreation.

Figure 11.3 graphs the production of cordwood (most of which is pulpwood). In recent years the cut has been much greater than shown because of the increased use of fuel wood. Both sawtimber production and pulpwood production have been increasing rapidly.

Pulpwood is destined for the pulp and paper industry. Pulpwood is processed chemically and mechanically into a substance called wood pulp, which becomes the raw material for paper. In an average year more than 90% of Vermont's pulpwood is sent to pulp and paper mills in New Hampshire, New York and Maine. Only one Vermont plant (in Sheldon Springs) processes locally-produced pulpwood, about 20,000 cords annually. Most Vermont paper mills now receive their raw material from Maine, Canada and other places, or receive already-manufactured paper and convert it for other uses. For example, Christmas-wrapping paper is produced in Bennington.

The largest pulp mill in Vermont was probably the one at Readsboro. This mill was the primary reason for the building of the Hoosic Tunnel and Wilmington Railroad. In order to supply pulp for the growing paper industry at Holyoke, Massachusetts, the Deerfield River Company was formed in 1882. For $60,000 it constructed a large mill powered by water from a dam 57 feet high. At that time, the dam was reported to have been the highest in the United States. The dam is still there, but the pulp mill burned to the ground in 1922.

Many years ago, softwoods were the only source of wood pulp and Essex County has been cut over repeatedly for that resource. With improved wood-processing technology, large amounts of hardwoods have been chipped and made into wood pulp so that now almost half of the cordwood cut is hardwood. Of the 1982 total pulpwood production in Vermont, 109,000 cords came from spruce and fir, followed by hard maple with 32,681 cords and yellow birch with 25,694. As recently as 1960, 139,000 cords of spruce and fir went into pulpwood, compared to only 50,000 cords of all hardwoods (Figure 11.3). The cut of hemlock pulpwood has grown 15 fold in the last 10 years.

In contrast to sawlog cutting which tends to be widespread, pulpwood comes mainly from northeastern Vermont. Table 11.3 shows Essex County as by far the most important, followed by Caledonia and Orleans.

TABLE 11.3

Pulpwood Cut Per Square Mile, 1984

County	*Hardwood Cords*	*Softwood Cords*	*Total Cords Harvested*
Addison	*	*	1,025
Bennington	*	*	6,330
Caledonia	35.2	61.2	59,007
Chittenden	*	*	3,358
Essex	106.1	77.6	122,093
Franklin	*	10.0	9,296
Grand Isle	---	---	---
Lamoille	*	12.8	7,207
Orange	*	11.1	8,155
Orleans	22.0	38.0	42,814
Rutland	*	*	7,474
Washington	*	*	4,290
Windham	*	11.8	12,771
Windsor	*	*	6,923
STATE	13.4	18.0	290,743[a] 328,878[b]

*Less than 10 cords per square mile
[a]Pulpwood only
[b]Total cordwood
Source: *Vermont Pumpwood, Boltwood and Particleboard Summary, 1984.* Compiled by William G. Gove, Vermont Department of Forests, Parks and Recreation.

The earliest paper mills used rags as their raw material, and as people "produced" rags, it was essential that the mills be located near a large population center. The first Vermont paper mill was built in Bennington in 1784. Other early mills were in Fair Haven (1794), which was the first mill in the country to use some wood in the process, Middlebury (1800), Sharon (1801), Montpelier (1806) and Berlin (1810). At one time or another mills were found in Milton, Bradford, Guilford, Wells River, Brattleboro, Burlington, Putney and Bellows Falls. This last once may had been the most important pulp- and paper-mill town in the United States.

William A. Russell, who later became the first president of the International Paper Company perfected a process there in 1869 to use wood pulp in the manufacture of paper. Even today there are four small plants in Bellows Falls producing a variety of paper products, four in Bennington (another old paper center), two small concerns in Putney and others widely scattered around the state (Figure 11.4).

Many smaller plants owe their particular location to either historic ties, such as those in Bennington and Bellows Falls, or individual managerial decisions, such as the large container plant in St. Albans. Vermont does not illustrate clearly the process of industrial agglomeration (like industries attracting like industries) that is common elsewhere, although the association of the printing and publishing industries in Brattleboro are possibly related to the new large Erving Paper Company plant.

The largest purely paper and paperboard-manufacturing plants are in northern Vermont or along the Connecticut River. Their location was related originally to the accessibility of raw pulp, either directly from the northern softwood forests, or from low-cost transportation in log rafts on the rivers. The largest paper mill in Vermont (manufacturing with both pulp and paperboard) is the Boise Cascade operation in Sheldon Springs, where water-power is available, and where for years logs were floated down the Missisquoi easily. The large Georgia Pacific Company plant at Gilman (in Lunenburg) is adjacent to the Connecticut River, and is next to the great forests of Essex County and northern New Hampshire. A paperboard mill is in St. Johnsbury on the Passumpsic River, and other paper-only mills are in East Ryegate, Wells River and Putney.

Woodchips

For many years, Vermont sawmills had many tons of wood slabs and sawdust—waste material to be disposed of. Sawdust burners once took care of the problem, but commercial markets have developed. Some of this residue went into pressed board, but in Vermont most sawdust is used for dairy cattle bedding. The current interest in this resource is focused on chipped slabs

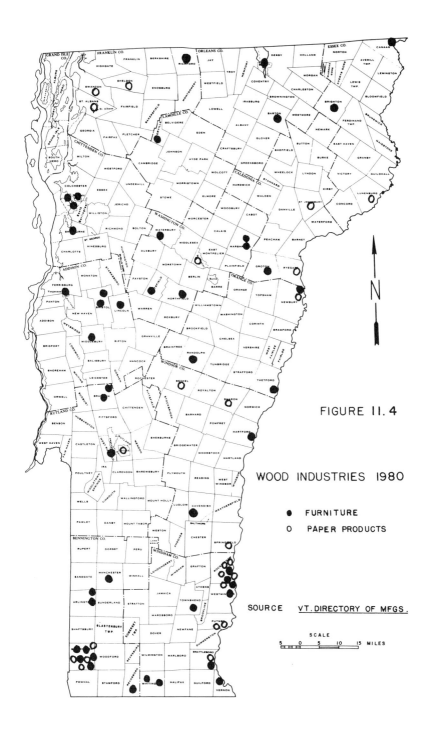

FIGURE II.4

WOOD INDUSTRIES 1980

● FURNITURE

○ PAPER PRODUCTS

SOURCE   VT. DIRECTORY OF MFGS.

SCALE
5   0   5   10   15 MILES

for electrical generation and for the pulp and paper industry.

Besides woodchips produced from sawmill scraps the other major source is from whole-tree chipping operations. The importance of the latter stems from successful demonstration projects in Duxbury and Victory in 1974. Whole-tree chipping is now carried on at several localities. Table 11.4 shows the growing importance of green woodchip harvesting.

TABLE 11.4

Green Woodchip Production: 1977, 1984		
	1977	*1984*
Hardwood chips produced by Vermont sawmills	123,083 tons	106,449 tons
Softwood chips produced by Vermont sawmills	66,837 tons	109,861 tons
TOTAL Vermont sawmill production	189,920 tons	216,310 tons
Whole-tree chips produced	66,055 tons	333,327 tons
TOTAL GREEN WOODCHIPS	255,975 tons	549,637 tons
Equivalent number of cords	(112,275)	(230,548)

Note: In 1984, an additional 211,252 tons were imported from New York, New Hampshire and Canada.

Source: William G. Gove, Vermont Department of Forests, Parks and Recreation.

In 1984 the most important use of green woodchips was in the pulp and paper industry, with 63% of the sawmill chips going for that use, and 53% of the production from whole-tree chipping. The remainder went for industrial fuel and electrical generation. Total woodchip production from all sources in 1977 would have been sufficient to fuel a 50 Mw generating plant for 241 days, and in 1984, for over 13 months. But this resource is scattered throughout all of Vermont. Burlington Electric has an annual need for more than 500,000 tons of green woodchips (Chapter

9). Since the plant began operation in March 1984, a considerable amount of the 1984 woodchip production (and importation) is accounted for by electrical fuel demand.

Bowls, Bobbins and Furniture

The many sawmills in Vermont—the primary fabricators of wood products—produce boards, structural timbers, flooring, chips and other wood products which are used much as they come from the mill. The paper mills utilize either domestically-produced or imported wood pulp, but most paper-manufacturing plants in Vermont are smaller and often further finish papers produced in paper-only mills, often outside of the state. The largest employer of workers, and the largest number of plants in the general category of wood-products industries, are in what are called the "secondary" mills. Those innumerable establishments fashion bowls, cutting boards, baskets, covered-bridge bird feeders, "antique" maple sap buckets, tabletops, childrens' toys, implement handles, and of course, furniture. As there has been a steady decline in the primary sawmills, the increase in tourism has given rise to many small cottage industries all producing products made from native wood. In 1980, there were nine plants doing millwork (molding strips, door jams, window frames), five making plywood and veneer board, five making boxes, 12 manufacturing wooden pallets, one manufacturer of mobile homes, 13 producing prefabricated buildings, 45 furniture plants, and 55 miscellaneous plants that defy classification. The last group includes basket makers, a manufacturer of duck decoys, a small operation which makes wooden puzzles, a maker of hand-carved wooden signs and a clothespin plant.

These secondary industries are usually very small operations, each employing few people. In the "miscellaneous" category above, only three operations employ more than 100 workers; those are Basketville, Carris Reels in Rutland, and Boise Cascade Specialty Paperboard Division in Brattleboro. More than half the manufacturing plants in that class employ fewer than 10 people. The three largest plywood-veneer mills are in Hancock, Newport, and Rutland.

Furniture-manufacturing plants rank next to the host of small miscellaneous wood-product firms, with a total of 45 listed in the *1980-1981 Directory of Vermont Manufacturers* (Figure 11.4). These plants employed 2,600 workers in 1980, or six percent of all manufacturing workers in the state. Small furniture operations have been increasing in recent years, partly from tourism. In 1970 there were only 25 plants.

Ethan Allen Inc. is easily the largest furniture manufacturer in Vermont with operations in Canaan (Beecher Falls), Orleans, Brighton (Island Pond) and Randolph. The plants in Beecher Falls and Orleans each employ more than 500 people and represent the largest employment in northeastern Vermont as well as nearly half the total furniture-manufacturing employment in the state. Located close to large supplies of timber in an economically-distressed region, the plants are vital to the economic well-being of the Northeast Kingdom.

The raw materials of the forests have played an important role in the development of Vermont's economy. The earliest settlers worked the forests for logs to construct their homes. Later they used wood to produce potash which brought the only cash income to many early Vermonters. As settlement spread and waterpower sites were developed, early sawmills provided the first cut lumber for clapboards, flooring, beams, doors and windows. Long before the coming of the stone industries, Vermont lumber was the most significant export of the state, to be exchanged for manufactured products produced elsewhere.

Now after a period of relative decline, the industry is experiencing healthy growth. While the number of sawmills continues to shrink, the number of Vermonters engaged in wood-related occupations is rising. The 1960 United States Census listed Vermont employment in the lumber and wood industries as 4,100 in 1960. That had fallen to 2,800 by 1970, but had increased to 3,600 in 1983. Employment in pulp and paper manufacturing has gone from 2,400 in 1960 to 2,600 in 1983. And the work force in all phases of furniture manufacturing has increased from 1,800 to approximately 2,600 over the same period. Total employment then in the three wood industry categories has risen

The employment base of Essex County is almost entirely based on wood processing. Above is the large Ethan Allen furniture plant in Beecher Falls, below the Georgia Pacific paper mill in Gilman on the frozen Connecticut River.

from 7,900 in 1960 to about 8,800 in 1983. For 1983 the Vermont Department of Forests, Parks and Recreation has estimated a total employment of 9,300, placing the industry second only to electrical machinery.

The future? Those associated with the Vermont Department of Forests, Parks and Recreation are optimistic that growth will continue. On the other hand, much timberland in the state needs better management, especially that under small private ownership. Some of that may be withdrawn from timber production, and high land prices restrict the ability of companies to acquire or control more acres. Certainly the greater sawlog cut, especially on softwoods which are in short supply, is of concern as is the rapidly growing cordwood harvest for electrical generation (Chapter 9). The industry is in a period of transition and it may be another decade or more before trends become clear.

The Soil Resource

Landforms, climate, water, vegetation, and minerals constitute parts of Vermont's natural environment and resource base. Electric energy is tied closely with water resources and climate, and wood industries are based upon the vegetation resource. The remaining major natural resource element is soil. It is overlooked frequently, but is an item of critical importance in the state's past and present land use.

Most of Vermont has poor soils for farming and/or development. Farming has retrenched, and now is concentrated in the better-soil areas, generally the stone-free valleys with heavy glacial lake bed clays. Community development, on the other hand, has avoided the clays, and instead has concentrated on the sandy glacial deltas where available. Most of the best development sites have been utilized and now building is being forced into poorer-soil areas. One of the major reasons for Vermont's strict land-use legislation was development on poor soils for building purposes in southern Vermont.

Soils and Agriculture

In a national or global perspective, one of the great misalignments of resources and people is that soils in humid areas, like Vermont, tend to be agriculturally poor. Conversely, in dry areas, where there is insufficient rainfall for crops, soils tend to be excellent. The task of the farmer is to make the soils as much like the better dry-land soils as possible. This involves considerable expense.

In general, most commercial crops prefer a soil which is approximately neutral in reaction, in other words, neither excessively acid (pH 4.5) or excessive alkaline or salty (pH 8.0). Neutral soils are widespread throughout the central United States but are rare in the east. One exception is the fertile soils of the Pennsylvania Dutch country, underlaid by limestone. Soils over most of Vermont tend to be acidic, but less so in the Champlain Valley where limestones and marbles are common. In all areas of the state, lime must be added to counteract the natural acidity. This knowledge was important even in the 1860s in the establishment of many small lime kilns (Chapter 6). The state geologist in the 1861 *Report* devotes considerable attention to the subject, and even provides a table showing the requirements of various crops for lime and other minerals.

For example, 1,000 pounds of potatoes contains 81.90 pounds of potassium, 129.70 pounds of lime, 17 pounds of phosphorus and 5 pounds of chlorine. The message is clear; if you want to grow potatoes, the material has to be in the soil. With nearly all the crops listed in the 1861 *Report* lime becomes the single most important commodity. The *Report* glowingly refers to Vermont's Champlain Valley limestones:

> as a large tract of land in the state . . . east of the Green Mountains, is destitute of good limestone, the value of these deposits is greatly enhanced. Every crop taken from the land, and every animal fattened for market, diminishes the quantity of lime in the soil. . . . much land, in the granitic and green slate region, has already diminished in fertility.

Declining fertility, measured in this case by a lack of liming, probably was important in hastening the disappearance of many Vermont hill farms in eastern and central portions of the state. Today, as many large farms grow alfalfa hay with its high lime requirements, the need for agricultural limestone rises, even with a continuing decrease in the number of commercial farms.

It may be hard to separate "fertility" from lime, but strictly speaking lime counteracts the natural acidity of native soils while other minerals are critical for crop growth. Vermont soils, along with those of most of the humid eastern United States, are greatly deficient in necessary minerals. This is because in any area where there is adequate rainfall for crop production much water percolates through the soil (leaching) and dissolves and removes the soluble minerals. Insoluble minerals are left behind and a Vermont soil profile often will show a gray-colored layer just below a narrow zone of darker organic material, followed by a reddish brown layer. The colors indicate strong leaching, removing the soluble minerals, and leaving behind silica (white to grey in color) and iron and aluminium compounds (yellow to red to brown in color). Soil scientists call these poor but colorful soils *podzols,* from a Russian word meaning ash, in reference to the gray, leached layer near the top of the soil profile.

Soluble minerals in Vermont soils must be provided artifically. The three critical ones are nitrogen, potassium and phosphorus. Bags of commercial fertilizer have numbers like 10-10-10 or 10-6-4, which represent the percentages of these minerals in the mix. Commercial agriculture in Vermont requires that large amounts of prepared fertilizers be purchased.

Many people feel that natural fertilizers are better than commercial brands. However, the only naturally-occurring fertilizer is nitrogen in the form of manure, and while manure from whatever source is important, it alone cannot make up for the lack of potassium and phosphorus. In 1861 the Vermont state geologist went to considerable lengths to extoll the virture of manure:

> . . . it is doubtless . . . that the sources of manure available to every farmer, are, through the benevolence of Providence, adequate to the wants of every soil in Vermont. . . . the natural resources of manure are not exceeded, if equalled by any other [State] .

There is a footnote on page 727 of the 1861 *Report.* After a discussion of cow dung, the writer turns to the subject of liquid wastes, and recommends cow urine as a more concentrated form of fertilizer than manure. After noting that a person voids about 1,000 pounds a year, and a cow 13,000 pounds, there is a suggestion that the farm family use the fields instead of the privy.

Vermont soils, naturally deficient in lime, and also deficient in the primary mineral fertilizers, require large amounts of both to make them agriculturally competitive with better soil and climate areas of the country. A third factor, while less important than these, is the amount of organic material incorporated in the soil. As vegetation dies it decomposes, and the decomposed material, whether it be pine needles, maple leaves or dead annual grasses, is added to the soil from the top down gradually over a period of time. Soils developing under a natural grassland have a large amount of humus, as this type of vegetation annually con- tributes the most organic material. Soils developing under forests, such as those in Vermont, lack humus, and here again is a com- modity which in many cases has to be added artificially.

Organic material mainly provides greater friability to a soil; that is, thoroughly mixed, it creates more air spaces and loosens the soil so that bacterial decomposition increases and there is an easier penetration of lime and fertilizer. Some organic material may add nitrogen as well. Sawdust, which once was burned in many sawmills, is trucked away now by farmers and others to mix with their soil. Bags of Quebec, Michigan and Vermont peat are purchased each year to dump in small gardens.

Back in 1861, there was some attention paid to Vermont "muck." While there is no way of determining what muck meant at the time, the references probably refer to what we now call peat. A Mr. Solomon Steel of Derby wrote a long epistle to the state geologist extolling the virtues of this substance:

> In the fall previous, I had prepared a heap of compost, one-third swamp muck, and the balance decomposed manure taken from the cow-yard . . . I also prepared another heap of swamp muck in the back yard near the house . . . To this we applied all the soap suds, chamber water, etc., from the house during the win- ter. In the spring I had about five loads of manure in my hog yard.
>
>   . . . on the 14th of May the . . . planting commenced. First with the hog manure, second with the heap of saturated muck, third, from the heap of compost. The whole field was finished on the 19th of May . . . After the first hoeing I applied one hun- dred pounds plaster (quicklime) to the acre. Result as follows:
>
>   The best corn and the greatest yield was taken from that portion where the muck was applied; second from that portion

over the hog manure; third that portion over the compost.

Such are the facts of the case, and if it be true that twenty loads of muck can be rendered more valuable than the same amount of any other manure, by the process above mentioned, and as we know that the muck required is to be found in abundance upon almost every lot of land in Orleans County, we really see no good reason why our young men should leave the graves of their fathers, and wander in the far West in search of a better country than our own.

Such is a testimonial to peat, and a plea to remain in Vermont because of its abundant resources. It may be that the added chamber water supplied the muck with its mystical qualities, but the point is that peat can be important in raising the productivity of farmland, replacing the natural humus which is lacking.

The fourth factor determining the agricultural potential of land is drainage, and here generalizations are difficult since this factor can vary over an area of a few miles and even a few yards. At the two extremes are excessively sandy soils and excessively clay-like soils. The light sands common on glacial deltas and kame terraces often require irrigation if they are to be used effectively, but they tend to warm up much faster in the spring than do other soils, making them particularly valuable for early vegetables. Also, they often are more receptive to fertilizer because of their porosity. The small truck farms around Burlington are on sandy loams. These soils, however, have their chief value as soils capable of handling septic systems and thus are excellent for non-agricultural use.

At the other extreme are heavy clays. Many of the soils in Vermont river valleys are of this type as they represent old glacial lake bed deposits; this is especially true in the Champlain basin, but nearly all large valleys in the state have clay soils (Chapter 3). Clays impede drainage and often delay the time that crops can be planted in the spring. On the other hand, since they tend to retain water far better than the sands, irrigation usually is not required and crops will do well on the clays while they often will dry out on coarser soils. Some crops even will get waterlogged on heavy soils, and the yellow among the stands of green corn sometimes indicates this condition. In general, clay soils are better agriculturally than those excessively sandy. Soils somewhere between the extremes are best. They are called loams.

In Vermont, as over the rest of New England, there are large areas of rough, rocky glacial till; probably about 70% of the state is so covered. These bouldery hillsides probably were used as sheep and cow pastures as it is unlikely that many upland till fields surrounded by stone walls were used for crop farming. At lower elevations the till usually is thicker, stones smaller, and the soils reasonably good, although often rather well-drained. The important dairy region around Randolph is on thick glacial till and large boulders are rare. The same is true in the moraine complex of Orleans and Caledonia Counties (Chapter 6).

Vermont's agricultural soils then are acid, infertile, low in organic content, and often either poorly or excessively drained. In a word, they are generally poor soils, especially in a national context, and their quality, of lack of it, certainly was one factor in the great westward migration. In a New England context, the soils of the Champlain Valley are some of the best in the region; but they too suffer by comparison with those of most of the Middle West.

The Soil Conservation Service periodically inventories soils nationally for agricultural use. Eight classes have been established, with the highest capability Class I, decreasing to unusable agricultural soils, Class VIII. For most purposes, Class I and Class II soils can be considered the best in the country ("prime"). Class III has moderate limitations while Classes IV–VIII are increasingly

TABLE 12.1

Area	Agricultural Land Capability			
	Class I %	*Class II %*	*Class III %*	*Class IV-VIII %*
United States	2.1	12.7	13.1	72.1
Vermont	.7	9.9	9.2	80.2
Iowa	11.3	39.9	26.9	21.9

Source: Calculated from Soil Conservation Service.

marginal. The place of Vermont in a national ranking is shown in Table 12.1. When recent figures indicate that only about 20% or so of the state is being farmed, it seems to be consistent with land-capability estimates. One of Vermont's finest agricultural counties, Addison, contains 3,092 acres of Class I land and 95,004 acres of Class II, which together amount to 19.7% of the total area of the county. Orange County, on the other hand, is only 8.2% prime farmland, and there is a total of only 635,000 acres of Class I and II land in the state. With a climate similar to that of southern Wisconsin, Minnesota and parts of Iowa, Illinois and Indiana, soils become the determining factor in the generally poorer agriculture of Vermont. This is why many crops, including milk, can be produced at lower cost in other areas.

To make a general soil map is almost impossible. Vermont soils vary with elevation, slope and the materials in which they are formed. Only in the relatively flat Champlain Lowland do individual soils extend over fairly large areas. This complexity is a reason why recently developed maps of land capability have little utility; they are based upon very general soil maps which do not show the tremendous variations which may occur in a small geographic area. Vermont's soils are a hodgepodge and are very complex, but an understanding of them is basic to an understanding of Vermont agriculture both past and present, and the increasing development pressures on the land resource for non-farm use.

The first real soil survey of Vermont was made in 1930 by the U.S. Department of Agriculture, Bureau of Chemistry and Soils. The Soil Conservation Service was not born until 1932. The survey mapped and assessed soils purely for agricultural use, and included a summary map of agricultural land classes. The small map on page 21 of the survey is a map which attempted, on a very small scale, to class Vermont soils by their agricultural potential. While it is generalized, the map is reproduced here with those soils ranked Class I and Class II for agricultural use darkened (Figure 12.1). Only a very small area of the state shows as really high-quality farmland, that in the Champlain Valley, the Valley of Vermont, and in scattered locations along the Connecticut River floodplain.

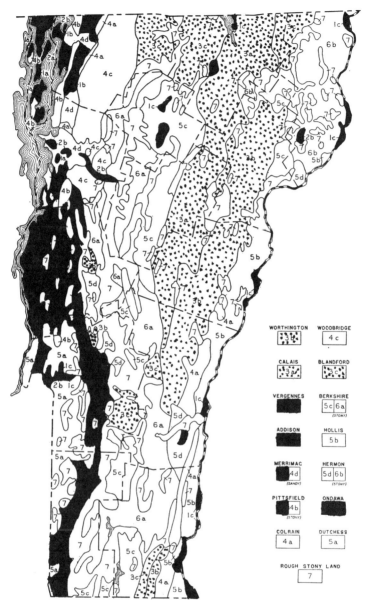

Figure 12.1. An early ranking of Vermont soils in terms of agricultural capability. Class I and Class II soils are shown as black, Class III soils by a dot pattern. Source: *Soil Survey Reconnaissance of Vermont*, U.S. Department of Agriculture, Bureau of Chemistry and Soils, Series 1930, Number 43.

Soils and Community Development

Until the 1950s, the farmer was the only consumer of soil information provided by the Soil Conservation Service. But the number of farmers continued to shrink in Vermont and elsewhere in New England as the climate, poor soils and topography prevented local farmers from competing with better-favored farming areas. Advice was dispensed increasingly to other users, and while a section of a new *County Soil Survey* is devoted to agricultural use, far more space is concerned with engineering properties of soils, soil limitations for community development, and forestry and wildlife uses. Detailed soil surveys (1984) are available for Grand Isle, Chittenden, Addison, Lamoille, Franklin and Orange Counties, and work is progressing rapidly in other areas. The new surveys build upon major soils identified in the 1930s but are far more detailed and useful to the public.

Soils and topography are the key items in the capability of an area to sustain commercial development, and more than 80% of Vermont has soils with limitations on such use. Excessive slope, shallow depths to bedrock, wet conditions, stability and erosion are all problems. As a general rule, steep slopes of more than 15 to 20% tend to have shallow soils and a great tendency to erode once the vegetative cover has been removed. To a builder, shallow soils, no matter what their texture and drainage characteristics, present two significant problems. One is the difficulty of on-site sewage disposal. The second is the cost of excavating a basement and even a foundation. Excess soil moisture may make a site nearly impossible to develop. Unless expensive engineering is done, such soils can cause footings, foundations walls, underground piping, and roads to fail.

Soils also have a natural tendency to compact and compress. This characteristic of stability, or lack of it, in a soil is determined by two factors—bearing capacity and shear strength. Bearing capacity is the result of both soil texture and soil moisture, and measures the ability of a soil to support structures. Fine-grained soils, such as clays and silts, have a poor bearing capacity and tend to shift and settle under loads. Coarse-grained soils, on the other hand, are much better. Soils also exhibit shearing, especially on hillsides where a soil mass of insufficient strength will collapse and slide downhill. This is also typical of clays and silts. Poor development soils include the Vergennes soils of Chittenden and Addison Counties, and the widespread Belgrade and Hartland soils common in eastern Vermont.

Construction on unsuitable soils is expensive, and can continue to be expensive over the years. But cracking foundations and wet basements are nuisance factors compared to a downright hazardous health problem which could emerge with improperly-designed septic systems, or systems installed in soils and on sites unfavorable for this sort of use. More than 200,000 rural Vermonters were without municipal waste-treatment facilities in 1982 and had to have their own means of getting rid of effluent. The number of people so affected is bound to increase, and to increase predominantly on soils poor for waste disposal.

Traditional methods of waste disposal include the inevitable privies, cesspools, septic systems and "straight pipes" to any nearby stream. Several years ago in Franklin County I followed a straight pipe until it went through the window of a wrecked automobile. Most of the rural population today uses a septic system; and certainly all rural homes constructed after 1950 use this method. The system itself is simple. There are two components—the tank and the soil-absorption system or leach field. The leach field consists of a series of perforated pipes, or tile lines, laid in beds of gravel or crushed stone. Effluent enters the tank where anaerobic bacteria accomplish biological decomposition. The now-liquid material overflows into the leach field. At this point the effluent is odoriferous and contains large quantities of anaerobic bacteria, nutrients, salts, suspended solids and even pathogens.

The capacity of the whole system is determined by the soil-absorptive ability in the leach field because waste water cannot be discharged faster than the soil can absorb it. Here is where the desirability of a coarse soil is obvious. During the absorption, the soil and gravel filter the organic material, and further decomposition takes place by more bacterial activity. The chemical reactions are complex, but the water which eventually percolates to the surface, usually some distance away, is clean as it enters the surface runoff. There is no possible way that fine-clay soils can work because those soils have no permeability. That is, they can hold water, but water and effluent cannot pass through. In a similar fashion, areas which have a high water table cannot handle the effluent, nor can areas in which the soil is shallow to bedrock. Areas which have slopes greater than about eight percent allow the effluent to percolate through the soil at a too-rapid pace, resulting in incomplete decomposition. This is a severe problem with mountain developments.

If one could calculate (1) the areas of impermeable clays in Vermont, (2) the areas of shallow soils, (3) the areas with a slope greater than eight percent, and (4) areas with a seasonally- or permanently-high water table, there is little land left. Such a map was included in the 1973 *Land Capability Plan* but was too generalized to be of much use.

Strictly speaking, at least 80% of Vermont suffers limitations of one kind or another for what the Soil Survey refers to as "community development." The problems of leach-field absorption can be overcome by large amounts of coarse fill. It is done, however, at additional expense to the person who wants to live in the country and limits the ability of many lower-income people to enjoy more rural environments as a place to live.

In addition to producing small-scale state maps of land capability for development, the State Planning Office produced a series of larger-scale county maps in the early 1970s using generalized soil maps, some going back to the 1930 soil mapping program, as a basis. A section of one of those maps is included here, and those areas of "few or moderate" limitations are emphasized (Figure 12.2). They still are available and often can be of some use, although the detailed soil maps contained in the new surveys are far superior for local planning purposes.

As Vermont's population growth began to accelerate above the national average in the 1960s, pressures on the physical-resource base multiplied so rapidly that state and local authorities could not cope. The local population explosion coincided with a national environmental movement, and far-reaching environmental legislation was passed by the State Legislature dramatically affecting where people were going to live, and how much land they would have to live on. The immediate stimulus to what is called Act 250 was severe soil erosion and waste-disposal problems occurring in vacation-home developments in West Dover.

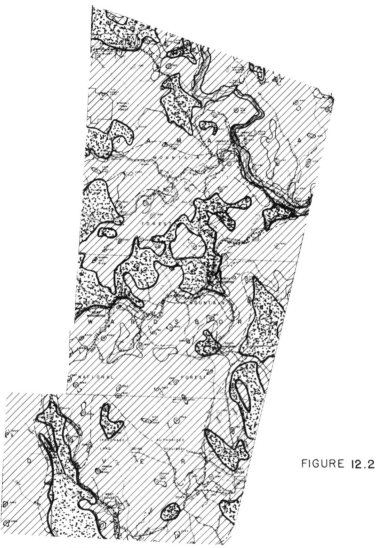

FIGURE 12.2

AREAS WITH FEW AND MODERATE DEVELOPMENT LIMITATIONS

IN JAMAICA, WARDSBORO AND DOVER

SOURCE: WINDHAM COUNTY SHEET,

VERMONT LAND CAPABILITY PLAN, 1972

Land Use Legislation

Vermont's natural resource base has influenced economic activity in the state greatly. Mineral and forest-products industries have been tied directly to the resources of the environment. Power production historically was based on water. Agriculture cannot be divorced from climate, soils or topography. The recreation industry, responsible for about 15% of Vermont's gross state product, certainly is based to some extent on the character of the land. Where would skiing be without snow and slopes?

As the state's population grew during the 1960s an interest and concern for the environment developed. Many people forgot that it was the *use* of the environment which had brought Vermont to its present state of being; instead they urged that environment use must stop because it endangered a prized quality-of-life image. While that is another story, it is certainly true that over many years some Vermont resources were poorly managed and perhaps controls over land use were necessary to preserve natural-environment quality.

While there were attempts at getting a state land-use plan enacted in the early 1970s, citizens were unwilling to have Vermont divided up into urban and village areas, rural areas, natural resource areas and conservation areas, all placing severe restrictions on land use within the designated areas. But while a state land-use plan was frowned upon, other legislation was passed which continues to have a profound impact on Vermont's geography. Three major pieces of legislation were enacted.

285

The first land-use legislation passed was the Vermont Municipal Regional Planning and Development Act (VSA, Title 24, Chapter 117) which became effective in March 1968. This legislation required every town and municipality to develop a local plan and zoning ordinance and established regional planning commissions with instructions to prepare regional plans. The Act gives local and regional planning commissions wide-ranging powers.

Planning History

It is hard to believe that Vermont did not have any coherent planning until the late 1960s. There was a short-lived Vermont State Planning Board in the 1930s which produced several reports, but it ended with the outbreak of World War II. Between about 1938 and 1960 few paid much attention to Vermont land use. The Agricultural Experiment Station at the University of Vermont continued to publish bulletins to help the remaining farmers, and various reports on manufacturing, tourism and economic development continued to emanate from Montpelier. But no real inventory of the state's economy, physical resources, population, and development was done until the enactment of the Federal Housing and Urban Development Act in 1954, variously referred to as "HUD" or, relating to the number of the legislation originally providing planning funds, "701."

HUD funds originally were designed to go to the decaying urban regions of America; but such a storm of protest reached Washington from more rural areas that HUD monies have been channeled into every state to aid in local, state and regional planning. Every state now has a central planning office, partially funded by 701 funds, and Vermont has 12 regional planning commissions. The Central Planning Office, now called the State Planning Office, was created in the early 1960s with HUD funds, and the various regional commissions came along shortly thereafter. The first step in any sort of planning involves an inventory of what exists, and the state and regional planning commissions in Vermont and elsewhere produced, and are still producing, a flood of statistical, land use, economic, social and miscellaneous material. But as a result of the planning activities of the 1960s, there is a good knowledge today of what Vermont and its various regions are like.

As the inventory phase of planning got underway, many reports on Vermont population, recreation, agriculture, natural resources, and so forth were prepared by and for the Central Planning Office. All the research showed Vermont changing from an agricultural state to a manufacturing-recreation-urban-suburban region with mounting pressures on the available land and water resources. The inventory was completed essentially in a summary statement called *Vision and Choice: Vermont's Future* issued by the Central Planning Office in 1968. This milestone report predicted rapid changes in Vermont's geography, and urged greater planning and possibly legislation to channel growth into areas most appropriate to handle growth and change. Predictions of increasing urbanization and declining agricultural land use were certainly of concern to old and new Vermonters alike, and the Vermont Legislature was in a receptive mood to enact appropriate legal constraints on indiscriminate development.

Vermont Land Use and Development Law
(Act 250)

The late 1960s saw a national environmental movement in full swing. While environmental concerns dominated activities in all parts of the country, in some ways the wave of feeling reached a peak in Vermont. Bumper stickers proclaimed "Split Wood, Not Atoms," and "Don't Do It In The Lake," while even the native Vermonter went so far as to urge the following motorists to: "Save A Tree, Eat A Beaver." With an active, environmentally-aware population, or at least a vocal part of it; with prophecies of doom contained in *Vision and Choice,* and with many studies showing rapid development and change, the state began to respond. A *Vacation Home Survey,* produced in 1968 (and updated again in 1973), pinpointed some towns in Vermont where second-home developments greatly exceeded the number of preexisting homes. Developments were springing up on steep mountainsides with no regard to soil limitation factors; lakeshores were being turned into strip developments precluding public access. Towns without any adequate planning or zoning were being transformed overnight. Most activity was concentrated in the southern part of the state or in areas close to skiing. The Wilmington-Dover area was both and developments were causing significant erosion and effluent disposal problems. Poor development here was the straw that broke the camel's back and was the immediate stimulus to the resulting legislation.

In May 1969, Governor Deane C. Davis established the Commission on Environmental Control chaired by Representative Arthur Gibb of Weybridge. The so-called Gibb Commission developed a set of recommendations which were drafted into bill form and submitted to the 1970 Legislature. Perhaps to the surprise of many, the 250th Act passed in the session was Title 10, Vermont Statutes Annotated, Chapter 151, which were the Gibb Commission recommendations. Vermont had adopted "Act 250" which was at the time pioneer environmental legislation for the country, and was the second major piece of legislation of this period of great change.

Haystack Corporation filed one of the first permit applications after the passage of the act. The corporation's plans called for 2,200 homes and an 18-hole golf course, a 700-room hotel and various recreational facilities on the side of Haystack Mountain in Wilmington. These plans were one of the reasons the law came into being. For $12,000, a person could purchase a lot on the mountain and after building a dream home would have the snow plowed away, garbage removed and sewage and water hooked up to a common system serving the development.

It took only three days of formal hearings before the local district environmental commission for Haystack to get approval for the development in an era of experimentation with the new law.

That should have been the end of it, but the State Water Resources Board, an automatic party-of-interest to the application, was able to limit the amount of effluent that the town of Wilmington, plus Haystack, could discharge into a tributary of the Deerfield River to 500,000 gallons a day. This limitation allowed the State Environmental Board to restrict the number of lots that could be developed.

This was bad news for the owners of many of the 1,300 lots

that had been sold, but even worse news for the Haystack Corporation. The buyers found they could not build on their lots, and only 71 vacation homes eventually were constructed. That could hardly support a golf course. The marginally-financed Haystack Corporation collapsed in bankruptcy. It collapsed because of the action of the State Environmental Board rather than the local district commission. Since then, local commissions have gained much more expertise and now are capable of handling most of the applications which come before them in an adequate fashion. Such was not always the case in the formative years of environmental legislation.

Act 250, to use the common term, has had a tremendous impact on Vermont land use. Its future impact may be less, depending upon how the legislation is modified or challenged in the courts. The Act is a complex piece of legislation and some of the best legal minds in the state still do not really understand what some of the words mean (i.e., how do you define phrases like "undue water pollution"?).

What it does is require those wishing to develop most parcels of land to go through a hearing review process before a permit may be granted. This is in addition to review by a local planning commission, zoning board, or board of selectmen. Nine district environmental commissions hear testimony and render opinions.

The word "development" has precise definitions in the Vermont Statutes, but for all intents and purposes it relates to nearly any change on any piece of land in the state. Specifically excepted from Act 250 are forestry operations, farming, and facilities relating to electrical generation or transmission. The latter, however, require permits under other legislation. The criteria under which a permit will be granted are listed in Section 6086 of the law. The applicant has to prove conformance with Subsections 1, 2, 3, 4, 9 and 10. Any party in opposition must prove Subsections 5, 6, 7, and 8. Copies of the legislation are available at Vermont regional planning commission offices.

10 Criteria for Act 250

Before granting a permit, the District Commission must insure that the development or subdivision meets the following criteria:

(1)   Will not result in undue water or air pollution.

This criterion deals with water and air pollution potential generally and such specific matters relating to water pollution as:

(A) Headwaters; (B) Waste disposal; (C) Water conservation; (D) Floodways; (E) Streams; and (F) Shorelines.

(2)   Has sufficient water available for the needs of the subdivision or development.

(3)   Will not unreasonably burden any existing water supply.

(4)   Will not cause unreasonable soil erosion or affect the capacity of the land to hold water.

(5)   Will not cause unreasonably dangerous or congested conditions with respect to highways or other means of transportation.

(6)   Will not create an unreasonable burden on the educational facilities of the municipality.

(7)   Will not create an unreasonable burden on the municipality in providing governmental services.

(8)   Will not adversely affect the aesthetics, scenic beauty, historic sites or natural areas, and necessary wildlife habitat and endangered species in the immediate area.

(9)   Conforms with the *Capability and Development Plan* which includes the following considerations:

(A) The impact the project will have on the growth of the town or region; (B) Primary agricultural soils; (C) Forest and secondary agricultural soils; (D) Earth resources; (E) Extraction of earth resources; (F) Energy conservation; (G) Private utility services; (H) Costs of scattered developments; (J) Public utility services; (K) Development affecting public investments; and, (L) Rural growth areas.

(10) Is in conformance with local or regional plans.

When Act 250 was passed it was fairly straightforward legislation, but as the years have passed, various items have been added so that it is now very complex, and much broader in scope than drafted originally. There is no doubt that it has discouraged some development in Vermont, and has certainly increased the cost of developments which have had to go through the hearing process. It has hurt chiefly the smaller Vermont builder who lacks sufficient capital to get through the red tape. It also discourages any landowner who wants to subdivide land, and this led to perhaps the most unfortunate geographic effect of the law. This was the "10-acre loophole," which was a means of avoiding the legislation by subdividing land in plots of 10 acres or more.

Vermont statutes consider that land split up into lots less than 10 acres in size constitutes a subdivision which requires a permit. With the recent demand for land, owners had little trouble in disposing of 10-acre lots, and 10 acre plus lots rapidly began to dominate the Vermont landscape. In Chittenden County alone approximately one-third of all lots sold between 1968 and 1981 were more than 10 acres. Before the passage of Act 250, 10-acre lots amounted to only one percent of all land parcels sold. In the county, total land involved amounted to nearly 11,000 acres, equivalent to a third of an average-size town. One dwelling after another along many rural roads are found a few hundred feet apart fronting on the highway with a narrow, deep 10 acres extending back some distance from the road. This is an unfortunate type of development and terribly wasteful of land, yet it was the answer to avoid a long and expensive hearing process. Fortunately, the 1984 Vermont Legislature eliminated the 10-acre clause, but this has produced more paperwork for district environmental commissions.

Most people agree that Act 250 has resulted in better-quality development in Vermont; a fact acknowledged by even its bitterest opponents. State agencies working to attract investment in Vermont tout the legislation as a factor in retaining the charm of the state and ensuring a quality environment. On the other hand, it caused some areas to be broken up into 10-acre lots for one home when all that was required was an acre or two, and has contributed significantly to the high cost of land and development. While many new residents are able to afford country living, many native Vermonters are unable to, and perhaps are being priced out of housing in their own state. In 1974 Governor Thomas Salmon was quoted by the *Burlington Free Press* as stating that the legislation would "embark Vermont on the road toward an exclusive society where only the affluent could live."

The Land Capability and Development Plan

The legislative debates over Act 250 occupied a great deal of time during the early 1970s, largely because the original legislation called for a Land Capability and Development Plan and a State Land Use Plan. After an Interim Land Capability Plan was adopted in 1971, the State Planning Office worked on a permanent Land Capability and Development Plan which was completed in 1973. The plan as developed included detailed maps of each county with major limitations for development, and a recognition of unique natural areas.

The 1973 Legislature debated the merits of the Land Capability and Development Plan. Several elements of the plan are incorporated now in Subsection 9 of Section 6086 of Act 250 already referred to; but the bulk of the Land Capability and Development Plan can be found presently as Section 6042 of Act 250. There it is somewhat of a paper tiger as the 1973 Legislature directed that "this act shall not be used as a criteria in the consideration of applications by a district commission or the environmental board."

This probably reflects a slight waning of the environmental surge of the late 1960s and early 1970s. The same probably is true of the state land-use plan also required in the original law. A land-use plan may be enacted eventually, but it probably will not have very many teeth, and probably will have little effect on altering the geography of the state. In all fairness though, the Land Capability and Development Plan (Section 6042) was without doubt the third major bit of environmental legislation passed in this era of a changing Vermont.

Perhaps it is just as well that the 1973 Legislature saw fit to render parts of the Land Capability and Development Plan harmless. The work that went into the plan as put together by the State Planning Office has provided an   excellent inventory of

Vermont's lands and waters, material which is useful for nearly everyone interested in the state. In September 1974 the State Planning Office produced a seventy-page booklet entitled *Vermont Land Capability*, which remains the premier source of information for anyone interested in this aspect of Vermont. But in retrospect, if all the standards of the Vermont Land Capability and Development Plan had been added as required burden-of-proof elements in the Act 250 hearing processes, the effect on development in Vermont would have been catastrophic. At this writing (1985), the future of a State Land Use Plan is questionable. Either some sort of plan must be approved by the Legislature, or references to a State Land Use Plan should be removed from the original Act.

Act 250 Cases

More than 3,500 Act 250 applications were filed with Vermont's nine district environmental commissions during the 1970s. Nearly all were approved, some with considerable modifications. Less than 100 were disapproved outright and three important ones are discussed below. When one of the district commissions refuses to grant a permit the applicant can go to the State Environmental Board or go through the courts, whichever is most convenient.

The first major denial was for a "Wildlife Wonderland" to be located along Route 103 in the town of Mt. Holly. In that case, the district environmental commission ruled that the development would cause undue water pollution, unreasonable soil erosion, and reduction in the capacity of the land to hold water. An appeal of this decision went to the Vermont Supreme Court which upheld the ruling of the district environmental commission in October 1975. Wildlife Wonderland was dead.

Two important decisions were handed down by district environmental commissions in 1978. One dealt with a large shopping mall planned for Williston, not far from downtown Burlington. Proposed was an 84-store, 494,000 square-foot structure on more than 94 acres of land adjacent to I-89. The application was filed on July 22, 1977, and hearings and testimony dragged on until October 12, 1978 when the permit was denied. Basis for denial as stated in the Findings of Fact was "that the project described in the application . . . is detrimental to the public health, safety and general welfare." Specifically, the commission ruled that the application did not meet the requirements of parts of Subsections 9 and 10 of Section 6086.

In Subsection 9, the commission took into account the regional traffic congestion which would occur, noting that it would require large amounts of public funds to solve anticipated bottlenecks. Furthermore, it was ruled that the mall would not be "contiguous" to existing facilities, and the extension of facilities to serve the development would cost the public funds in excess of tax revenues. Another specific reason for denial was that communities in the region would lose tax revenues because of forced store closings due to increasing competition, this especially true of Burlington.

In Subsection 10, the district commission ruled that the mall would not be in conformance with the regional plan adopted by the Chittenden County Regional Planning Commission.

What is interesting in the commission's findings is that the denials were based mainly on factors other than the natural environment. They emphasized economic impact upon the region itself and the greater public costs which would accrue if the mall were built. The Findings of Fact encompasses 66 pages with an additional nine pages of appendix, listing all the testimony taken during the hearings. Burlington itself spent considerable money in opposing the plan, and the cost to the regional planning commission was approximately $100,000 in consulting fees alone. The investment of the mall company itself was more than $1 million. This is an illustration of the considerable expenses generated by Act 250 hearings.

Another major Act 250 decision was the denial of an expansion to a vacation-home complex in Pittsfield. There a second-home community of 262 residential lots on about 585 acres of land was proposed. This in a town with a 1978 population of 300 and a total town budget of $162,000. After hearings spanning a period of 20 active days between January and November 1978, the application was denied rather completely, largely because of a negative environmental impact on the mountainside and the impact it would have on the small community of Pittsfield.

The Summary of the decision is as follows:

> The application is denied because we find, as stated in detail below: that the project does not satisfy the following criteria of Section 6086(a): 1. Water pollution, 1A. Headwaters, 1 B. Waste Disposal, 1 E. Streams, 4. Soil erosion and the capacity of the land to hold water, 5. Highway Congestion and Safety, 7. Burden on the municipality to provide highway services, 8. Scenic and natural beauty of the area and aesthetics, 8A. Necessary wildlife habitat and endangered species, 9C. Forest and secondary agricultural soils, 9G. Private utility services, 9J. Public utility services, 9K. Development affecting public investments, and 10. Conformance with the regional plan.

The Summary reads like a litany of nearly all the points of Act 250. Very steep slopes were to be graded for house lots and roads, and the spectre of really excessive erosion was a major factor in the decision. The 262 lots were estimated to generate a large amount of traffic which the commission did not think the "upper section of Liberty Hill Road" could handle, and the town in no uncertain terms indicated it "has no present intention of making such improvements to Liberty Hill Road, and the applicant has refused to bear the costs of improvements." In fact, the commission felt there was no way in which a town with a total budget of $162,000, $40,000 of which was for highways, could possibly handle such an addition of homes and people. The large quantities of silt to flow into the White River during and after construction were enough to persuade the District Environmental Commission that the development would imperil the habitat of the Atlantic salmon, just now returning to Vermont streams.

Of these three landmark decisions of the '70s, two were denied primarily on grounds of a detrimental impact upon the natural environment, the third was denied largely on the basis of economic criteria, something the original designers of the legislation probably did not have in mind.

Geographic Impacts

Environmental legislation has altered Vermont's geography in several ways. In terms of land use the act probably has had a negative effect in scattering population over 10-acre lots, using up irreplaceable land and resulting in higher energy and service costs, and of course, inflating the price of land beyond the reach of many. But on the other hand, sewage no longers runs down hillsides and development tends to be of much higher quality, albeit more expensive. A study in Chittenden County reviewed all Act 250 developments filed up to 1976 and found that of those completed in 1976, 92 were built essentially according to the permit granted, and only 15 were in some violation, usually minor. Most violations involved landscaping and aesthetics. For example, a community park development had relocated a bathroom and a basketball court in a different place than specified on the original approved plan. One lumber company was piling wood higher than the 10 feet allowed.

Whether the legislation has slowed development is impossible to really measure. With a burgeoning population the increase in permits is to be expected, and probably many people find Vermont an attractive place to live simply because the state has strict environmental laws. This may in fact contribute to growth rather than depress it.

Since enactment of Act 250, Vermont's economy has prospered incredibly when compared to the pre-Act economy (Table 13.1). But how much of the change is attributable to national prosperity, and how much to the legislation itself is impossible to measure. It would seem, however, that as companies increasingly seek pleasant surroundings and a satisfied work force, the efforts to protect and ensure envirnmental quality have been a positive force in attracting economic development.

Purely from a land use point of view, the decisions on suburban shopping malls (unless overturned in the courts) probably ensure the survival of Vermont's largest urban cores with the result that large urban renewal grants may not be needed in the future to revitalize downtown areas. As energy supplies become more expensive centralized business districts in downtown areas make more sense, although frequently awkward and unpleasant to use.

TABLE 13.1

Economic Development and Act 250		
	1963-1969	*1970-1977*
New jobs created	1,577	10,813
New companies	91	121
Plant expansions	563	2,147

Source: Former Governor Deane C. Davis in the *Burlington Free Press,* June 1, 1980.

There is a lot of land in Vermont still capable, at least physic-ally, of supporting more community development. But as district environmental commissions increasingly use economic-impact criteria in their decisions, a lot of that suitable land may remain in a more natural state. Recent decisions suggest that Act 250 itself is in fact channeling developments into a certain type of area, and perhaps a state land-use plan would not be needed. One problem, however, with channeling development into suitable areas involves the whole question of prime agricultural land. There is very little of that in Vermont—perhaps up to 10% of the state's area, but definitions are not too precise. All Act 250 says is that primary agricultural soils means "soils which have a potential for growing food and forage (i.e., hay), are sufficiently well-drained to allow sowing and harvesting with mechanized equipment, are well-supplied with plant nutrients, or highly re-sponsive to the use of fertilizer, and have few limitations for cultivation. . . ." Furthermore, in order to qualify, "the average slope of the land . . . does not exceed 15%, and such land is of a size capable of supporting or contributing to an economic agri-cultural operation." Commenting on such a definition is fruit-less, but ironically, a gravel pit operator in Stowe a few years ago was denied a permit for excavation because of its being designated primary agricultural soil.

As the Vermont legislature responded to an awakening need for environmental control with enactment of state-wide regula-tions, local planning commissions operating under Title 117, the Vermont Municipal Regional Planning and Development Act, were also busy. Town plans were called for, and Vermont towns

now have their own plans, translated into legal zoning regulations for administration by a local zoning board of adjustment.
As a rule, most towns in Vermont do not want high-density
lower-income development, translated into higher school enroll-
ments with higher school taxes. Senior-citizens housing is great—
no children, little use of services, and a contribution to the local
tax base! The fear of higher school taxes though, is enough to
make many local planning commissions draw up plans which include restrictions on multi-family homes, apartments, subdivisions of small-lot size, mobile-home parks and any other type of
residential development which would concentrate a large number
of families on a small area of land. One community near Burlington has set a 10-acre-minimum lot size for any additional
single-family development.

Mobile homes are a case in point. As traditional housing becomes more expensive, mobile homes are the only affordable
type of shelter for many families. Yet until the state acted in
1975, 25 towns in Vermont banned mobile homes in their zoning ordinances. Paying minimal property taxes, and often housing young, lower-income families with several children, mobile
homes and "trailer parks" were (and are) often frowned upon
by other citizens. Yet the placing of mobile homes continues to
be important and even as early as 1970 more mobile homes than
traditional stick-built houses were "constructed" in more than
75 towns in Vermont. Few mobile-home parks have been developed in recent years, in general because of Act 250 red tape
as well as a public prejudice toward such developments. This has
forced such homes onto larger pieces of land in more rural areas
and led to other cries of frustration from scenery buffs. Has anyone ever seen a mobile home in a *Vermont Life* magazine spread?

Other legislation banned billboards and any sort of off-premise
advertising signs. Several enterprising Vermonters have been trying to get around this by an appropriately-lettered permanently-
parked truck. Other concerns have large signs across the Connecticut River in New Hampshire, easily seen by the traveller on
the interstate highway on the Vermont side of the river. When
one enters Vermont from nearly any direction one sees a host of
large signs just outside of the state line, telling one that Holiday
Inns and the like are only 100 miles away. In 1973, Vermont

was the second state in the country (after Oregon) to enact a returnable bottle/can law, and roadsides are much cleaner now, although the price of beer and soft drinks is higher. When beer was cheaper in 1972, Vermont ranked fifth in the United States in per capita consumption (24.1 gallons).

There is no question that Vermont is a beautiful state, and an awareness of this beauty, especially on the part of newcomers, has been a powerful force in efforts to ensure that this beauty and quality of life is maintained. But as one native Vermonter once told me, "it sure is expensive to live in a park." Environmental quality does not come cheaply, and residents of the state pay for every lengthy Act 250 hearing in high home prices as they do with lower wages once a new plant is built, Yet the environment is being treated with respect, and that ensures that the attractiveness of Vermont will be as great in the future as it was in the past when the first settlers moved into the virgin wilderness.

Selected References

Chapter 1

Allen, Farrow, et al. *Vermont Trout Streams*. Burlington, Vt.: Northern Cartographic, 1985.

Jacobs, E. C. *The Physical Features of Vermont*. Montpelier, Vt.: Vermont Development Department, 1950.

Jorgensen, Neil. *A Guide to New England's Landscape*. Chester, Ct.: Globe Pequot Press, 1977.

Thornbury, William D. *Regional Geomorphology of the United States*. New York: John Wiley and Sons, 1965.

Vermont Land Capability. Montpelier, Vt.: Vermont State Planning Office, 1974.

Chapter 2
(see also references for Chapter 3)

Jacobs, E. C. *The Physical Features of Vermont*. Montpelier, Vt: Vermont Development Department, 1950.

Johnson, Charles W. *The Nature of Vermont*. Hanover, N.H.: University Press of New England, 1980.

Jorgensen, Neil. *A Guide to New England's Landscape*. Chester, Ct.: Globe Pequot Press, 1977.

Meyer, H. A., and Marion Hubbell. "Erosional Landforms of Eastern and Central Vermont," *Annual Report of the Vermont State Geologist, 1927-1928*. Montpelier, Vt.: Office of the State Geologist, 1928.

Thornbury, William D. *Regional Geomorphology of the United States*. New York: John Wiley and Sons, 1965.

Chapter 3
(see also references for Chapter 2)

Chapman, D. H. "Late Glacial and Post-Glacial History of the Champlain Valley." *Annual Report of the Vermont State Geologist*, 1941-1942.

Doolan, Barry, and Rolfe Stanley, eds. *Guidebook for Field Trips in Vermont*, 64th Annual Meeting, New England Intercollegiate Geological Conference, Burlington, Vt., University of Vermont, 1972.

Flint, Richard F. *The Earth and Its History.* New York: W. W. Norton, 1973.
Flint, Richard F. *Glacial and Pleistocene Geology.* New York: John Wiley and Sons, 1957.
Flint, Richard F. *Glacial and Quaternary Geology.* New York: John Wiley and Sons, 1971.
Haviland, William A., and Marjory W. Power. *The Original Vermonters.* Hanover, N.H.: University Press of New England, 1981.
Jacobs, E. C. "The Great Ice Age in Vermont." *Annual Report of the Vermont State Geologist,* 1941-1942.
Prest, V. K. *Quaternary Geology of Canada.* Economic Geology Report Series, Geological Survey of Canada. Ottawa: Dept. of Mines and Resources, 1970.
Stewart, D. P. "The Glacial Geology of Vermont." *Vermont Geological Survey, Bulletin 19.* Montpelier, Vt.: Vermont Geological Survey, 1961.
Stewart, D. P., and P. MacClintock. *Surficial Geologic Map of Vermont.* Montpelier, Vt.: Vermont Geological Survey, 1970.
Stewart, D. P., and P. MacClintock. "The Surficial Geology and Pleistocene History of Vermont." *Vermont Geological Survey, Bulletin 31.* Montpelier, Vt.: Vermont Geological Survey, 1969.

Chapter 4

Doll, C. G., et al. Compilers and Editors. *Centennial Geologic Map of Vermont.* Montpelier, Vt.: Vermont Geological Survey, 1961.
Doolin, Barry, and Rolfe Stanley, eds. *Guidebook for Field Trips in Vermont.* 64th Annual Meeting, New England Intercollegiate Geological Conference, Burlington, Vt., University of Vermont, 1972.
Jacobs, E. C. *The Physical Features of Vermont.* Montpelier, Vt.: Vermont Development Department, 1950.
Jorgensen, Neil. *A Guide to New England's Landscape.* Chester, Ct.: Globe Pequot Press, 1977.
Vermont, A Guide to the Green Mountain State. American Guide Series, Federal Writers Project. Boston: Houghton Mifflin, 1937.

Chapter 5
(see also references for Chapter 6)

Abbott, Collamer M. *Green Mountain Copper.* Randolph, Vt.: Published by the author, 1973.
Adams, C. B. *First Annual Report on the Geology of the State of Vermont.* Burlington, Vt.: C. Goodrich, 1845. (This volume is often titled *Adams*

Geology of Vermont when it also contains the *Second Annual Report* (1846) and a section entitled "The North American Miscellaney." The *First Report* is 92 pages long; the *Second Report* is 263 pages long.)

Allen, Richard S. "Furnaces, Forges and Foundries." *Vermont Life,* Vol. 40, No. 2, Winter 1956-7.

Caverly, A. M. *History of the Town of Pittsfield, Vt.* Rutland, Vt., 1872. Reprinted by the Pittsfield Historical Society, 1976.

Gates, William B., Jr. *Michigan Copper and Boston Dollars.* Cambridge: Harvard University Press, 1951.

Grant, Raymond W. "Mineral Collecting in Vermont." *Special Publication No. 2.* Montpelier, Vt.: Vermont Geological Survey, 1968.

Hitchcock, Edward, et al. *Report on the Geology of Vermont.* 2 volumes. Claremont, N.H.: Albert D. Hagar (Proctorsville, Vt.), 1861. (This is often referred to as *Hitchcock's Geology of Vermont.* Its authors were Edward Hitchcock, Edward Hitchcock, Jr., Albert D. Hager, and Charles H. Hitchcock. Volume I is concerned chiefly with geology, Volume II with mineral resources and topography.)

Ingham, Adella. *A History of the Monkton Iron Company, 1807-1830.* Unpublished manuscript in Bixby Library, Vergennes, Vt.

Jacobs, E. C. "Reopening of the Vermont Copper Mines." *Annual Report of the Vermont State Geologist,* 1941-1942.

Jacobs, E. C. "The Vermont Copper Company." *Annual Report of the Vermont State Geologist,* 1943-1944.

Meeks, Harold A. *Marginal Agriculture in Michigan's Copper Country.* Unpublished Ph.D. dissertation, University of Minnesota, 1964.

"Mineral Deposits and Occurrences in Vermont Exclusive of Clay, Sand and Gravel, and Peat." *Mineral Investigations Resource Map MR5.* Washington, D.C.: U.S. Geological Survey, 1957.

Morrill, Philip, and Robert G. Chaffee. *Vermont Mines and Mineral Localities.* Hanover, N.H.: Dartmouth College Museum, 1964.

Rolando, Victor R. *Ironmaking in Vermont, 1775-1890.* Master of Arts thesis, College of St. Rose, Albany, New York, 1980.

Smith, Beth R. "The Plymouth Gold Rush." *Vermont Life,* Vol. 6, No. 2, Winter 1951-52.

Chapter 6
(see also references for Chapter 5)

Annual Report of the Vermont State Geologist. These *Reports* all contain relevant material on Vermont mineral resource development. Some of the more important articles include:

Dale, T. N. "The Granites of Vermont." *Report,* 1907-1908.

Dale, T. N. "The Granites of Vermont." *Report,* 1908-1909.

Dale, T. N. "The Commerical Marbles of Western Vermont, *Report,* 1913-1914.

Jacobs, E. C. "The Clay Deposits and Clay Industry of Vermont." *Report,* 1925-1926.

Jacobs, E. C. "Copper Mining in Vermont." *Report,* 1915-1916.

Jacobs, E. C. "The Talc and Serpentine Deposits of Vermont." *Report,* 1915-1916.

Jacobs, E. C. "Talc and Talc Deposits of Vermont." *Report,* 1913-1914.

Perkins, G. H. "History of the Marble Industry in Vermont." *Report,* 1913-1914.

Perkins, G. H. "The Marble Industry of Vermont." *Report,* 1931-1932.

Richardson, C. H. "Asbestos in Vermont." *Report,* 1908-1909.

Bertolas, Randy J. *Slate: A Geographic Study with Emphasis on Vermont.* Master of Arts thesis, Department of Geography, University of Vermot, Burlington, Vt., October, 1982.

Crane, Charles E. "Silk from Stone." *Vermont Life,* Vol. 8, No. 3, Summer 1954.

Emley, Warren E. "Manufacture and Use of Lime." *Mineral Resources of the United States 1913.* Washington, D.C.: U.S. Geological Survey, 1914.

Gay, Leon S. "Dwellings from the Hills." *Vermont Life,* Vol. 5, No. 1, Autumn 1950.

Glover, Waldo F. "Old Scotland in Vermont." *Vermont History,* Vol. 23, No. 2, April, 1955.

Hill, Ralph N., Jr. "Pure, White and Plenty." *Vermont Life,* Vol. 16, No. 1, Autumn 1961.

Leland, Ernest S. "Barre." *Vermont Life,* Vol. 2, No. 1, Autumn 1947.

Marshall, Philip. "Roofing Slate of the Vermont-New York Slate Belt." A research project in Historic Preservation, University of Vermont. Burlington, Vt., January, 1979.

McDonald, Marion. *The Granite Years: Barre, Vt., 1880-1900.* Unpublished Master of Arts thesis, Department of History, University of Vermont, Burlington, Vt., 1978.

"Minerals in the Economy of Vermont." *State Mineral Profiles (SMP-2).* Washington, D.C.: Bureau of Mines, U.S. Department of the Interior, April, 1978.

Mineral Resources of the United States, Part II, Non-Metals, 1913. Washington, D.C.: U.S. Geological Survey, 1914. (This is only one of the annual volumes published by the U.S. Geological Survey. They are a significant source of data on mining and quarrying operations.)

Morrow, John A. *A Century of Hard Rock: The Story of the Rising and Nelson Slate Company.* Granville, N.Y.: Grastorf Press, 1970.

Orton, Vrest. "Talcum Powder Under Our Mountains." *Vermont Life,* Vol. 6, No. 2, Winter 1951-52.

Rogers, Frank R. "Vermont Slate." *Vermont Life,* Vol. 10, No. 2, Winter 1955-56.

"Soils and Men." *U.S. Department of Agriculture Yearbook.* Washington, D.C.: U.S. Government Printing Office, 1938.

Tillman, David A. *Mining in Vermont.* Portland, Me.: Tower Publishing Company, 1974.

Tomasi, Mari. "The Italian Story in Vermont." *Vermont History,* Vol. 28, No. 1, January, 1960.

Chapter 7

"Climate and Man." *U.S. Department of Agriculture Yearbook.* Washington, D.C.: U.S. Government Printing Office, 1941.

Hopp, Richard J., et al. "Growing Degree Days in Vermont." *Bulletin 654,* University of Vermont, Vermont Agricultural Experiment Station, Burlington, Vt., 1968.

Hopp, Richard J., et al. "Late Spring and Early Fall Low Temperatures in Vermont." *Bulletin 639,* University of Vermont, Vermont Agricultural Experiment Station, Burlington, Vt., 1964.

Ingram, Robert S., and Samuel C. Wiggins. "Climate of Burlington, Vt." *M.P. 53,* University of Vermont, Vermont Agricultural Experiment Station, Vt., October, 1968.

Ludlum, David. *The Country Journal New England Weather Book.* Boston: Houghton Mifflin, 1976.

Ludlum, David. *The Vermont Weather Book.* Montpelier, Vt.: Vermont Historical Society, 1985.

Chapter 8

Johnson, Luther B. *Vermont in Floodtime.* Randolph, Vt.: Ray L. Johnson Company, 1928.

Ludlum, David. *The Country Journal New England Weather Book.* Boston: Houghton Mifflin, 1976.

Merrill, Perry H. *Vermont Under Four Flags.* Montpelier, Vt.: Published by the author, 1975.

Regulation of Lake Champlain and the Upper Richelieu River. Report to the International Joint Commission by the International Champlain-Richelieu Board, Office of the Chairmen, Hull, Quebec, and Albany, New York, 1978.

Water and Related Land Resources of Vermont. State of Vermont and New England River Basins Commission, Agency of Environmental Conservation, June, 1974.

Chapter 9

Note: Nearly all the material incorporated in this chapter has come from widely scattered documents including *Annual Reports* of Vermont's major power companies, documents on file with the Vermont Public Service Board, newspaper clippings from the *Burlington Free Press* and the *Rutland Herald*, and technical publications made available by the Vermont State Energy Office. Robert Hartnett, a graduate student at the University of Vermont provided data on fuel wood pricing, and Charles Ryerson helped with material on solar energy. Other sources of data include publications of the New England Power Company and Northeast Utilities. The Federal Energy Office (formerly the Federal Power Commission) and the Edison Electric Institute provided information on typical electric bills.

Energy Use in Vermont and the Public Interest. Montpelier, Vt.: Vermont Department of Public Service, 1984.

Khouri, Lance. "Vermont's Great Oil Boom." *Vermont Life,* Vol. 31, No. 3, Spring 1977.

Merrill, Perry H. *Vermont Under Four Flags.* Montpelier, Vt.: Published by the author, 1975.

Water and Related Land Resources of Vermont. State of Vermont and New England River Basins Commission, Agency of Environmental Conservation, June, 1974.

Wright, John K. ed. *New England's Prospect, 1933.* Special Publication No. 16. New York: American Geographical Society, 1933.

Chapter 10

Atlas of United States Trees, Volume I: Conifers and Important Hardwoods. Miscellaneous Publication 1146. U.S. Department of Agriculture, Forest Service. Washington, D.C.: U.S. Government Printing Office, 1971.

Johnson, Charles W. *The Nature of Vermont.* Hanover, N.H.: University Press of New England, 1980.

Jorgensen, Neil. *A Guide to New England's Landscapes.* Chester, Ct.: Globe Pequot Press, 1977.

Siccama, Thomas G. "Presettlement and Present Forest Vegetation in Northern Vermont with Special Reference to Chittenden County." *The American Midland Naturalist*, Vol. 85, No. 1, January, 1971.

Vermont Land Capability. Montpelier, Vt.: Vermont State Planning Office, 1974.

Vogelmann, Hubert W. *Natural Areas of Vermont*. Report No. 1, Vermont Resources Research Center. Burlington, Vt.: University of Vermont, 1964.

Vogelmann, Hubert W. *Vermont Natural Areas*. Montpelier, Vt.: Central Planning Office, 1969.

Chapter 11

Armstrong, Frank H. *Valuation of Vermont Forests, 1968-1974*. Unpublished report, Department of Forestry, University of Vermont, June, 1975.

Bonyai, Susan, and Paul Sendak. *Vermont's Timber Economy, A Review of the Statistics*. Montpelier, Vt.: USDA Forest Service and Vermont Agency of Environmental Conservation, 1982.

Industrial Survey of Vermont, Summary Report, 1930. Prepared by New England Power Company, The Connecticut River Power Company of New Hampshire, Bellows Falls Hydroelectric Corporation, Grafton Power Company, and the New England Power Corporation of Vermont, December, 1930.

Kingsley, Neal. "The Forest Resources of Vermont." *U.S. Forest Service Bulletin NE-46*. Northeast Forest Experiment Station, Upper Darby, PA., 1977. (Excellent most-recent source on annual growth and inventory.)

Kingsley, Neal, and Joseph E. Barnard. "The Timber Resources of Vermont." *U.S. Forest Service Bulletin NE-12*. Northeast Forest Experiment Station, Upper Darby, PA., 1968.

Merrill, Perry H. *Vermont Under Four Flags*. Montpelier, Vt.: Published by the author, 1975.

Opportunities and Choices: The Future of Vermont's Forests. A report prepared by the Resouce Policy Team of the Vermont Forest Advisory Council, Montpelier, Vt.: Agency of Environmental Conservation, June, 1981.

Orr, David W. "Historical Geography of the Lakeport of Burlington, Vermont." *The Vermont Geographer* (Department of Geography, University of Vermont), No. 2, 1975.

Orr, David W. *Port of Burlington, Vermont: Site and Situation, A Study in Historical Geography.* Master of Arts thesis, Department of Geography, University of Vermont, 1972.

Policies for the Use of New England's Forested Lands. American Forest Institute and the New England Natural Resources Center. Eight-page brochure, no date.

Vermont Forest Exchange and Information Bulletin. Vermont Department of Forests, Parks and Recreation. Agency of Environmental Conservation. Montpelier, Vt. (This monthly publication contains annual summaries of Vermont forest cut and use. Detailed annual surveys are available from the Department.)

Whitmore, Roy A. "Lumber Marketing by Vermont Sawmills." *Bulletin 630.* University of Vermont, Vermont Agricultural Experiment Station, Burlington, Vt., September, 1962.

Whitmore, Roy A. "Marketing of Lumber by Vermont Retail Lumber Yards." *Bulletin 651.* University of Vermont, Vermont Agricultural Experiment Station, Burlington, Vt., September, 1967.

Chapter 12

Meeks, Harold A. *The Geographic Regions of Vermont* (Special Publication No. 10). Hanover, N.H.: Dartmouth College, 1975.

Basic Statistics, National Inventory of Soil and Water Conservation Needs. Statistical Bulletin 461. U.S. Department of Agriculture. Washington, D.C.: U.S. Government Printing Office, 1967.

"Soils and Men." *U.S. Department of Agriculture Yearbook.* Washington, D.C.: U.S. Government Printing Office, 1938.

Soil Survey Reconnaissance of Vermont. Number 43. U.S. Department of Agriculture, Bureau of Chemistry and Soils, Series 1930.

Vermont Land Capability. Montpelier, Vt.: Vermont State Planning Office, September, 1974.

Chapter 13

Note: The Agency of Environmental Conservation, State of Vermont, and the staff of the Chittenden County Regional Planning Commission furnished much of the information used in this chapter.

Meeks, Harold A. *The Geographic Regions of Vermont* (Special Publication No. 10). Hanover, N.H.: Dartmouth College, 1975.

Index